MW01657135

Water the Snot Out of It and Other Gardening Tips

ISBN: 978-0-9981476-1-1
Second Printing January 2017

Art work by Zoe Black

Format/Cover Design by Minion Editing & Design
www.joyminion.com

Printed in the United States of America

Order from:

Bev Johnson
27490 289th Avenue
Underwood, MN 56586
(218) 826-6476

Also available at:
U of M Extension office
505 S. Court
Fergus Falls, MN

Dedication

To Arlen, who for 61 years was my husband and best friend.
He would be so proud.

Foreword

Bev Johnson is best known for gardening wit and wisdom—with a few wisecracks thrown in. You may have read her articles—she writes one every week for publications with a combined circulation of well over 61,000, including the *Fergus Falls Daily Journal*, the *Midweek*, the *Pelican Rapids Press*, *Senior Perspective*, the *Battle Lake Review*, the *Grant County Herald*, the *Ashby-Dalton Post*, and the *McLean County Independent* (Garrison, ND).

Perhaps you've heard her on the radio. All year long she heads to KBRF in Fergus Falls, Minnesota, to record a quick weekly spot, except for during the growing season when she does a one-hour program every Saturday morning.

She gives workshops on gardening: *Seed Starting*, *How to Build a Greenhouse*, *Growing Vegetables*, whatever. She's made Bunkey famous for his gardening misadventures. ("Bunkey" is the Challenged Gardener, who never quite gets it right.)

Bev is a Master Gardener. She completed the University of Minnesota Extension course-work in 1999 and continues to meet the volunteer and continuing education commitment to maintain her status. She in fact far exceeds the minimum 25-hour commitment per year—she's logged more than 3,000 volunteer hours over the 17 years she's been in the program.

Sometimes you can catch her at City Bakery answering horticulture questions. She's in the U of MN Extension office in Fergus Falls once a week to return phone calls to people who have gardening questions, or to visit with people who have brought in samples of their problem plants. (And she brings gorgeous bouquets of flowers from her garden!)

But it's not all about being an Extension Master Gardener. When she can't be in the garden, she sews the most adorable doll outfits, all of which she either donates or gives as gifts to young relatives. No rocking chair for this retired nurse, even though SHE ROCKS! She's "Bev the Gardener," Bev Johnson, University of Minnesota Extension Master Gardener, from West Otter Tail County, Minnesota.

But Bev's gardening wisdom didn't begin when she became a Master Gardener. She had a grandmother who gardened and raised a family of six kids on what she grew. "My mother was the same way," Bev recalls. "She always had a garden, and I've gardened since I was a little kid."

Bev's other grandmother was high society, Bev recalls, the type who used napkin rings for lunch. Her grandmother was Methodist and there was no Methodist church in Underwood. The closest was Fergus Falls…a long way to go to hook up the horses back during World War II. So she went to the Lutheran church, Bev says. One day the church women asked her to join Ladies Aid. "No, I can't do that," said her grandmother. "To do that I'd have to be stone cold sober, fully dressed, wearing a hat and carrying a cake." So THAT explains Bev's wisecracking.

Bev grew up in Underwood and graduated from Underwood High School. It wasn't long after graduation that she married Arlen Johnson. I ask if Arlen was from Underwood too. "No," Bev says, "he grew up in Fergus. When I was sixteen I went on a date with his cousin and met Arlen. He was better looking, so I took him."

Arlen worked for a heating company in Fergus, which then moved to Underwood. Eventually the company went out of business, and he took at job with a company in Wisconsin. "I would never live in Wisconsin again," Bev says. "By the time we left, my son Kelly was telling his sisters to 'tie my shoes because that's what girls do.'" That attitude didn't last long.

From Wisconsin, the family moved to Red Wing and then St. Cloud. The next move would have been Minneapolis and an office job, so in 1979 the family moved back to Underwood.

Bev's dad had given them land with a cabin on Little Pleasant Lake. Bev created the plans to turn the cabin into a home, and they began building. These many years later, Bev looks around satisfied. "When the kids were at home," she says, "the place was a bit small—now it's the perfect size for the two of us."

Perfect indeed. The dining area looks out onto the front deck where finch and orioles flock to a row of bird feeders. The living room comfortably accommodates Bev's indoor interests: reading (sci fi, mysteries, biographies and anything on plants), knitting and listening to classical music. The floor plan is open and inviting. Missing from the scene is anything high tech. I ask how Bev writes her columns. "I use a word processor," she replies. If I need something, I call one of my kids."

Her "kids" gladly accommodate their mom with the Internet, but favors go both ways. Across the drive, on the shore of Little Pleasant Lake, sits a homemade greenhouse. Each spring Bev starts plants from seeds. When plants are mature, she gives some to her kids (I've inoculated all four of them with gardening," Bev says), some to her brother and uses the rest for her own flower and vegetable gardens.

But there is more to Bev than gardening. In Wisconsin, once all four kids were in school, Bev worked as a home health aide. She continued working in that field in Red Wing and St. Cloud—16 years total over the three locations. She's taught knitting to adults and 4-H, makes baby sweaters for Public Health and afghans for the cancer center. "Keeps me out of bars," Bev says.

Once her children were through high school, Bev started thinking about her future. She'd known a couple of widows living on social security and decided she needed more stability than that. She signed up for career assessment at the college: "What do you want to be when you grow up?" Bev quips. The answer came back: cop, horticulturist or nurse.

Bev chose nurse. She worked at Lake Region on the surgical floor and started nursing school at the college in Fergus Falls, a program out of Brainerd. "So you were older than most of the students?" I ask. "Heck…I was older than the teachers," Bev replies. "The older students were always wrecking the bell curve, she says, so the younger ones didn't like having us in class."

Bev recalls a paper she wrote for English Comp: "Why do we say it's colder than brass balls on a monkey?" I look at her to see if she's serious. She is. She explains: in the old days when ships had cannons on board, the cannon balls would be kept on a brass plate, called a brass monkey. The balls were piled in a pyramid on the plate. When it got really cold, the plate would contract and the balls would roll off. "Whenever I ran into my teacher after I graduated, he remembered me," Bev says. No doubt.

After graduating as an RN, Bev worked at the Regional Treatment Center (RTC) in Fergus. Patients made the job interesting: bipolar patients were fun when they were "up," and schizophrenics walked down the hall talking to themselves. "I recall a patient who started himself on fire," Bev says, "and other patient—one who had been a paramedic—put him out."

Although Bev is retired from nursing, she teaches gardening classes to cardiac rehab patients. Her kids are grown: Christa, the oldest, graduated in forestry; Kelly is an electrical inspector; Melissa, a lawyer; and Kala, the youngest, is a teacher and has a Masters Degree. Bev's life is full. She enjoys family and friends. She grows vegetables, cans and freezes. She tends her flowerbeds. She teaches, writes columns and offers gardening advice on the radio. She knits, reads and listens to classical music. She volunteers. She does it all with wit and wisdom… and oh yes…with a few wisecracks thrown in.

— Reba Gilliand
Master Gardener

Preface

You're holding in your hands a loosely-organized, occasionally repetitious collection of my gardening articles and snippets of advice.

This book would never have been born without some very pushy people who believed I had it in me when I wasn't so sure.

To Diane Johnson, fellow Master Gardener, who nagged me to, "Just do it!"

To Jan Brooberg and later Sharon Funk, both secretaries beyond compare, who removed all those extra commas, repaired spellings, questioned questionable sentences and got the articles off to the proper newspapers on time each week.

To the editor of the *Fergus Falls Daily Journal*, who took a chance on an unknown and very amateur writer and printed my articles every week.

To my editor, Joy Minion, who waded hip deep through years of articles to find the few reprintable ones.

To an excellent artist, Zoe Black, who gave my characters a face.

And last, but never least, to my kids: Christa Peterson, Kelly Johnson, Melissa DeGroff and Kala Richards. They are often embarrassed by the word choices in my articles. And they insist no one can possibly write anything without a computer, the Internet and a smart phone. Can too. I did it with a word processor and a flip phone. So there!

My characters are figments of my imagination. They are quite lively for figments, as they often sneak into my articles.

So, who are these people?

Bunkey's real name is Richard. He got his nickname from an old song, *Gramma's Lye Soap*. It has the recurring phrase, "*Is that what's bothering you, Bunkey?*" Seemed to fit. In other words, *Bunkey* is shorthand for *Joe/Jane Gardener.*

Bunkey and Petunia, his wife, are city people who moved to a small town of about 4,000 for Petunia's job. She is some kind of manager, very bossy and a bit of a nag. Never got her hands dirty in her life, but she's trying. Bunkey had a job cleaning the Metrodome in Minneapolis. Since it collapsed in a snowstorm, he's been a house husband. Now he is determined to raise all of their food and make their new "estate" (a 250-foot lot) perfect. Unfortunately, he knows nothing about gardening and makes every mistake possible.

Enter neighbor George, an older gentleman who has been a Master Gardener for 30 years. He enjoys sharing his expertise, but often despairs of Bunkey ever becoming any kind of a gardener, let alone a Master Gardener.

A picture of these characters will introduce full articles. A tiny trio of garden objects will indicate the end. A watering can with flowers tells you that this is just a snippet. Do pay attention!

Bev Johnson, a.k.a. Bev the Gardener

Contents

A Few Basics

You can't rollerskate in a buffalo herd, and you can't put a garden just anywhere.

What Is In Your Soil?

With the price of gas and groceries on a constant rise, more people are thinking about planting a garden this year. Here are a few tips for the novice gardener.

First, start small. You may find that gardening is just not your thing.

Second, do a soil test in the area you are thinking about planting. The garden should be in full sun, that is from 8 a.m. to 6 p.m. If the soil is good, you can start removing the grass from your plot. If you simply till it in, you will fight grass and weeds for as long as you garden there. If you find that the soil will need a lot of renovation, build raised beds. They only need to be about two feet deep, three feet if you hate to bend over to garden.

Now to plant. Peas, potatoes, carrots, lettuce and all the cabbage plants can go in as soon as the frost is gone from the soil. Corn, tomatoes, and peppers need air and soil temps of 55. Beans and the vine crops, cucumbers, melons, pumpkins, need soil temps of 60.

Rows should run north and south, but that is not set in stone. Just be sure your corn isn't shading your tomatoes. Lettuce likes the cool side of corn. Never plant tomatoes where you had potatoes last year and vice versa. They are cousins and are sensitive to the same diseases. Don't crowd plants. Good air circulation can prevent many diseases.

Mulch. Lay 4 to 6 layers of newspapers on the soil and cover them with grass clippings, straw, leaves or hay. This does several good things for your garden. It keeps the weeds from sprouting from seeds in the soil. Any seeds that fly in with the wind can't get to the soil to sprout. It keeps the moisture in the soil. It keeps the roots cool and when it rots, as it will by the end of the season, it adds micronutrients to the soil.

When you buy seeds, check the days to maturity. We have a very short growing season. Ninety (90) days is a good time to look for. Plant corn that ripens at different times, which will stretch your season. Plant radishes every two weeks until July to have a continual supply. Lettuce and spinach will bolt (flower in the hot weather), but can be replanted in late August for a fall treat.

Give gardening a try. It is not only good for the table, but good exercise for the gardener.

Do you know what is crawling around in your soil? Well, according to Jeff Gillman, Associate Professor of Horticulture at the University of Minnesota, our garden soil is full of creepy crawlies. We have all dug up worms, so we will start with them. In our gardens, their burrowing activities reduce compaction, letting air and water move through the soil. They digest organic materials in the soil, breaking them down into smaller parts that release nutrients more easily. Their castings are full of nutrients which is why you can often buy worm castings in seed catalogs.

While worms are good for the garden, they aren't good for our forests. Most worms are not native, having come from the "old country," often as ship's ballast. They came with the soil around the plants gardeners brought with them to make this strange place a little bit like home.

Worms & Fungi

There is growing concern among experts that earthworms are infesting our forests and devouring the litter that decays and feeds the soil. This could well change the soil, and perhaps, the forests themselves.

Worm castings (poop) have high levels of potassium, nitrogen and phosphorus, the very same minerals we buy in manufactured forms to put on our gardens.

Worms are used by medical researchers because their bodies have nervous systems, blood vessels, hemoglobin and a sort of kidney that produces urine. It is safer for the scientist to use them, as worms can't sue if an experiment goes wrong and they end up with extra appendages. Don't get too upset about having worms as weird relatives you never knew you had. Worms have five hearts, have both male and female reproductive organs, and breathe through their skins. To eat, they stick their throats out of their mouths to grab food.

It is a myth that if you cut a worm in half it will be perfectly happy. It will continue to wiggle, but so would you if you were stabbed. If you have all those worm lumps in your yard, use an aerating machine that makes cuts in the lawn that kills the worms, thus reducing the lumps.

Fussy people hate mushrooms in their lawns, but fungi are important. A very important one is *mycorrhizal fungi*, a naturally-occurring fungus that connects to the roots of plants through the soil and collects minerals, especially phosphorus. They deliver the minerals to the plant and receive carbohydrates in return. When you dig a tree or plant, you should take some of the surrounding soil with it. The fungi in the soil are already friends to that plant.

Another soil helper is *rhizobia bacteria*. It lives in the roots of the legume family (peas, beans, etc.), and some trees where they have an easy living environment. Nitrogen is the nutrient plants need most. The air is full of it, but not in a form that plants can use. The soil needs this bacteria to convert nitrogen into a form plants can use. There are other nitrogen-fixing bacteria that are important in healthy soil where they supply other forms of nitrogen.

To ensure your soil stays healthy, use very little synthetic fertilizer. A little will benefit the soil by adding extra nutrients, but is packed with salts. Large amounts of synthetic fertilizer will make plants or grass look greener, but it will weaken the soil and the plants will be less able to survive when stressed. If you must use it, limit applications to two per year. Better yet, use organic fertilizers. They add natural nutrients to the soil.

The moral for this day is, feed your soil and it will feed you. But do not dump your fishing worms in the woods.

Understanding Soil pH

Do you know the pH of your soil? Do you even know what the heck pH is? The chemist's definition is, "A number expressing the acidity or alkalinity of soil equal to the logarithm to the base of 10 of the reciprocal of the effective concentration of hydrogen ions." OOOooof! In plain English, pH stands for power of hydrogen. The pH scale goes from 1 to 14, with 7 being neutral. The higher the concentration of hydrogen ions in the soil solution, the lower the pH. Easy to remember. Just think of vinegar. It is 5% acid. Lower than neutral. One step on the scale, for instance from 6 to 5, means that the soil measuring 5 is 10 times as acid as the soil measuring at 6. Most plants grow best in the 6 to 7.5 range. Soil in Otter Tail County runs alkaline, 7 and up.

Because plants take up nutrients only in solution, the pH of that solution determines what dissolves and what doesn't. For instance, iron and aluminum dissolve in acid soil—perfect for blueberries, but deadly for tomatoes. This is why soil sulfur is used to acidify soil. It helps the soil release iron. Not enough iron and leaves turn yellow. Too much rain (think *Seattle*) washes the calcium, magnesium and potassium out of the soil, making it acid. Not enough rain and calcium and other bases predominate, making alkaline soil. You can temporarily modify the pH of your soil by adding sulfur or limestone, but it will revert quite quickly.

Compost acts as a buffer, helping to keep soil pH stable by binding to plant nutrients and holding them until they are needed. Even if you don't have a formal compost pile, sheet composting will help your soil. A layer of leaves tilled into your garden or just piled on and left to rot in a flowerbed will lead to healthier plants. In the spring, simply dig a trench in the garden and bury your food scraps—no meat, or the dogs and raccoons will dig it up. By the fall, your scraps will have rotted and can be tilled in.

So, how do you find out what the pH is of your soil? Simple. Visit your local Extension office and get a bag for your soil and an information sheet on how to sample it. Then send it in to the address provided, along with the proper fee. They do all the work and send you back a list of what you need to add, the amount of compost in your soil and the pH.

Knowing the pH of your garden will make you a better gardener. Just think of the fun you can have at those coffee klatches. "What's the pH of your garden? You don't know? No wonder you have those little tomatoes."

Water Has pH Too!

As gardeners, we worry about the pH of our soil. We never think about the pH of our water. We think of rainwater as "pure" water, naturally neutral. Not so. Carbon dioxide in the atmosphere lowers the pH of rainwater to about 5.6, nearly as acid as vinegar. So what about city water? If you get your water from a city system, it will be alkaline. It has to be, or it would eat up the older lead water pipes that deliver water to many of our houses.

To find out what the pH of your city water is, call your local water department. For instance, in St. Paul, MN, water is 8.2. To make it fit for watering houseplants, St. Paul gardeners need to add 1½ teaspoons of vinegar to 5 gallons of water to bring the pH to 5.6.

Take a look at your houseplants. We used to think it was the chlorine in city water that gave our plants brown leaf tips and prevented them from doing well. Maybe not.

Well water might not be all that great either. It can have significant amounts of calcium and magnesium in it. This will take even more vinegar to lower the pH. One way to know if you have these salts in your water is to look at your flower pots. Do they have white crud around the top of the pot? You won't see that sort of stuff in your flower garden. So what do you do? There is a pH monitor called *Sunleaves* that hydroponic growers use. It costs about $10.00. It changes color to tell you how acid or alkaline your water is.

An easy way to lower the pH of your water is to use vinegar. It's cheap, safe and easy to get. If you have trouble growing houseplants, maybe all you need is a pH meter and jug of vinegar.

Houseplants are a must in most homes. Not only are they decorative, they also clean up the air in our closed up, winter homes. Call your water department, get a jug of vinegar, and in a few months you may need a machete to get to your bedroom.

It Tastes Like Dirt!

Have you ever complained that your tomatoes don't taste as good your neighbor's? Do your carrots lack that sweet taste they should have? How about melons? Have you quit growing some vegetables because they just don't taste good from your garden? There is a word wine growers use about their soil: *terroir*. It means *taste of earth*. It's a flavor one can get from a specific geographical place, attributable to the mix of minerals and micronutrients in the soil.

If you read many gardening magazines, they often encourage you to add lime, gypsum, ashes, dolomitic limestone, greensand, cottonseed meal, rock powder or other soil amendments to your garden. At the extension office, we often get questions about putting wood ashes on the garden because an article said it would "sweeten up" the soil. Wood ashes are extremely alkaline. Here in western Minnesota, our soil is already alkaline. Putting ashes on it would make the soil so toxic, not much of anything would grow very well.

Before you add anything to your soil, get a soil test. This is one test you don't even need to study for. And, better yet, it is easy to do. Just stop in the Extension office for the supplies and directions. What soil needs on the east coast, where many of those articles are written, may not be what your garden needs. Here, you may need to add sulfur to acidify your soil. Probably the test will tell you that you need more organic material and a bit of nitrogen.

If you have raised beds, you've had soil hauled in. While it may be great looking stuff, you need to know if it has the proper balance of micronutrients, and what the pH is. You probably don't need to get your soil tested every year in your regular garden. If your produce doesn't have the flavor you think it should, however, a soil test will tell you what, if anything, is missing and what and how much to add.

It is not easy to amend soil. For instance, if you want to grow blueberries, you will need to add soil sulfur to the soil almost every year to get any berries. If you insist on having a blue hydrangea, you need to keep the soil around it acid. Our alkaline soil will keep attempting to modify that acid. Some modification is fairly simple. Adding finished compost or tilling in leaves and last summer's lettuce, cabbage, untreated grass clippings and alfalfa in the fall will eventually make your soil light and fluffy and full of micronutrients and organic material. *Alfalfa*, you ask? Sure. Any feed mill sells it in pellets or a sort of dust for cattle food. It is full of micronutrients. Of course, if you live on a farm, you might be able to get the unprocessed stuff.

Test your garden soil in the spring to get on the right track to have the bragging rights to the best tasting tomatoes on the block.

Adding sand to clay soil will not make the soil any "lighter." To make the pores of clay wide enough for water to drain, add copious amounts of compost.

The Ephemeral Nutrient

If you have ever taken a soil sample (and if not, why not?), the information you get back from the University indicates the proportion of potassium and phosphorus in the soil, how acidic or alkaline it is and what percentage of humus your soil contains.

There is no mention of nitrogen in the report. There is a good reason for that. The availability of nitrogen depends on many factors, including the temperature and moisture of the air, the soil composition and condition, and the activity of soil organisms. As these conditions can change so rapidly, labs can't test for it. Since nitrogen is critical for plant growth, there is always a suggestion from the lab as to how much should be added to your soil.

Signs of nitrogen deficiency are usually easy for even the most inexperienced gardener to see: yellowing of older leaves, and slow growth even in the best growing conditions.

Heavy users of nitrogen are corn, lettuce, squash and roses. Vine crops love it, but will attempt to cover the garden with vines and forget to set fruit. Since nitrogen is necessary, and usually lacking in heavy enough percentages to encourage the best growth, the gardener must replace it each year.

There are many amendments that do just that. Organic materials (particularly those that contain proteins), include grains, seeds, legumes and animal by-products.

Composted manure can be purchased in bags like potting soil, or you can gather your own raw manure. Do compost manures at least six months to kill weed seeds and reduce the amount of ammonia in the manure.

Too much ammonia can "burn" your plants. You can apply the fresh stuff to your garden in the fall after harvest and till it in a month before planting in the spring. This can be an iffy project if the soil is too wet in the spring. Till wet soil and you have a problem all summer.

Another option is blood meal. It too can burn seedlings, so either mix it with water and add to your irrigation system or water it well after applying.

Fish emulsion is really stinky and needs to be reapplied monthly. It can be used as a foliar spray.

Feather meal (dried pelleted feathers) doesn't break down readily, so it is an excellent long-term source of nitrogen. Alfalfa meal not only adds nitrogen but also micronutrients to the soil. Soybean meal is another fairly slow-release source.

Of course, you can always buy a bag of chemical nitrogen and send organic gardeners into the vapors. Just add some nitrogen for your best-ever garden.

Fertilizer—Organic or Chemical?

It's fertilizer time. Time to decide what type, how much and what to fertilize. Walking down the fertilizer aisle can make your head hurt. What the heck is organic, and is it really better than the other stuff?

Let's start with organic. It's made from plants, manure or by-products of once living organisms. It can even include feathers. Microorganisms in it help break down and transform organic material into food your plants can use. This makes organic fertilizer slow-release so you don't have to apply it as often. And, unlike the chemical types, it's much less apt to burn or damage your plants. Another advantage of organics is that they add micro-nutrients to the soil, improving the actual soil structure. They do, however, contain smaller amounts of the three major chemicals than synthetics do.

Synthetics are manufactured from minerals, gases and waste products. They are quickly released unless coated or encapsulated and are available to the plants in a form they can readily absorb. This means if you don't read the directions, you can easily burn your plants. You will need to apply smaller amounts and more often than with organics.

Before applying any fertilizer, you should know what those numbers are on the front of the bag and what each does for your plants. The first is *nitrogen*. This is the chemical that promotes leaf and stem growth. A plant lacking in nitrogen will be pale and yellowed.

The second number is *phosphorus*. Plants need this chemical for fruiting and blooming. It also promotes good root growth. Unfortunately, if it gets into our lakes, it makes for lush water weed growth. For this reason, synthetic fertilizers meant for lawns have no phosphorus in them in my state and many others.

The third chemical on the fertilizer bag is *potassium*. Potassium increases hardiness, as well as drought and disease resistance. A balanced fertilizer has the same percentage of all three of these nutrients, thus 10- 10- 10. This used to be the answer to all fertilizer; however, both phosphorus and potassium tend to stay in the soil. They can accumulate in the soil to such an extent that they interfere with the uptake of other nutrients, including the micronutrients that all plants need. Most gardens that have been fertilized every year will show this problem. Most plants need yearly nitrogen as it doesn't stay in the soil and plants need more of it than the other two.

There well may be other terms on your fertilizer bag. *WIN* is the percent of water insoluble nitrogen. It is the percentage of slow-release nitrogen in the mix. Soluble nitrogen may be described as *fast-acting* or *quick release*, or just *water soluble*. If the chemicals are coated or encapsulated, they will be labeled as *slow release*, *timed release*, or *controlled release*. Organic fertilizers are automatically slow release.

The back of the bag usually will give you information on rates of application. This is generic information. It may or may not apply to your gardens. This is why Master Gardeners stress soil sampling. A soil sample will let you know exactly how much of each of these three chemicals are in your soil and what you need to add, if anything, to ensure a good crop. So, take your soil test report and hie thee to the garden center, prepared to get exactly the right fertilizer for your gardens.

How to Improve Your Soil

As a gardener, one is always making tough choices about the soil. Should I just have some black dirt hauled in to spread on top of the native soil and call it good? The thinking is that we have now provided a good spot for our perennials. While that may do for a year or so, it is not a permanent solution. To really do the job, and do it properly, the gardener must mulch.

Mulching reduces the weed population by shading the soil. Most seeds need light to germinate. If thick enough, mulch prevents seeds falling on it from getting to the soil to root. Seeds that germinate on top of the mulch are easily pulled out. Often, if left, they die because they can't root properly. As the mulch rots, it provides micro nutrients. This is especially true of any mulch that contains alfalfa. Mulch also keeps the roots of the surrounding plants cool and holds moisture—especially important during the heat of the day and in dry periods.

Why go to all the trouble to spread leaves, straw—or in the case of trees, bark—when you can just lay down fabric weed barriers? This stuff was originally designed to place behind rock or block walls to prevent soil erosion and prevent weeds growing in said walls. Yes, it does hold weeds down for about 2 years. After that, annual weeds will land on it and take root. Perennials will eventually push their way through it, tough as it is. Worse yet, it reduces oxygenation of the soil and prohibits spread of groundcovers or plants you want to self-seed. If it is laid under rock mulch, it will eventually get full of litter and dirt and have to be removed. It is a nightmare to plant through. And, it slows or even prevents moisture from getting through it.

Never, never use rock mulch around live plants. Even worse, is rock on top of the weed fabric. The rock heats in the summer and fries the small feeder roots just under it. If you must use rock, put your plants in pots and set them on top of the mulch. You will need to water them much more often as the hot rocks will heat up the soil in the pots, drying them out much more quickly than if they were on the deck or, better yet, on bare soil. Putting rock on top of fabric makes everything worse. The fabric lets dirt and debris stay on top of the soil. As a consequence, the rock needs to be cleaned periodically. This entails removing the rock, hosing off the fabric and returning the rock to the area.

Organic mulch—composted compost, chopped leaves, pine straw, cocoa hulls, anything that once was alive—will eventually rot and improve the soil. It even will make clay soil loose and fluffy. After several years of mulching soil, you will be able to plant peas by simply pushing them into the soil. And as mulch also adds to the fertility of the soil, those peas will fly out of the ground and grow like Jack's beanstalk. Plant and run.

Using damp newspapers under the mulch will not only help prevent weeds from popping though, but when tilled in with the mulch in the fall also helps lighten the soil. After all, paper is a wood product. Just don't use the colored section. That ink may or may not be soy-based, as is the black ink.

Gardeners come from the earth, and eventually, like mulch, return to the earth. In between, we garden.

Have you ever wondered what was in the city compost, and what is it good for? Since it usually is strictly yard waste with no added soil or manure, it is very low in nitrogen, high in potassium and moderate in phosphorus and calcium. This compost is very high in organic content, averaging 70%. Add this to heavy soil to improve the texture. Add to sandy soil to improve water retention. Add to the flower garden to improve blooming. Add to the vegetable garden and the calcium will help prevent blossom end rot on tomatoes (the calcium content). In other words, this is good stuff.

And speaking about fertilizers, don't get stung. Take kelp, for instance. It is usually a major ingredient in "bioenhancers." It is supposed to boost plant growth, make the plant more resistant to disease, pests and stress. It's snake oil. Doesn't do a thing. How about extra phosphate for bigger flowers and better roots? In this case, yes, but a little goes a long way. Too much and the plant can't take up enough iron, causing yellow leaves. And how about Epsom salts, which is really only magnesium sulfate? Most garden soils have enough already. Then there are the dusts one is supposed to put on pea seeds to enhance mycorrhizal spores. Healthy soil has plenty of them. If your soil is so damaged it has none, adding packaged spores won't help. Instead, add compost. It has all sorts of healthy components.

Much of this information about fertilizers came from Linda Chalker-Scott, an extension urban horticulturist at Washington State University. If you want to learn more about fertilizers and soil conditioners, look for her book *How Plants Work*.

Many gardeners swear by beer as a fertilizer. It is supposed to be good for root growth. Others just drink it.

Mulching

Petunia put Bunkey in charge of raising vegetables, she does the flowers. That being the case, you would have found Bunkey on his hands and knees these early spring mornings, mulching the garden. He first lays 4 to 6 layers of damp newspapers between the rows, then covers them in leaves. The newspapers have been marinating outside the back door since he started collecting them around Halloween. He bundles them up and hopes he has enough damp papers by spring to cover the garden. The leaves have been piled behind a fence all winter too. To get enough, he regularly picks up his neighbors' leaves. It takes him about 20 hours to completely mulch the garden. He is willing to do the work now so he can go fishing and forget the garden the rest of the summer. The only weeding that will need to be done are weeds that pop up in the vegetable rows and they can be pulled as he is harvesting. Bunkey is not a lazy gardener, he just hates working in the garden when it is 95 degrees with matching humidity, as often happen in the summer. There are better ways to spend those days. Inside an air-conditioned house reading, for instance.

Bunkey learned several things at Garden Day. (You mean you didn't see him? He had a Hawaiian shirt on with his long chartreuse shorts, flip flops and a big floppy hat as a disguise.) Most mulch doesn't remove nitrogen from the soil. The exception is bark or sawdust. Sawdust isn't recommended, as it forms a crust and the water runs off it.

You only need to mulch a tree to the drip line. Be careful not to get close to the trunk as this can cause rot resulting in the loss of the tree.

Keep It Cool

Bunkey isn't too fond of weeding, especially when the air temperatures are in triple digits and the humidity is not far behind. Shortly after he moved to his present home, his neighbor, George the Master Gardener, tipped him off to mulching. George quoted Jill Clapperton, the principal scientist for a company called Rhizoterra in Florence, Montana. She maintains that providing shade to the soil, that is, by mulching, you not only reduce evaporation but also keep "underground livestock, (earth worms, soil microbes and other beneficials), cool and working for the gardener." If the soil gets too hot, worms will migrate deep in the soil to find water and avoid the heat.

Another expert, J.J. McEntire, a USDA scientist, said as early as 1956 that 100% of moisture is used by the plant for growth when the soil temp is 70 degrees. When the soil temp hits 100, only 15% is used for growth. The rest is lost to evaporation and plant transpiration. When the soil reaches 130 degrees, all moisture is lost and at 140 degrees, most of the soil bacteria die.

McEntire contends that when the soil temp is 68 degrees, most organisms in the soil have "fully functioning populations and are actively reproducing. There is lots of mineralization going on and plant roots are taking full advantage of this activity. Mycorrhizal fungi also work at the same optimal temp so there is high speed transport of nutrients going on." In plain English, the plants are growing like weeds.

Bunkey has been mulching, using 4 to 6 layers of damp newspaper under his mulch. Last week he was poking around a hardware store (guys do this for entertainment, you know), when he discovered a shortcut. There, right in front of him was a roll of heavy brown paper, 3 feet wide. This building paper is thick enough to prevent seed sprouting and sturdier than wet newspaper. (He had put his knee though newspaper more often than he wanted to admit.) Not only that, if he laid newsprint on a stick, the stick popped right through it, leaving a nice hole for a weed to pop up. He still needed the newspaper in some spots, but rolling out feet of paper cover rather than laying a few feet at a time made for quick work of mulching.

When mulching, don't put the mulch right up to your plants. This can lead to rotting of the plant. Of course, this means that there will be weeds in the rows but Bunkey, (or more often, Petunia) simply pulls the weeds as she harvests. Even though there may be enough moisture in the soil now, we know there will be weeks with no rain. Since Bunkey waters with city water (and he is so tight with money, the buffalo on his nickels bellow), he wants to conserve any moisture he has. Mulching in a dry period can reduce soil evaporation by as much as 2 inches, and that is a 2-weeks supply of moisture.

Get down on your knees and mulch. Your back may be achy and your knees worn out of your jeans at the end of the day, but you will be able to sit under a tree and have a cold one when it's 100 above and so wet that moss is growing on your north side.

Gardeners, Should You Use Peat Moss?

The use of peat moss in gardening is fairly recent. Before the mid-1900s it was mostly unavailable. Then Canada discovered that about 11% of its land is covered in peatlands, about 279 million acres of the stuff. So why should gardeners be concerned about using it if there is so much of it and Canada can surely use the money?

First of all, sphagnum moss grows less than 3 inches in a century. This means that, to amass the 2-meter depth needed to justify the costs of harvest, a fully-mined peat bog will not be able to be harvested again for at least 3,000 years.

Second, not every bog can be harvested. It must have moss deep enough, be in an area that has dry spells occasionally, and the bog must drain readily. Only a dry bog can be harvested, and then only with very specialized machines. The bog must also have access to roads, a work force and electricity. There are few areas in Canada where all these things come together.

And third, consider the carbon load of peat moss. Peat is the partially-decomposed remains of plants, most commonly sphagnum moss. The moss grows on the surface of the bog. The older parts of the plant are underwater in oxygen-poor water. This lack of oxygen slows decomposition dramatically, preserving the moss and anything that might fall or be pushed into it. Remember the bodies found nearly intact in Ireland's bogs? They were thousands of years old, but almost perfectly preserved.

It takes millions of years before the dense, absorbent material gardeners buy by the bag is usable. If left alone, the process doesn't stop there. A few eons down the road it will become coal, and we all know about dirty coal. In other words, peat moss is a baby fossil fuel, rich in carbon. A 2009 article in the journal *Science* claimed that "meter for meter, peatlands store more carbon than any other terrestrial ecosystem," approximately 562 million tons of the stuff. That carbon is released when peat decays, just as coal does when burned. When the bog is drained, it releases carbon. Some mined bogs continue to exhale carbon even long after mining, often despite habitat-restoration attempts.

There are other options. *Coir* is a fiber found on coconut shells. The coconut tree stores carbon, as other trees do. The fiber is harvested from the outside of coconut shells. While it still may produce carbon as it rots, it is a much more sustainable material as coconuts only take months, not eons to become usable.

The use of peat moss won't stop any time soon, but "green" gardeners will reduce their use of it, or at least look for more sustainable substitutes. Coconut trees grow in wide areas of the world—even in Ireland, believe it or not.

Rock Shock

Did you buy into the rock-as-mulch movement? Don Engebretson, a landscaper, notes that nowhere on earth do plants spring from beds of 1- to 1½- inch gravel. It just looks "bizarrely unnatural," he says.

The movement to rock mulch started in the 1950s and 60s, and unfortunately continues to this day. Engebretson calls rock mulch on top of black plastic *horticultural homicide*, or maybe it should be *planticide*. Even though holes are cut in the plastic to stick the plants in, the holes are too small for the plant to get either enough water or oxygen for proper growth. This lack actually kills off the essential microbial activity needed, resulting in a nearly dead environment for anything planted in such conditions. The plants attempt to send out roots, but the soil has no food for them. Then to really put the cap on the planticide, the sun heats the rock, raising the soil temperatures near the surface to abnormal levels and killing any roots that may have sprouted there. Any roots attempting to grow under the plastic are stunted by the heat.

So the gardener switches the plastic to landscape cloth. That solves the problem, right? Wrong! The stuff is only minimally porous and the rock still heats up the soil. Not only that, "Martha" types have to rake off the rock and wash the dirt from rock and plastic about once a year. The solution? Get rid of the rock. Engebretson apparently has dealt with the problem. Here are his suggestions.

- Determine how much rock you need to get rid of, that is if you can't pawn it off on an unsuspecting neighbor. Dig by hand in 3 or 4 places to see how deep the stuff actually is. If you have a lot of it, rent a roll-off dumpster. A 10-yard dumpster should have an end gate that swings open. Make a ramp up to it for your wheelbarrow. Maybe you should also rent a few football players, as rock is not light.
- Wrap your shrubs in six-inch shrink wrap. Start at the bottom, tie the end of the wrap to a sturdy branch and wrap to make it as small as possible.
- If the rock hasn't been "Martha-ed" it will be stuck together with dirt. You will need to rake this into piles first. A straight-edged shovel works best if the rock is reasonably clean.
- Pull up the plastic or fabric, add some organic fertilizer and water it in. Now mulch with organic mulch, shredded bark, wood chips, leaves or pine straw. You will have much happier plants. The down side is they may grow too big for their space. Another reason not to plant shrubs too close to the house.

While this can't be done in the winter, it is something to look forward to in the spring. By the way, this doesn't apply to rock gardens. They aren't usually mulched with rock.

Beware the Freebie!

Or in other words, never accept a plant that comes from a filled wheelbarrow.

There are some plants a smart gardener never plants, that is, unless you are planning to cover a cliff. They go under the unassuming name of "groundcover," and boy do they! They start out as cute little mounds, but turn your back and they are half an acre away, climbing the neighbor's fence and heading for the nearest freeway.

Here is a partial list of obnoxious plants.

- Bishop's weed or snow-on-the-mountain (*Aegopodium podagraia Variegeta*). This plant has very pretty green and white leaves and nondescript flowers. It will grow in full sun to dark shade. The roots are very aggressive and difficult to get rid of. It has been seen growing 2 feet out on a cement walk.
- Gooseneck loosestrife (*Lysimachia clethroides*). A very pretty, 2- to 3-foot-tall perennial. It has arching white flowers, thus the gooseneck name. It has fast-spreading roots and grows in full sun to part shade. Actually, you should beware of any plant that has "loosestrife" in its name.
- Japanese knotweed (*Fallopia japonica*). She also has arching stems, but with cluster of airy pink flowers. Again, 2 to 3 feet tall, spreads by root and very hard to kill once established.
- Oriental limelight (*Artemisia Artemisia vulgaris Janlim*). Truly vulgar, this is a perennial with yellow-streaked green leaves. It grows in full sun, is 2 feet to 3 feet tall and up to 30 inches wide. It spreads by underground runners.

- Ribbon grass (*phalaris arundinacea picta*). Why anyone would plant grass is a mystery to Bunkey. He spends most of the summer pulling the stuff out of flowerbeds. However, there is no accounting for taste. Ribbon grass is a variegated green and white grass that spreads very quickly by roots. It will grow to 4 feet tall and 5 feet wide right before your eyes. Like other grasses, it's very difficult to eradicate.

There are other monster plants out there, including monarda (spreads underground), hardy geranium (she loves to hide in taller plants), Canada white violet, and a bellflower (looks like a drumstick). These all spread, most often in places it is difficult for you to reach to murder them. Sometimes, planticide is the only option.

Types of Gardens

You didn't know there was more than one?

Your Own Greenhouse

Bunkey decided he has enough "gardening smarts" to start his plants in his own greenhouse. Before he starts, there are a few things he needs to know. For instance, he may or may not recover the cost of the building for years, especially if he is only supplying his own garden. If that is not a problem, here are a few tips to help him build the best, most efficient greenhouse he can afford.

One of the most important things Bunkey needs to do is site the building properly. For best results, it needs to have full sun on 3 sides, east, west and south. If he must choose only 2, drop west. Full sun, remember, is from 8 to 5, business hours. Ideally the north side should be protected with either another building, the landscape, a hill or a copse of trees.

Now, what to build it of? Sliding doors work well, as they have double panes. Storm windows work, but will leak more heat. A commercial greenhouse usually has all 4 sides clear. In Minnesota, that's not the best use of clear material. A kit will allow Bunkey to build a building with 3 clear sides, saving the extra material to make it a bit larger.

Kits and commercial greenhouses can either be glass—a bit tricky here in hail and strong wind country (think *flying tree branches*)—or polycarbonate, a better choice. It comes in either single sheets, twin or triple wall. The latter 2 look like clear corrugated cardboard and are quite heat saving.

If Bunkey were planning a 3-season building, it should be at least 4 feet wide, 8 if possible. This will allow for grow lights. They are just fluorescent shop lights with 1 bathroom/kitchen bulb (warm) and 1 regular blue one (cool).

Now, for heat. Electricity can be iffy. In storms, it can go out and leave your plants to freeze. Propane is more reliable. Do vent it through the roof to prevent CO build up if the wind changes.

Flooring should be a heat sink (bricks, tile, etc.) that will hold heat once heated up. It should be easy to sweep, as planting is a messy job. Another heat source is heat tape. Build your main shelf with a 2-inch-high edge. Fill the resulting trough with sand and bury a heat tape in the sand. This will keep the plants' feet warm even if it is cool on their leaves.

The very best use of the north side of the building is as a potting shed. It needs shelves, a table to pot on and soil storage. Bunkey has let his neighbors know his building plans and asked them to save used pots. By fall, he will find huge garbage bags of pots appearing, apparently by magic.

Every gardener would love a home greenhouse. What a great Christmas or birthday gift from a gardener's partner.

Better Beds

Why would anyone go to the work and expense of building raised beds? Lets' start with backaches. We are all getting older and getting down on your knees to weed or pull carrots can be, quite literally, a pain. Or maybe, you are a "competitive" gardener. You want the first ripe tomatoes in the neighborhood.

It could be the soil you have been dealt. Heavy clay—or its opposite, sand—can be difficult to grow in. Raised beds not only warm up earlier in the spring, they also have excellent drainage, especially nice if you have been dealing with clay in the past. A raised bed prevents creeping charlie, crabgrass or other sneaky weeds from getting into the garden. Even charlie can't climb a 2-foot wall. However, snow-on-the-mountain would sure make a try at it.

If you have no place or desire for a regular garden, a raised bed will give you fresh vegetables or a bouquet of flowers and the hummingbirds and butterflies that come with them.

If you actually do have great soil, but are dealing with drainage problems, a raised bed could be only 6 inches high. If, however, it's the stooping that gets you, shoot for at least 2 feet. Most plants need at least 12 to 18 inches of good soil to do well. Small shrubs will demand 2 feet of soil, and forget about a raised bed for a tree. There just is not enough soil in one, unless it's huge, to protect the roots from our freezing winters. Make the bed at least 18 inches wide so you can reach all of it. It can be 6 feet wide if you can get at it from all sides.

Now, what materials are available?

- *Pressure treated lumber.* Never use this for anything you plan to eat. The chemicals it is treated with can leach into the soil. Wear a dust mask and goggles when you cut it, wash your hands right away to prevent ingestion and never burn the scraps. The good part: it lasts about 20 years and is quite cheap.
- *Cedar, redwood and other rot-resistant woods.* Can be expensive and hard to find in needed dimensions. It should be treated with deck sealer to prolong life. The good part is that it is beautiful and long-lasting.
- *Landscape timbers, not railroad ties.* They are expensive if you are building a large bed, and they need reinforcing rods if you have more than 2 layers. The good part: they are easy to place as they are big and heavy (get a football player to help lay them).
- *Raised bed kits.* Expensive for what you get, but quick to assemble and great for square-foot gardening.
- *Brick.* Gorgeous, classic and versatile. You can curve the bed or make it round. Always use brick fired for outdoor use. The other kind crumbles. The bad thing: it's expensive and takes time and expertise to do well.
- *Flagstones or boulders.* Flat flagstones stack easily. Boulders or field rocks, not so much. Can be very attractive. The bed will need to be lined with landscape fabric to prevent leakage of soil. The bad part: smashed fingers, lots of time to get them to fit tightly. You don't want them rolling off the wall. Can be expensive if you need to buy them.

- *Concrete block.* Cheap, easy to stack but not very attractive, and you should use metal rods if stacked over 2 high.
- *Landscape block.* Cheap, easy to use, comes in the shape of bricks or cut stones or the pie-shaped pieces that can make curves. Do buy the cap pieces to make the bed look more finished.

The Ultimate Raised Bed

If you have wanted a raised bed but didn't want to buy the cement blocks or treated lumber or railroad ties (the last two need liners)—or just don't have the energy to build one—this may be a solution for you.

An Austrian farmer, Sepp Holzer, made a name for himself by taking very poor land in an area called the "Siberia" of Europe and turning it into one of the most productive farms in his country, and he did it the easy way.

It's called *Hugelkultur.*

Simply take a pile of logs, stumps and brush and cover it with good soil. You now have a raised bed loaded with organic material, nutrients, and air pockets. As the years pass, the soil becomes extremely rich. The wood shrinks as it ages, making smaller air pockets and becomes almost self-tilling. The first few years, the pile will heat as it composts. Use this to your advantage by planting a bit earlier than you normally would.

What a neat way to get rid of unwanted, dead trees. If you put live branches in the pile, it should heat more quickly. Add some grass clippings or green weeds: almost instant hot compost. The pile has natural air pockets encouraging composting and you have no after-care.

If you don't have trees and branches to start this type of plantable compost pile, or don't have room for a pile like this, start small. A whiskey barrel is an excellent planter. Because it is quite deep, most people fill it at least half full with empty pop cans, Styrofoam or even old planting containers.

Start by filling your container about half full with cardboard, newspaper, grass clippings, old blue jeans and manure, keeping in mind that you want three parts brown to one-part green. Now fill the top half with potting soil. You should get the same effect as the woodpile: the compost will heat and decompose. You will need to have a way for the bottom half to get aerated. A perforated pipe stuck in the middle of your barrel should do the trick. You can add water to the planter through the pipe, ensuring it gets all the way to the bottom of the planter. Do have good drainage in your barrel or your plants will need rubber boots in rainy weather.

It's worth a try. Even if it takes several years to compost, you have gotten rid of a lot of paper and had fun experimenting.

What Goes In a Raised Bed?

Now that you have your raised bed built, what are you going to put in it? Start with the soil. You know we all go back to the soil eventually, but only the garden does it while still alive. We want live soil in our beds. Start with the best soil you can buy. If it doesn't look and smell good, refuse it.

Mix as much compost into the soil as you can get your hands on. Don't just layer different soils or compost in your bed. Different soils have different pore sizes and water has a difficult time passing between them. Mix it before you put it in the bed. Forget rocks or gravel or anything else in the bottom of the bed. Again, it may just stop the water from draining. If the bed is to be on top of moderately good soil, dig lots of compost into it before you add soil on top. This will help any roots that get that far down.

Next, consider what type of plants are going into the bed. Most annuals, including tomatoes, need from 12 to 18 inches of soil to grow well. A small ornamental shrub needs more, up to 3 feet deep and 3 feet wide and long.

If you are in a wheelchair, don't make the bed wider than you can reach sitting down. That is usually 18 inches in all directions. If you can find a good builder, have a cut-out built into the bed for the chair to fit under. The shallower sides can be planted to annuals while the middles can take deeper-rooted plants.

Tomatoes and vine crops can be trained to grow on a trellis or some type of frame. This will give you more room for plants below and around the vines. Bush cucumbers are short enough to hang over a 2- to 3-foot-tall bed. Because you won't have a lot of room to deal with, plan on succession planting. Start with radishes, lettuce and spinach. When they are done, the carrots planted with the radishes will take over. A celery plant can grow in the lettuce row and spread when the lettuce is pulled out and composted. The tomato will be small enough to go in back of the radishes. Peas can be on a trellis, pulled in late June and replanted the first part of July for a fall crop. The spring vegetables, radish and lettuce can be replanted then too—if the tomatoes haven't taken over. You can plant almost every vegetable or flower (other than corn) in a planter.

If you are planting flowers, keep them deadheaded, and if they get scraggly trim them to keep the planter looking good all summer. Plan for fall when you plant—an annual grass or late bloomer is the base for a fall show. Pull out any tired annuals, add a potted mum or two and maybe a gourd and you have a whole new look to your bed. For winter, evergreen boughs or tree tops with or without lights, a Christmas deer or snowman, or whatever you can find for a Christmas display and you are golden. Pull the Christmas ornament in January, add some bird suet balls or dry cookies or other bird treats and you have a fresh look. It all comes out in April when you add a fresh layer of soil and plant.

Because the planter has a limited amount of soil in it, you will need to fertilize your bed. Use a liquid fertilizer at half strength weekly, along with a long-acting granular fertilizer dug into the soil. This will keep all your plants fat and happy. Happy plants make for a happy gardener.

Horse Trough Gardening

Most gardeners are cautious people. While they are willing to try new things, they also want to be sure that whatever the new thing is, it is not damaging to the environment or their health. That is why there were questions about using galvanized cattle watering containers for raised beds. What is in the coating, and will it leach into the soil? If it does leach, what are the consequences for the person eating the tomato that grew in the container?

The answer is, yes, the compounds in the galvanizing process will leach into the soil. How much leaching is determined by climate and soil conditions, like moisture and salinity. The amount of leaching of zinc and other materials is usually not a concern, since zinc is an essential micronutrient that occurs naturally in our soil. An average background level is 0.07 milligrams per gram of soil. Not a whole heck of a lot since our daily need for it, established by the FDA, is 8 to 11 milligrams for a full grown gardener.

Zinc is the main ingredient in the galvanizing bath used to coat and prolong the life of steel. Increased levels of it have been found in the soil next to the walls of the galvanized container, the level comparable to normal soil background levels and within EPA guidelines. It doesn't readily migrate through soil, so the elevated levels of zinc tend to be only in the immediate area of the wall of the container.

Soil pH, organic matter and other soil characteristics affect zinc's ability to be taken up by plant roots. As much as 90% of zinc in the soil may be unavailable for the plant to take up. This means there is little chance that you will get too much of the mineral from eating that carrot that grew next to the container wall. Actually, you won't even get your needed daily amount from it. Other metals found in galvanized surfaces are bismuth and nickel. These too are typically so low that you probably would never see any difference in the amount you ingest, other than what is normally found in your garden.

There are plants you don't want to plant in your horse trough. Blueberries, for instance. They need an acid soil, and acid will corrode the galvanized metal much faster as the pH decreases.

One consideration is the health of beneficial soil microorganisms that are exposed to galvanization. Zinc can kill some of the soil's microbes and others just love it.

Jeff Lowelfels, the author of *Teaming with Microbes: The Organic Gardener's Guide to Optimizing Plant Nutrition* (say that one twice) says, "I am willing to let arbuscular mycorrhizal fungi take up excess zinc, feed the plants and hold the rest" (of the zinc). He feels that any damage done to the soil food web by excess zinc is quickly corrected by it if the soil is healthy.

The takeaway here is to go ahead and fill your horse watering trough with good soil, plant it and eat any produce without fear that you will not need to be embalmed because you are full of chemicals. Of course, that is only true if you don't make a habit of eating lots of artificial foods, like corn curls. Then you might even glow in the dark.

Lazy Gardeners Love Shade

So you can't grow grass in that shady spot—so what? It's a perfect place to make the most enchanting and visually alluring part of your landscape.

Start by amending the soil with compost and/or composted manure and peat. Most shady spots are also dry, so you want the soil to hold moisture. Then decide on a centerpiece. It can be a small patio, a fountain, garden art, a large rock or even an interesting stump.

The next step is to pick plants that have contrasting shapes, color and sizes. Huge hostas can add large spots of subtle color. The blue ones especially do well in shade. The lighter colors—the yellows, chartreuse, and white spotted or striped hostas—will not be as bright, but still will be an accent. Add some ferns and you have an exotic background for a bench. If you want more color, throw in some coleus. They come in all kinds of colors and mixes.

There are many flowering plants that do quite well in full or light shade. If you are a rock collector, it's a perfect place to display them. Large rocks should be partially buried to look natural. A few smaller ones scattered here and there can accent a special plant. A large flat rock can be a stage for a piece of garden art that otherwise would be too small to see well. An old watering can, a child's toy or an odd piece of metal all painted a bright blue and scattered in your new planting can bring it all together. Use your imagination.

Anything can be garden art if you want it to be. One thing you do not want to do is cover any tree roots with soil. Instead, dig between the roots for a planting hole. Amend the soil and pop in a plant.

Rock walls will develop a nice touch of moss in the shade. Fountains don't turn green as fast and don't run dry as quickly as they do in full sun. Birds are more apt to use a shaded bird bath—they can zip up to the tree it's under for the rest of its toilet. It takes time to get all those feathers back in the proper place after all.

If you enjoy watching the birds, install a water feature. Leave one area quite shallow with lots of noise from water running over rocks. Robins love this. They will do the breast stroke across a shallow spot. Many birds that are too shy to come to a regular bird bath are attracted to the sound of running water.

What Does Well In the Shade?

Many gardeners have no idea that there are so many plants that do well in shade. Impatiens are the first flower that comes to most minds. Some years there is a problem with that most popular plant—it has been decimated by downy mildew. The symptoms: yellow or stippled leaves, leaves that curl downward, white downy growth on the undersides of the leaves, leaf and flower drop and total plant collapse. At this time, there is no cure. They may have been infected before you brought them home and the mildew developed once they have been planted. If your plants are affected, dig the plants up, roots and all, put them in a sealed bag and drop them in the trash. Don't try to compost them. The pile just doesn't get hot enough to kill the *Plasmopara obducens*.

There are many alternatives. *Sunpatiens* for one. They are not affected by the disease. They are easy to grow and spread more widely than the regular impatiens. Then there are the begonias. The wax leaf begonia has small flowers in pink, red and white. Tuberous begonias have a much larger flower and in more colors.

Coleus come in multiple colors, leaf shapes and sizes. Some will even do well in full sun. Cut the blooms off as soon as you can since the plants tend to go downhill after blooming. Another plant with colorful leaves is the caladium. It can be pink, red, white, green or a combination of those colors.

If you need trailing plants, think fuchsia. It too comes in many color combinations. There is also a dwarf bedding type. The only drawback to the trailing type of fuchsia is their tendency to break off in a strong wind. The hanging begonias also have this weakness.

Looking for blue? Wishbone flower (*Torenia*) is a blue/purple front-of-the-border flower that will grow in shade. *Nicotiana* or flowering tobacco is another flowering annual to consider for your dark spaces.

There are always houseplants that like shade—Wandering Jew, croton, Dracaena, philodendron and Chinese evergreen for instance. Of course, all your houseplants love a summer vacation outside in the dense shade. Why not use them for shade accent? Leave them in the pots (bury the pots or conceal them with bedding plants). Two birds with one pot!

If you are looking for perennials (the others were all annuals), there are more choices than hostas. Coral bells (*Heuchera*) have a wide range of leaf colors from greens, browns, pinks, speckled and shades of gold. Wegiela is a small shrub that has pink or red blooms. Get adventurous. Put some color in those dark spaces.

That Difficult Shady Area

Bunkey noticed last week that the patch of grass under his oak tree looks bare. Petunia reminded him that it has looked that way ever since they moved there. Although he isn't a grass fanatic like Olaf down the street, Bunkey does like to keep the place looking good. His neighbor, George, has planted *ajuga*, a shade-tolerant groundcover, under his oak tree.

In the next block, Marion has transformed a problem of only patchy sun by building slightly-raised beds around clumps of three oaks in one spot and five maples in another. These beds are a riot of color and texture. The maples have dappled shade, so she was able to put plants that will tolerate some shade in that bed. It is full of lilies, exotic ferns, wild-colored Heucheras, interesting rocks and light colored hostas. The deeply-shaded beds around the oak also have hostas and ferns, along with brunnera, astilbe, bleeding heart and lamium around the edge for a silvery accent.

There are many groundcovers that are plant-and-forget, other than to keep them from heading for the neighbors. Native violets,

White Canada violet, ajuga in one of its several colors, yellow or silver lamium, and sweet woodruff are all low growing. For a fuller look, pachysandra is six to ten inches tall. A simple ring of wide-leaved hostas in the bare area around a single tree makes an elegant fix for a problem spot.

Do not add soil around a tree. Instead, dig pockets between the roots and add better soil to those areas.

Do be aware that groundcovers do just that, they cover the ground—sometimes very rapidly and more widely than you may like. Just think of creeping charlie, an excellent groundcover for poor, shady soil that everyone loves to hate.

Depending on your tolerance, you can just let them fly or confine them to a definite area. The best thing about groundcovers is that you don't have to mow them. You may have to weed them until they get well established, however.

September is a good time to get started on this project, as the weather is cooler for the gardener. You only sweat a gallon an hour, not buckets. And better yet, plants are on sale now and have enough time to get very well established for a nice look in the spring.

Dark Corners

One corner of Bunkey and Petunia's lot is very shady. There is an old spruce tree on the north side of it and a maple on the west, making for a very dark, dank area where nothing except an occasional mushroom grows. Petunia loves flowers and has always decried the fact that she couldn't grow anything in that area. Then, last week, the wind tore down the spruce, taking a fence and a corner of the garage with it. While Bunkey called the insurance company, Petunia was planning the new garden for that corner.

There was still shade once the spruce was removed, but the area was no longer deep, dense and dank. A trip to the nursery resulted in a car full of plants Petunia had only dreamed of having. Her neighbor George, the Master Gardener, cautioned her not to get in too much of a hurry to plant. To start, she would need to amend the soil with compost, as the trees had probably depleted it of much of the nutrients needed for new plantings. Also, trees are greedy, keeping most of the resources to themselves. And she needed to be careful planting under trees as too much disturbance of the roots can hurt or even kill a tree, maples and oaks being most susceptible. The trick is to get small plants, dig holes no larger than needed and don't add soil on top of the tree's roots.

Now, what to plant. It seems many shade plants are mounds (think *hostas*). To make a planting interesting you need color, contrast and texture. More vertical and/or flowering plants are needed. (Think *ferns.*) A hybrid called *Ghost* is a standout. The deep burgundy midribs contrast with the silver-sparked leaves of this Japanese painted fern. Another vertical but little-used plant is our native Solomon's seal. The variegated cultivar has a bright green oval leaf with a thin yellow white edge. For color, try one of the hellebores. They take a little TLC to get going, as do many long-lived plants, but the spring show is worth it. They can be pale pink, dark pink, white with pink edges, or yellow with orange or red tips. Eventually the clump will be about 2 feet wide and 18 inches tall with blooms up to 3 inches wide. Astilbe, a frothy spire of blooms, come in white and shades of red and pink and from 2 to 5 feet tall.

Another plant with texture is Canadian wild ginger. A cultivar to look for is *Asarum Saruma*. It gets 2 feet tall and has a showy, soft yellow flower that starts in late May and continues off and on through June. The native bloodroot has a similar leaf shape. It also blooms in May with round white flowers held above the leaves. Both plants stay green all summer, unlike some spring bloomers. Spring bulbs can give that corner a bright start. Daffs and the minor bulbs will be done blooming by the time the trees leaf out. For fall color, look to toad lilies, an ugly name for an interesting flower. Plant her where she won't get killed by an early frost and she will bloom in September. The flowers are carried up and down an arched stem and spotted as a freckled redhead. A more durable cultivar than most is *Tricyrtis hirta*.

There are many other flowers and foliage plants available for that dark spot in your yard. Limbing up trees to introduce dappled shade will give you a larger selection to plant, especially if you want blooming plants. You don't have to relegate those dark corners to toads and their furniture.

It's Just Plain Yukky Out

In mid-April in Minnesota, everything is either tan or brown—yukky! The bare spots you have been trying to ignore stand out like kneecaps on a Chickadee.

If you are dealing with dense shade, under an oak tree for instance, about all you can do is mulch the area. Dress it up with stepping stones and people will think you are a great landscaper.

If, however, the bare area gets some sun, either all over for a few hours, or dappled shade all day, there are options. If you have an east-facing slope, vinca is the answer. All it needs is a few hours of sun, then shade for the rest of the day. It spreads by roots, is easy to pull up if it creeps into a forbidden area, and best of all, it blooms with small bright blue flowers held just above shiny oval leaves.

There are always the natives. Bloodroot has large-lobed leaves that persist all summer. It blooms with a pretty white flower in early spring. Add Solomon's seal, either variegated or all green for the mid height, and native ferns for the tall background. All the care you will need is to keep the area watered in the hot days of summer. The 3 shades of green are very soothing to the eye when it's 95 above and no end in sight.

If you want a little sparkle under the trees, look for *Lamium maculatum, Pink Pewter.* The leaves on this shade plant are silver with green edges. It blooms in early summer with pale pink flowers. It spreads fast and is a great groundcover. If it starts looking tacky, just cut back hard. The light color of the leaves and blooms really stand out in the shade. It likes part shade, but will tolerate nearly full shade.

Another silver-leaved plant is *Brunnera*. It blooms in early spring with airy blue flowers. This part-shade plant takes a bit more care. The flowers should be cut back after blooming to encourage the plant to form a nice mound of leaves. It can get 18 inches tall and each plant will be 18 to 24 inches wide

Hostas are always an option. They come in every size from 2 inches tall and wide, to *Empress Wo* who spreads many feet tall and wide. Picture her filling that empty spot in the shady corner. One plant and you're done.

Japanese painted fern will grow in dry shade. Most other shade plants need moist soil. This fern has silvery fringed leaves and can lend a light, airy look to the shaded area.

All these plants will do better with a mulch to keep the soil cool, damp and weed free. Leaves make the most natural looking mulch. Bark is usually too bold a look.

If you have had issues with slugs, you will want to treat your shady groundcovers early in the spring, as soon as you see green sprouts. Most treatments only need to be applied once. Look for the iron-based granules. They are safe for the pets, that is unless your pet is a banana slug. Make your shady spot an accent, not a detriment.

A shady garden will grow fewer weeds and take less water, so it will take less time to keep it looking great. Build a pergola or a gazebo in your shaded corner. It is a perfect place to not only bird watch, but to curl up with a good book and pitcher of lemonade on a hot day. Love your shady spot. It makes for easy gardening.

A No-Weed Garden

Yes, there is actually one garden you never have to weed: a water garden. Water gardens are the perfect solution for the gardener who no longer can get down on his/her knees to weed and get up again without a crane.

Your garden can be in anything that holds water. Go hunting. That old metal wagon your kids loved so much you just couldn't part with, the metal wheelbarrow propped up in the corner, an old washtub, or how about that huge punchbowl that sits in the back of the closet. Or, go bigger and more complicated—dig out that flowerbed that never did well and landscape it with a series of ponds with waterfalls, lighting and a sitting area where you can enjoy the splashing water after a long hot day. If you are one for instant gratification, there are pond liners made for whiskey barrels, or even ready-to-go water gardens already planted. Don't use an unlined wood container. It can harbor bacteria that can harm both plants and the animals that are attracted to it.

Now to plant your new garden. What will do well depends on how much water your container holds, its diameter and depth, where it is located (shade or sun), and your pocketbook. Ponds do best when about 1/3 of their water surface is plant covered. A smaller container can hold more, but do read and follow the instructions on the plant tag. You want to be able to see water.

Many plants float serenely on the water surface; however, you may want some grasses or even miniature cattails in your pond. It not necessary to buy special pots for these plants. Any plastic or clay pot will do. Do be careful of soil type. If there is peat in it, you will very shortly have a nice tan to brown pool.

Clay is often the best for water plants. Cover the clay with rocks or sand to help it stay where you want it. You will need to fertilize these plants just as you would with regular garden plants. Get the pellets where you got your plants.

If you feel no pond is complete without fish, you will be adding some work. They are pets and need food and care. They need the right water conditions, not too hot or cold. If the water is too shallow, the rapid change of temperature on a hot day will bake them nicely. Some materials are toxic to fish.

And then there are the predators. Raccoons, cats and some birds will really enjoy an easy meal of your flashy pets. Then there is the problem with what to do with them in the winter. If the pond is deep enough, a cattle heater will keep a hole in the ice open for oxygen in the winter. Or a tub with a bubbler and light in the corner off the basement may do it. If nothing else, it will keep your cats entertained.

Some water lilies can be perennial if properly over-wintered, or you can just plan on them being annuals. In a pond you will need plants that add oxygen and help maintain the proper pH of the water. Two to look for are parrot feather and hornwort. For floaters, there are water lettuce and water hyacinth. Your seller should be able to help you choose the proper plants for your garden.

Never dump unwanted pond plants in lakes. They may become invasive pests.

While you never need to weed a water garden, you will still have gardening chores to do to keep it healthy and looking good. After all, you don't want to sit and rust out. You're a gardener and we don't do *sit, stay* well.

Bernice's Water Garden

It took nearly 18 years, loads of rocks, and lots of digging, engineering and plumbing to make Tim and Bernice Overland's backyard "water noisy." The noise is from an artificial stream and two ponds with accompanying waterfalls, a very pleasant noise on hot days. The stream and a bridge over it are a late addition, adding motion to the water.

The ponds are home to colorful koi, tropical water lilies and a few potted water plants. The ponds are surrounded by beautiful plantings. There are ferns that Bernice dug locally, "pass on plants" from her mother-in-law and mulched beds of perennials. There are yellow and orange Asiatic lilies, purple liatris, a creeping, yellow-flowering sedum, blue veronica and a yellow daisy, the yellow and purple blooms accented by bright fuchsia petunias. All around the ponds are oriental lanterns. Flat rocks arranged as stepping stones allow one to admire the ponds at close range. Other interestingly-shaped rocks are placed here and there on the mulch as accents. A pair of metal herons oversee one pond and a ceramic frog spits water into the other one. The Oriental theme honors their Chinese-born daughter.

One pond is quite deep. Bernice said she thought Tim would never quit digging that one. It is deep enough that with a heater in the winter, the pond Koi and the tropical water lilies don't have to be removed from it in each fall. They used to put both into a stock tank in the garage for the winter, but lost some of the fish. The Koi are tame enough to nibble at fingers dipped in the water, almost pets— and like any pet, it hurts to lose one.

There is an arbor covered with orange trumpet vine, with pots of multicolored petunias hanging from its eaves. A bridge over the stream is a perfect spot for admiring the water features from comfortable chairs. In the background, several boulders are arranged around a fire pit for toasting marshmallows on summer nights. A hummingbird feeder is hung near one pond to attract the little fliers.

Behind the ponds are huge hostas. On one side, a row of conifers surrounds the ponds. A birch tree makes a beautiful accent against the blue spruces behind it.

A block retaining wall has more of the small yellow sedums flowing over the top of it and sneaking out of the cracks here and there. There are also more of the fuchsia petunias adding their color to the wall. It encloses several globe conifers, providing a windbreak for one side of the pond.

All this water is too much for the local mallards. They love the ponds for courting in the spring. The Overlands don't have problems with other wildlife, even though the bright-colored koi look like lunch to hungry herons and raccoons. Fortunately their dog polices the ponds, preventing wildlife from dining on live sushi.

What a beautiful oasis these water features are for lounging around during the heat of the Minnesota summers.

Green Roofs

When Bunkey was on vacation this winter, he saw quite a few buildings with green roofs—they were planted, not shingled. Since he had built a sandbox without too much trouble, he decided his dog was going to get a green roof on his dog house.

Since the roof has a south exposure, the dog seldom stays in it in the summer, preferring to dig a hole in the soft soil of the flowerbed. Bunkey's thinking is that the plants and soil will insulate the roof better than the fiberglass, making it more comfortable for Muttly and, hopefully, keeping him out of the flowerbeds.

Bunkey started by getting together the materials he needed: treated lumber, half-inch staples, rubber pond liner, landscape cloth, and because the roof may sag, a precut piece of 5/8-inch pressure treated plywood.

To start, he pulled off the south facing side of the roof, then made a box 4 inches deep and 2 inches longer than the lowest eave. The next step was to put in the pond liner and landscape cloth. This was long and wide enough to flow over the top and sides of the box, making it waterproof. He stapled only the top and side edges as close to the top as possible. He didn't want the dog to get leaked on. He turned the box over and caulked the cracks in the frame. Next, he cut some slits in the liner at the bottom. Now the excess water will drain off the bottom of the eave. The finished box was then screwed to the roof, being careful not to make any holes in the liner.

Now for planting. Bunkey chose sedums as they can handle both drought and flooding. He filled the box with a soilless mix, covered as much of the soil as he could, then mulched it with shredded bark. The shredded stuff won't wash off in a hard rain.

To be sure the dog would use his house, and since Muttly is an elderly dog, Bunkey put a new cedar dog bed in the house for him. After a thorough examination, Muttly decided the remodeling passed the sniff test and, so far anyway, has stopped digging up the flowerbed for a nest.

That Darn Slope

It's easy to plant a flat space, but slopes can bring you to tears. It may be too steep to mow easily, or prone to erosion or just plain boring. If this is your problem, there are several solutions.

The first step is to determine what sort of soil you are dealing with. Next, orientation: which way does the slope face? If the slope is very steep, the best bet is to terrace it. You can use rocks, cement blocks designed for walls, or, in the last resort, treated wood—which will eventually need to be replaced.

Bunkey had a steep, south-facing slope. His material of choice was rock as that was readily available. Every farmer has a rock pile. The trick is to pick rock small enough to handle and oddly shaped enough to fit tightly to another rock.

The first course should be dug in about 1/3 its depth. Tilt the rock into the slope. Now, if you have a tiller handy, till the area right above the rocks. This will give you a flat terrace. Here is a proper place to use that weed barrier. Tuck it behind your rock wall. It will help keep your soil from running out the cracks. You can fill some of those cracks with smaller rocks. If the soil is poor, it is now easily amended or replaced. Set the next row of rocks on the rear of the tilled area. Continue until the last area is level with the top of the slope.

Now to plant. If the slope gets full sun, you can plant most any plant you want. The trick is to put the shortest plants on the lowest level, increasing the height as you go up. A north-facing slope is perfect for hostas, ferns, low growing junipers, bergenia, and if it is quite sandy, some of the creeping sedums. Do remember that you will be able to see the entire space at once. Groups of similar plants look much better than just one here and there. Fill in with shade annuals like begonias.

If the slope is not steep enough to terrace, you might want to plant it with a groundcover. You may need to stabilize the slope first. Pound-in edging will do that quite well. If you hate the looks of it, you can remove the stuff after your plants get well established.

Here is where you can plant those garden monsters. You know which ones they are. They start out small and cute, then turn into chewbaccas. They will take over the flower garden in two seasons. Perennial geraniums, wild violets, lily of the valley, wild ferns, lamium and periwinkle are a few. These are plants that tend to root along their stems, forming a thicket of roots.

If your slope has a tendency to wash in a strong rain, these are the plants for you.

Now that you have your terrace or gradual slope, you need to plan a way to weed it. If the slope is very steep, your path may need to be a switchback, weaving back and forth. Steps will do well for a less steep area.

Like all gardens, just plants can be a bit boring. On a shallow slope, an interesting rock here and there or a small sculpture or statue will add some piazzazz. A rocked terrace will probably have a few rocks with flat tops, perfect for fat cement frog or, if you are into that sort of thing, a garden gnome. Tuck 3 or 5 of your preferred eye-catchers in amongst the plants or perch them on rocks.

You may find that you are moving rocks, plants, gnomes and whatever you started with to new homes almost every year. That's gardening. Gardeners are always looking to next year, when everything will be perfect. After all, most gardeners are optimists. They would never plant a garden otherwise.

Front Door Follies

The first thing your guests see as they come to your house is the front door and the plantings—or the lack of them. You want that first look to be welcoming, to give your guests a hint of your taste, your style. That being said, there are a few things you perhaps want to avoid in front door plants, or even front-of-the-house plantings.

The first step is to stand where your guests do when they get a first look at your house. Can they actually see the front door? Too often, the cute little evergreen you planted 20 years ago has become a monster, partly covering the door and half of the front of the house. If you need to prune it every year just to be able to get through the door, whack it down and dig or grind it out. When you do replant a different shrub, move it at least 4 feet away from the house and make sure the tag says it is a dwarf. If your house is so ugly you need to hide it, either move or get some expert help to do something about that.

Check out that front door shrub. If it is thorny, your next guest may sue you for destroying her expensive silk suit as she entered your door. A shrub with thorns is perfect under a window. It's a great deterrent to anybody attempting to sneak into your house. Do keep it below the window. You don't want to look out through a forest. It makes the room dark, too.

Don't plant flowering shrubs near a door either—they attract bees. While that is a good thing, you don't want to get stung every time you brush past the shrub as you are carrying a bag of groceries. Spilt milk smells terrible in the hot sun.

If you have a flowerbed on the walk to the front door, make it behave. You don't want people tripping over a floppy plant that has decided it likes to lay on the walkway. Put that puppy in restraints or pull it out and plant a better-mannered one in its place.

Speaking about walkways... if you have a tree or shrub close to your walk, watch out for face scratchers or hat removers. Prune it high enough that your basketball-playing friend can safely walk under it without fear of being attacked by low branches. Your insurance provider will thank you.

Foundation plantings need circulation. Keep them well away from the foundation of your house. Nothing is uglier than a plant that looks nice and full front in the front and bare naked on its backside. And people will see that naked backside as they stand at the door. You probably planted that shrub 20 years ago and never really look at it anymore. Like looking at your spouse, you just don't see how scruffy things have gotten over the years.

Spring is renewal time, a good time to redo your planting mistakes and make your house look fresh and welcoming. Besides, it's a good excuse to stroll through the plant nurseries to see what the plant breeders have come up with this year. But just look. Give a new release at least 3 years before you invest in it. Remember *Endless Summer*? She looked great on paper. Not so good planted up here in the frozen north.

Lasagna Gardens

Bunkey came tearing into the house, his hair on fire. "How many times have I told you not to leave the hose in the yard? I'll either run over it with the lawn mower or the sun will rot it!"

Very calmly, Petunia asked, "Are you done now? I was using the hose to mark the shape of my new flowerbed. Since you refuse to dig me one, I'm going to use the lasagna method and build my own."

If you have ever made a new garden from scratch, you know how much work it is to dig up all the turf, kill off all the weeds and then till the area up, hoping all the time that the soil will be fit to grow something. The lasagna method not only saves your back, but ensures the soil is "good stuff."

The first step, naturally, is to consider the site. Depending on what you plan to grow, you will want full sun or part shade. Forget attempting to grow much in full shade. Now that you know where you want the plot, Roundup® the area. This will kill most of the plants. You can eliminate this step if you want, but it is helpful.

Now, using a hose, decide on the shape of the bed. If it is in an area you will be mowing around, mow around the hose to determine if you can actually maneuver the mower around the corners without either cutting some of the plants or leaving swaths of grass unmowed.

Next, cover the area with either 2 layers of wet cardboard or up to 10 layers of wet newspaper. Don't use the shiny stuff. It has too many chemicals in it and doesn't break down easily. Be sure to overlap the papers to eliminate any holes that grass or weeds could later sneak through. Cover the paper with 4 to 6 inches of the best soil you can obtain.

Cover this with 4 inches of mulch. Leaves, weed-free straw or rotted hay work very well. It will take 2 to 3 months of hot summer days for this cover to kill off any weeds or grass under it. Keep the bed damp to hasten the activity.

If you are doing this in the fall, you can add other organic matter to the bed to enrich it. Coffee grounds, chopped leaves, fruit or veggie peelings, tea bags and shredded newspaper all work well. Cover it well with mulch, and by spring it will be ready to till and plant.

Seeds & Plants

To start or to buy...that is the question

Seed Catalog Danger

This is the time of the year that gardeners are almost afraid to open their mailboxes for fear of an avalanche of seed catalogs. The first thing a good gardener does is look at the state the catalog is based in. If it is more than 250 miles south, round file it. If it is any further west than Montana, in the trash. East is usually OK and Canada is great. Why? Seeds grown in the warmer areas don't have enough time to ripen in our short growing season.

If you have a small garden, Pinetree Garden Seeds is the catalog for you. The seed packets are small, 1 oz. and 30 seeds is a norm. They also have many heirloom varieties of everything from beans to squash.

Vermont Bean Seed Company has most of a page of ornamental corn. Two varieties are even edible, one for making flour and the other for cooking and eating like regular sweet corn. Stokes Seeds Inc., is New York based and has many short-season seeds, as does Veseys Seeds of Maine.

Before you order seeds from any catalog, read not only the description of the seed but check the days to maturity. We have about 90 days of good growing weather here in west central Minnesota. A melon that takes 130 days to get ripe is just not going to do it here. Another thing you need to look for are the words, "good or excellent flavor." If a tomato grows great but tastes like the cardboard-flavored ones you get in the store, what have you gained for all your work?

Jung Seeds and Plants (Randolph, Wisconsin) has a tomato called *Pink Wonder*. They describe it as "meaty with a mouth-watering sweet and tangy flavor that makes you wish tomato season would never end." Now that sounds like a tomato worth planting. That's the kind of description you are looking for when you order seeds.

Buying plants, trees or shrubs from these catalogs is not recommended. The plants are much smaller than the same plant you can get at your local nursery. They have to be to ship them.

And, you are paying for shipping costs. Yes, you also pay for shipping at your local store, but it is probably charges for 20 trees or 50 plants divided for each plant. Also, if your tree dies, the local nursery will replace it if it is less than a year since you bought it. Try that with a catalog. A local nursery will not sell you a Granny Smith apple tree that is only hardy to zone 5 either.

Buy seeds through the mail, but forget buying live material. Buy from catalogs as soon as you can because they do run out of some of the more desired seeds. Enjoy the winter, but plant ahead for spring.

Using Seed Catalogs as Reference Material

Don't throw away your seed catalogs after you send in your seed orders. There is a plethora of information in those pages. For instance, you are planning to plant a tree this spring. Your seed catalog can tell you how high and wide that tree will be at maturity. It will also have descriptive information about the tree. For instance, "In cold climates, plant in a sheltered area." Red flag. This tree is probably not reliably hardy here. It will tell you the fall color (if any), if the tree is fruit-bearing (like flowering crab), and if the tree holds fruit through the winter.

Some trees are planted for their shape. The *Pagoda dogwood*, for instance, is a very horizontal tree. The flowering crabs can be very upright, round or more horizontal, depending on the cultivar. They can also have different colored flowers in the spring, ranging from dark pink, almost red, to light pink or white. If you have a red house, you probably don't want a dark pink tree close to it.

Even evergreens come in different shapes: columnar, round, weeping, or even flat to the ground. A picture of the tree you are looking for can make your eventual shopping locally much easier.

In the spring your local nursery will have many shrubs, some blooming, some not. If you want a shrub that blooms later or gets interesting berries in the fall, you probably don't want to wait until fall to buy it. A look through the catalog will show the shrub at its best, be it fall or spring.

If you are planting in a dry area, look for the words, "resists drought." Now this doesn't mean you never have to water it, it just means it will take less water than usual. "Adaptable" is another word to look for if you have a difficult site. Some trees and shrubs will grow in sand or clay, but many just say "rain on it" and belly up. Windy areas are very difficult for almost any tree or shrub. They lose so much water that it is difficult for them to live, let alone prosper.

Words to beware of are "fast growing." This usually means a weed tree that will grow for 15 years then fall on your house in a strong wind. "Slow growing" is fine if you are 20, but if you are 50 and want a shade tree, forget that one.

Your local nursery is the place to buy shrubs or trees. They will have a lot of information on their stock, but they absolutely love customers who come prepared, who know the growing conditions they are planting in and know what will or will not thrive there.

It is usually not the best idea to buy the newest tree or shrub out. Give it a few years to see if the plant actually lives up to its advertisements. Think of *Endless Summer* hydrangea, for instance. It does great in Minneapolis, but here, not so well. It never gets as big as advertised and can freeze if not heavily mulched.

The moral for the day: don't chuck your seed catalogs. Get educated in what you need and buy locally.

Keeping Seeds

Poor Mrs. Bunkey is in a tizzy. She's the kind of housekeeper who has the vacuum cleaner out before the guests are in the car. She just has to get the footprints out of the carpet before she can sit down. So you can imagine her distress seeing all those open seed packets lying all over her kitchen table. Bunkey is attempting to determine what seeds he needs to order this year. Like most thrifty gardeners, he keeps unused seeds from year to year.

Unfortunately, many seeds have a shelf life. Most seed companies have seed packets that are too large for the average home gardener. We only need a third or fourth of the packet, so we save the rest. Corn and pepper seeds are good for about 2 years. Asparagus, peas, beans and leeks about 3 years. You can keep beets, pumpkins and squash, rutabagas (although why would you want those?), tomato and watermelon seeds for 4 years. Cole seeds (cabbage, cauliflower, etc.), lettuce, radish, muskmelon and spinach seeds are viable up to 5 years.

If you can't find a date on your seed packet, here is how to determine if it pays to plant that seed. Put a line of 10 seeds on a sheet of damp paper towel. Roll the paper up, wrap with plastic wrap, and put in a warm place. The top of the fridge works very well. Every few days, check the rolls to see how many, if any, seeds have germinated. If you get 2, you have a 20% germination rate.

Don't throw old seeds in the trash—put them in the bird feeder. Some birds will eat anything! You may also get a pleasant surprise when you find an aster in the pea row or a tomato plant in with the marigolds, planted by the birds. The nice thing is that they are already fertilized. However, don't feed any seeds that have been coated. Corn seeds often come with a coating that prevents them from rotting in cold soil. Dyed seed is also iffy. Melon and squash seed may be dyed to let the gardener know to put one colored seed with one uncolored for proper germination.

To keep from ending up with a lot of old seeds, plan ahead. Talk to your gardening neighbors and share seed packets. Some packets have enough seeds to plant half the neighborhood. You might find yourself trying varieties you would not have otherwise. It could make for a friendlier neighborhood. By sharing, you may even get that grouch neighbor to be a bit more pleasant. However, if he comes to the door with a loaded shotgun, forget about it!

Starting Seeds

Why the heck would you start your own plants when in a few weeks you can buy them at any grocery, big box store or nursery? There are several reasons. The most important one is that you can grow plants not easily available or even found in those places. Another very good reason is the health of the plants. If you grow them yourself, you know they have not been starved of water or gotten bugs. And, you can plant them when you want to. If we have an early spring, peppers, for instance, may not have been shipped yet. The wholesaler sends plants depending on our "usual" spring temperature, not what it actually is.

Here are a few tips to get you started.

- To prevent damping off (a fungus that will kill your seedlings), everything they touch must not only be clean but sterile. If your planters have ever had soil in them, soak, then scrub them in a solution of 1 part bleach to 10 parts water. In other words, a couple of glugs in a sink full of water.
- Use only an unopened bag of soilless mix. Use bottom heat—the top of the fridge, a heating pad or heat tape will pop the seedlings out quickly.
- Put a cover on the flat, whether a commercial one or saran wrap, will keep the soil moist until the seeds germinate. Once they are up, remove the cover to prevent mold.

- Keep the soil damp by watering from the bottom.
- Pot them into a larger pot when the plants have two sets of true leaves. The knobs on tomato stems will sprout roots if in the soil. Bury them up to the bottom of the leaves each time you repot them. Fertilize seedlings with half strength fertilizer now.
- When the temperature is warm enough, harden off your plants by setting them outside, first in the shade for an hour, next day for two hours in part shade, and then continue until they are out all day in full sun.
- Before you set out any semi-tropicals (tomatoes, peppers or the vines), stroll out to your garden and sit on the soil in as few clothes as your neighbors will tolerate. If you don't get a cold, wet butt, it is warm enough to plant them.
- Do protect them for 7 to 10 days from spring winds and cutworms. A three-pound coffee can with the bottom cut off, pushed into the soil works very well.

Have fun getting your hands dirty!

Seed Starting Class

There are several reasons to start your own plants. Saving money isn't one of them. Most seed starters do it because they can't find the varieties of plants they like. Or, they want to have the option of planting their garden before the commercial plants are ready. Some years, you may be able to plant spuds on Good Friday and actually get a crop.

Start with the containers. Sure, egg shells, grapefruit halves and other assorted "stuff" shows up in magazines as containers—cute, cheap, but totally worthless. If you must use a container other than a regular plastic pot, a milk carton will work; however, it must be sterilized and have holes poked in the bottom for drainage. They also take up a lot of room. Instead, save your containers from the plants you have purchased or get the flat with a clear cover. It makes planting much easier.

If your container has ever had soil in it, you must sterilize it. Soak it in a solution of 1-part bleach to 10 parts of water (just add a couple of glugs of bleach to your water container). Soak plastic for about ½ hour to be sure you have killed any viruses or bacteria that can kill your new seedlings.

Next, never use last year's potting soil, or worse yet, garden soil or any combination of the two. Get seed starting mix. It is a sterile mix, usually combining coir, peat, compost and possibly, worm castings (worm poop). This mix has no nutrients in it as seedlings have all the food they need to get started. Using sterile mix in a sterile pot will ensure that your plants won't "damp off." This happens when a disease kills your seedlings by cutting off the plants right at the soil level. You think they have gotten too dry because they look as though they are wilting. Nope, they are DOA.

Now to plant. If you are planting in a flat, it's a good idea to make rows in the seed starter. That makes it easier to transplant the seedlings later. The mix should be damp, not soaking wet. Cover your container with saran or a plastic bag, or if you got a flat with a clear cover, use that. The idea is to keep the mix just damp. Uncovered, the moisture will evaporate. To give your babies a head start, warm their bottoms. Set your container on the radiator, the top of the fridge or invest in a heat tape designed for seed starting.

Your plants probably will need transplanting several times as they grow. Transplant the first time when the seedlings have 2 sets of true leaves. This container can be fairly small. Fill it with new potting soil—again, no leftovers. Let the plant get a good-sized root, then repot it into a larger container. The larger the second container (within reason), the more room the roots have to grow.

Your plants might get leggy. Not a problem. Simply pinch off the growing tip. This will force the plant to bush out. There is a chemical in that growing tip that tells the plant to get taller. If you remove it, the chemical migrates to the nearest set of leaves and gets busy growing again. This is an especially good practice with tomatoes and peppers. The more leaves and root, the bigger the crop.

When to plant is always a guess. Most plants that are started inside tell you to start them 4 to 6 weeks before planting out. This is true for most plants. Some, such as onions and peppers, need more time. To get peppers before Halloween, they should have buds on them when you set them out. Vine crops, such as melons, squash and cucumbers, need only about 3 weeks from starting to planting. Much longer and you will need to have a machete to get through them.

The Winter Blues

When we have a long cold spell (60 days below zero) it's really difficult for everybody, but even more so for gardeners. The mad desire to get our hands in dirt can lead to problems. Mid-to-late February is the time to start some plants, but, as in any endeavor, you must do it right or suffer the consequences: a flat of dead or dying seedlings.

Start with scrupulously sterile flats or pots. Use only freshly-purchased seed starting mix. The bag you got last spring has been open and may no longer be sterile—chuck it into the part of the garden that has heavy soil. Next, read the back of the seed packet. It will tell you how many days before planting out you need to start the seeds. Some seeds may need some additional treatment. Thick-coated seeds like sweet peas and lupine, for instance, may need to be soaked overnight or even have a nick cut in the seed. Nicking a seed can be very difficult as the darn seed tends to roll away, or squirt out of your fingers as you attempt to scratch a hole in it. Try a nail file or a small wood file to do the job. Other seeds need to be chilled before they will sprout. Some seeds need total dark to germinate. Or they are so small you just sprinkle them on top of the soil. All this information should be on the seed packet.

Water is as important as the soil or container. Never use softened water. It's toxic to most plants. If you have chlorinated water, let it sit a day or two. The warm room temperature will help dissipate the chemical. Melted clean snow is an excellent choice. Just be sure it doesn't have snow-melt or street salt in it.

Not everything should be started this early. Yes, you can start tomatoes now and have a 2-foot-tall, skinny plant to put out, but waiting until the second week in March (6 weeks to planting time) will give you a shorter plant that will have less transplant shock and start growing sooner that its lanky cousin.

You can start peppers now. They need to be ready to bloom shortly after planting if you are to get any crop. Keep them pinched off and stocky and when they get in the garden they will be ready to start blooming. Many flowers, such as snapdragons, need a long time indoors so they bloom in July, not August. They will keep blooming until a very heavy frost. Coleus can be started now. The first sprouts all look green. They need to get some size before you can determine what colors they actually will be. Celery should be started early, too. The trick with it is that it is actually a swamp plant, so it needs more water than most seedlings.

Wait until the first week in April to start the vines. Melons and cucumbers started to the 4-leaf stage will take off running in May when the soil is warm enough for them. They will be several weeks ahead of directly-sown seeds. Those weeks may mean the difference between having a ripe melon or having to compost them after the first freeze. Be that gardener who plans ahead. We love to gift our neighbor with a ripe cantaloupe when his are just starting to set flowers. Gloating isn't nice, but it sure is fun.

Thinking About Starting Your Own Plants?

Why not start your own tomatoes this year? You can buy 5 or 6 varieties of plants in the spring, the same old varieties every year. Did you know that there are approximately 100 varieties of tomato seeds available? Not just red, but pink, yellow, orange, brown, striped and every shape and size you could possible imagine. The trick to getting a better-tasting tomato is to carefully read the description of the fruit. The words to look for are "excellent taste," "good flavor," or some other word related to taste. Believe it or not, some tomatoes really taste icky or have very little taste at all. If you can your own fruit, you want a plant that produces meaty tomatoes. These are usually the smaller types, but not always. *Brandywine*, a big old honking fruit (ugly too), has a very small seed cavity, great for taste, too.

Peppers are another plant that comes in many colors, sizes and hotness. *Scovil units* measure the hotness of peppers. The higher, the hotter. Peppers can be listed as a sweet bell (your ordinary grocery green pepper), sweet cherry (a smaller type), sweet pimento or cheese type, sweet stuffing, and sweet banana. All have very low Scovil units. The hot peppers have their own listings. Habanero, cyanne, Anaheim, Serrano, Ancho/poblamo and jalapeno all mean hot. Again, read the description. Some packets will list the Scovil units, but that is rare.

Read the back of the packet to see how deep to plant your seeds. Rule of thumb is 2 times the size of the seed. To visualize that, a pea seed can be poked down as deep as your finger can go into the soil. Carrot seeds should be dusted with soil.

Another reason to start your own plants is if you want a big display of annual flowers. A 6-pack doesn't go very far if you want a wave of them through the flowerbed. A $1.00 packet of marigold seeds will give you dozens of seedlings. Let your imagination run wild. Pull out that green thumb and get planting.

Bare Naked Planting

No, not the gardener. That would be a very bad thing. (Think *sunburn in uncomfortable places, big bites and worst of all, the neighbors laughing at you.*) The bare we are discussing today is bare root plants.

If you have ever ordered plants from a catalog (not recommended by the way), you were probably pretty disgusted with what came. The plants come in little plastic bags filled with peat moss or sawdust, and look like nothing more than dead sticks. They might have a few green sprigs on them, a sign that they really are alive. First, unpack the poor little things. Look for mold or rot. Healthy plants will have white or off white roots that are nice and plump. A bit of gray or white mold on them is OK, but fuzzy blue-green mold, brown roots, mushy roots, roots that smell bad or are shriveled up are not okay. If the roots feel light for the size of the plant or look dried up, back they go. Even the best companies can have shipping problems: plants that have been held too long so they have dried up. Ship them back and ask for a replacement or if the rest of the shipment looks bad too, a refund and cross that company off your list.

A reputable company will either ask you when to ship your order or tell you when to expect the plants based on your local frost-free date. That's a good trick as we don't even know when that will be. Average is May 15th. If you get plants and we are still hip deep in snow, or the soil is too cold or too wet to plant, you have two options. Pot them up. Or dampen the stuff they were shipped in and put them in the refrigerator crisper box for no more than a week. If you are potting the plant, use a soilless mix, not garden soil. Give the plant a good soaking, an hour if possible. Pick a roomy pot that won't crowd the roots. The crown of the plant should be at soil level. This prevents water from pooling at the top of the crown, leading to rot. If you are really lucky, the plant will come with planting instructions.

Now, you are ready to plant these babies. Check for broken roots. Usually a few get broken in transit. Snip them off with a sharp knife so they don't rot after you plant them. A tip here: keep all your cutting tools sharp to prevent crushing plant material. It is a good thing to disinfect a tool after each cut to prevent transmitting diseases. Listerine® mouth wash works well and won't dull your edges. Now, pack the soil lightly to prevent air pockets and water until it runs out the bottom of the pot. Keep the plant in a cool bright area, 50 to 60 degrees is ideal. Don't water again until you see growth.

Planting outdoors is very similar. Prune off broken roots, soak the plant, then dig a wide hole. Spread the roots out, keep the crown at soil level and water. If the plant is dormant, you can plant it a bit deeper. Under-watering kills more transplants, whether bare root or potted, than any other practice. Give them an inch a week, a bit more if it is really windy and dry. Remember, these are still babies.

Surprisingly enough, bare root plants often take off faster than container grown.

If you must order plants from a catalog, do it early to be sure you get what you want. Some companies will send you a better plant if you okay a substitution. However, you never know what they may substitute. Five-foot-tall phlox for a creeping phlox? Ouch!

Why Doesn't My Garden Grow?

When we have a plant, tree or shrub that is not doing well, we often blame either insects or disease, when the actual cause may be our cultural practices. OK, what are those? Site selection, drainage, hardiness, watering, mechanical damage, animals, highly susceptible plants and maintenance practices.

Site Selection—This is particularly important for trees and shrubs, but applies to all plants. Does the plant need full sun, part shade, full shade? Will it do well in our alkaline soil? (Blueberries, for instance, won't.) Does it need protection from wind, sun or falling snow (off the roof for instance)? And last, does it want wet feet, just damp or well-drained soil?

Soil Drainage—All bulbs need good soil drainage. They evolved in dry areas, leading to water-retentive structures we call bulbs, rhizomes or corms. Too wet and they either rot or just fail to thrive. Other plants love that low, periodic puddle in the lawn. Think *rain gardens.* (Good drainage is like having good hair, you either have it or not.) Poorly drained soil stays wet long after the rain. The ground water table may be high, or you may have soil compaction. Bad grading or construction traffic can make soil drain poorly.

Plant Hardiness—Bunkey's friend George constantly harps on zones. Sure, you can plant a zone 5 apple tree and it may live a year or two, but it will never thrive or live long enough for you to get a good crop of apples. A plant "out of zone" will be chronically stressed, require protection, need more maintenance and will be more prone to diseases. Why go to all that fuss?

Transplant Stress—Root loss during transplanting, drying of roots, poor handling and storage of bare root trees, and planting too deep can lead to a dead tree or shrub. Not watering enough or long enough (five years for new trees), is another cause of stress or early death of trees.

Susceptible Plants—If you have white phlox, you know what this is all about. It seems to get powdery mildew no matter what the weather. Plants grown with a lot of water and fertilizer (to make them more attractive to the buyer) may last a month or so then fail—most gardeners have neither the time nor inclination to baby a newly-introduced plant that may or may not do well with normal care.

Weed and Insect Killers—The herbicide or insecticide can't tell a good plant from a weed or a good bug from a bad one. Take care when you spray. Know what you are killing.

Maintenance Practices—We kill our plants with kindness. We amend the soil, wrap, prune, over-fertilize, spray and paint, thinking we are doing the proper thing. Prune trees only at the proper time for the tree. Take only 1/4 of the plant a year. Do not paint the wound. It slows healing. Prune outside the branch collar. Trees don't need amended soil, and it will revert back to the original within a few years anyhow. Fertilize at the proper times of the year. Spring and fall for lawns, lightly at transplant for plants. Kill weeds in the fall, crabgrass and other annual weeds in the spring.

Follow these few rules and you will have the neighbors exclaiming, "I'll bet he could plant horse manure and grow a pony."

If you are unable to walk through the garden without stomping down a plant, you need to thin. Start with the flowers that are done blooming. If you have an invasive one like phlox, isolate it as much as possible. If a flower doesn't thrill you, dig it out. If it just isn't doing well, move it. Sometimes moving a plant only a foot will make it thrive. If you have moved a plant three times and it still looks crappy, dig it up. It just doesn't like you.

Understanding Plant Patents and Titles

Do you ever wonder why a plant would be patented? If you had spent 20 years crossing and re-crossing a plant to get *Endless Summer*, a hydrangea that blooms all summer instead of its cousin *Annabelle* that blooms only once, wouldn't you want to be paid?

The plant patent act of 1930 was an incentive for plant breeders to "invent" new and better plant cultivars. Patenting can be a long, expensive process, especially when there are no guaranties that gardeners will buy your "new and improved" plant. The upside for the patent holder is that he gets a royalty on every sale of his plant. Rates can be as low as 25¢ for a perennial, shrub or evergreen and 50¢ cents up to $1 for a tree.

So, how do you know if the plant you are buying is patented and why should you care? A protected plant will have a hang tag with the plant's name, *Endless Summer*, followed by PAF or PPAF, patent applied for. The patent is good only in the U.S. and for 20 years and is not renewable.

A trademark is different as it protects the plant's name. It is good for 10 years and can be renewed. A breeder can asexually reproduce this plant without a license, but can't use the trademark name. The plant can only be sold by its cultivar name. A federally-registered trademark is identified by an R within a circle (®). A small TM (™) means the name has been claimed but not officially registered by the U.S. Patent and Trademark office.

Now, why you should care? Say you've seen a dwarf variegated barberry, Latin name *Berberis thunbergii* "*Goruzam*" PP16203. The number shows that the plant is under patent. It also has a trademark name. *Golden Ruby*®. It can be propagated with permission under that name. However, once the patent expires anyone can propagate it but can only sell it as *Goruzam*. To sell it as *Golden Ruby*, the propagator would also need to get permission to use the Trademark name. Which name would catch your eye? If nothing else, you would wonder how a ruby can be yellow. *Goruzam* sounds more like a hungry stomach growling, not something you'd want to put in your garden.

To Plant or Not to Plant

Gardeners often don't know what to believe. We are supposed to use native plants, especially in rain gardens, but we are not to just go out and dig them up. Instead, we are told, buy native at your local nursery. But—don't buy a plant labeled "nursery grown." Isn't that what we are supposed to purchase?

Horticulturist Lynn Steiner tells us we must look for the label "nursery propagated." The difference? *Nursery grown* could mean that the plant was dug up in the wild and potted up. That is a no-no. The second label indicated that the nursery has actually grown the plant from seed, not collected it from the nearby wetland.

A reliable nursery will readily tell you the origin of the plant. If the answer is evasive or they hand you a bunch of gobbledygook, be very cautious about buying that plant. There are signs that a plant has not been legitimately propagated, but illegally dug up. The color is poor or abnormal. The foliage is thin, the stems are weak or it has wilted leaves. The plant is leggy, or off-centered in the pot. The soil is not regular potting soil. It may have stones in it or have different types of soil in the same pot. The plant is obviously mature, especially if it is normally a very slow-growing plant. And finally, there is more than one species in the pot. It is downright impossible to dig a plant up, in grass, for instance, and get just the preferred plant. The seller of such plants should probably be reported to the DNR.

Native plants should never be dug up unless they may be destroyed by road work or other development. Even then, you must get permission from the landowner to remove the plant or the seeds of one. If you get permission to collect seeds from a native plant, don't strip just one plant. Take a few seeds from several plants. This way, you don't endanger the whole population. The plant you stripped may be the only one surviving next summer.

There is a federal law that protects endangered native species; however, that only applies to federal lands. In Minnesota, we have three categories of plants, *endangered*, *threatened* and *special concern*. A species is considered endangered if it is threatened with extinction in all or a significant part of its range. A threatened plant is likely to become endangered in the foreseeable future. A special-concern species isn't endangered or threatened, but is very uncommon and has unique or very specific habitat requirements, such as the pink lady's slipper. It is illegal to "gather, take, buy or sell" plants in any of these categories without a special permit from the DNR.

A partial list of Minnesota's plants in these categories include prairie shooting star (*Dodecatheon meadia*), golden seal (*Hydratitis Canadensis*), nodding wild onion, (*Alluim cernum*), white prairie clover (*dalea candida*), eastern hemlock (*Tsuga Canadensis*) and butternut (*Juglans cinerea*) .

There are many native plants that aren't in any of these categories, like the ox-eye daisy. They look so nice there in the ditch that the unaware gardener digs a few and brings them home to her garden. Those pretty plants have been growing in conditions that would kill regular garden plants. Put them in good soil, water well, give them no competition from their normal neighbors and you will have an explosion of plants that are very difficult to get rid of. Never, never put ditch plants in your garden. You'll be sorry.

Why Plant Native Plants?

There are many reasons to plant natives. Not only are they tough, they are more tolerant of drought, poor soil and other crappy growing conditions. They can resist the damages from diseases and insects. They need less maintenance, consequently less dependence on fossil fuels used to pump water or run the lawn mower. They only need landscape conditions that match their cultural requirements. Think of milkweed. It will grow most places, but one type needs damp feet to do well.

Using native will certainly make your estate look different from your neighbor's manicured lawn and formal rose bed. For one thing, your plants will be a much livelier place, full of butterflies, birds and pollinating insects. This is very important, as the health of many populations of pollinating insects such as bees are in decline. The U.S. Fish and Wildlife Service has listed more than 50 pollinator species that are either threatened or endangered.

Why would you want your gardens crawling with bugs, you ask? Because the availability of native pollinators is as important as rain and sun to the reproductive success of almost half of the world's flowering plants. Even that neighbor's roses.

All native pollinators need native plants for their food, nesting and egg-laying sites. Indeed, some of them can't survive without a specific native plant that either the adult or its larvae feed on. This is the reason the monarch butterfly population has declined. Their caterpillar stage's sole food source is the various milkweeds. Farming fields edge-to-edge has reduced the area for milkweeds to grow.

Planting native plants helps preserve the natural heritage of an area. This results in a base of plants for plant geneticists to draw new and improved plants from. The genetic diversity of natives promotes the mixing of genes to form new combinations.

Your neighbors may not see eye-to-eyewith you if your yard is full of native plants—some of them are pretty weedy looking. You may need to start your native garden in a hidden corner. The rose aficionado may consider your plantings a bug-infested patch of weeds. Your job is to educate the poor soul.

What Not to Plant

Bunkey read every article he could find before he planted his flower gardens. Often, the article was a rave about several plants the author just loved. Bunkey swallowed them whole, believed every word. He loved the idea of "pass along plants," never stopping to wonder why a gardener had so many plants to share.

Bunkey's first disaster/mistake was accepting a clump of snow-on-the-mountain. It looked so innocent, just pretty green and white foliage. Bunkey broke the clump up and used it in a bare spot near his patio. Two years later, it was growing 2 feet onto the cement block patio. It took several years and gallons of sweat and Roundup® to get rid of the monster.

There are several other similar plants who start out as cute little puppies and grow into St. Bernards. Blue lyme grass (*Elymus arenarius*) and its cousin fountain grass (*Pennistum alopecuroides*) don't play well with others. They will spread by seed, rapidly.

Some monsters are root spreaders. Japanese knotweed, sometimes called bamboo, not only spreads like bamboo but kills anything in its path. The afore-mentioned snow-on-a-mountain is also a root spreader. Worse, its roots are brittle and break off when the gardener attempts to pull it out. Common daylilies don't spread as fast, but spread they do, making huge clumps of themselves. The blooms are pretty, but when done blooming leave ugly brown stalks and clumps of straggly leaves. Two other root spreaders are gooseneck loosestrife (*Lyisamachia clethrodies*) and chameleon plant (*Houttuynia corda*). Any farmer will tell you to avoid any plant with loosestrife in its name.

One professional gardener planted plume poppy (*Macleaya cordata*), a tall, big-leaved dramatic plant in the back of a bed. Two years later it popped up 5 feet away in a bed of iris. She had to dig up poppy plants for several years to get rid of it. Another planting mistake was planting a giant butterbur (*Petasities japonicas*) in a woodland garden. It not only moved, it came up seven feet away and across a cement path from the mother plant. A small native sedge (*Carex*) managed to smother the whole wildflower garden it was planted in.

If professional gardeners make mistakes like this, what can the average Bunkey do to prevent similar goof-ups? First, never, never accept a plant that arrives as a wheelbarrow full. Second, ask a gardener you trust before planting a "pass along" plant. Third, use your head. If the gardener is digging up a plant that is covering most of his garden, politely decline. And fourth, do some investigating. Check your seed catalog, or your computer if you are computer literate. If the description mentions "groundcover," "self-seeds readily" or "easy to grow," beware that cute little puppy. If you must have the plant, put it in an area all by itself, one you can easily get to with the Roundup®.

Do your homework. It will save both your back and your pocketbook.

The Dance of Seeds

Most gardeners have had the experience of moving favorite plant to a new garden at a new house and having it go belly up. Some plants are ornery that way. They liked where they were growing and if the gardener thought it was going to grow in the new flowerbed, she had another think coming. The trick is to plant seeds rather than attempting to move a plant that is quite happy just where it is.

A seed that has been left to get ripe and has no genetic mishaps or physical problems should be ready, willing and able to grow a new daughter plant. The trick is that everything has to be just right for it to do that.

Most seeds are designed to travel. They need elbow room away from their siblings and their parent plant, the right soil moisture, nutrients and just the right amount of sunlight. To do this, seeds have adapted several ways of leaving the neighborhood.

Hate it or put up with it, dandelions are a perfect example of fliers. They have a stalked plume that acts like a parasail. The fluffy top leaves the seeds dangling, ready to sprout in most any kind of soil. Another hated flier is the thistle. Their seeds have plumes coming off at all sorts of angles so rather than flying, they sort of tumble along. Some wind-dispersed seeds are either hollow or have a sort of air pocket.

Then there are the winged seeds. Watch the maple's seeds, called for some reason *samara*. They whirl around when the wind picks them up and promptly land in the rain gutters. Ash and elm trees have similar wings on their heavy seeds. The wings wither away once the seed finds a new home.

There are a few sailors in the seed kingdom, such as coconuts. They can travel long distances to beach themselves and get a new grove started. Water chestnuts are well named as they too will float. They are thorny, better to snag roots or the ankles of shoreline plants.

Then there are the exploding seeds. Some dry, shrink and tighten up. When the tension reaches a critical point, the seed capsule bursts open and throws seed far and wide. The seed cases of some tropical plants need humidity to pop. The capsule swells up until it can hold no more moisture, then the built-up pressure pops it open. Some seeds need a little push to burst open. It can be an animal, bird or person brushing by, or wind, rain or even its neighbor. One pod pops, hitting its neighbor and the whole colony starts exploding, one after another.

Anyone who has trekked through tall grass and weeds or has a long-haired dog knows all about hitch-hiking seeds. They will stick to fur, pant legs, car tires, farm machinery or bales of hay. Think about the burdock. It has bracts enclosing the burr end that holds the curved hooks. The seeds are inside. Attempt to remove them from your hunting pup, and the sheaths open and the seeds drop out, and all the while your dog is swearing at you. Some seeds are just sticky. All of them want to move to a suitable area and disembark and germinate. Some researchers think that a period of travel is built in to this type of seed. They need some time to move from the parent plant either to dry out or to ride out a winter or dry season.

All in all, seeds are very good at moving away from home. Like your kids, they need to "get their own place" to grow up and reproduce.

Trees & Shrubs

Ya gotta plant it right the first time—
they grow!

All About Trees

Each year, Americans plant 2.6 million acres of trees. The forest industry plants 45%, homeowners 42%, and the other 13% are planted by public institutions.

Oaks are the slowest-growing trees and don't produce acorns until they are of legal age, about 21. The mulberry tree is known to live 600 years. It's the last to leaf out in the spring. Wait until it is leafed out—it is then safe to plant tomatoes and the other semi-tropicals.

The horse chestnut is a native of Macedonia and Albania. During the two World Wars, horse chestnuts were processed for their starch content, which was used to manufacture *acetone* needed in the production of cordite for weapons. There are two stories of how it was named. One is that when you pick a leaf, the stem resembles a horse shoe. The other is that the Turks treated bruised horses with *aescin*, a natural chemical in the fruit.

We remember U.S. president Franklin Pierce mainly for being a drunk who once ran over a woman with his carriage while having imbibed a bottle or two of booze. On the other hand, he was the first president to have a Christmas tree in the white house.

Birch trees are relatively short-lived, doing well to reach 100. They are shallow rooted and when blown over in a storm the wood rots, but not the bark. They are one of several trees that make a particularly nice sound in the wind. The aspen is another.

Alder trees were prized up until World War ll for making charcoal used in making gunpowder. Because of its steady burning properties, it was used to make fuses for explosives. It's great for smoking fish and meat and making guitar bodies. However, if you are manufacturing a woodwind, use pear wood for the best quality.

Mountain ash trees (called Rowan trees in the U.K.) are loved by robins and cedar waxwings. The tree used to be carried on ships to ward off storms and planted on graves to prevent the dead from returning to haunt the living.

The ginkgo biloba tree is a living fossil. It is unique in being in a genus all alone. It's a tough one, mostly disease free and not bothered by insects. It will grow most any place and is especially suited to cities as even pollution doesn't bother them. Four ginkgos were near the atomic blast center in Hiroshima. A few weeks later they budded out. Two are still living. Tough indeed.

Trees need a lot of water. They will use about 2,000 quarts of water in a normal year, more in a dry one. Healthy fruit trees need air to circulate freely through their branches. This not only prevents fungal diseases but promotes ripening. If you see a green spot on your apple, it was shaded by a leaf. Plant fruit trees between 8 and 20 yards apart, prune them in February or early March and thin the small apples to one per clump in July to get the best from your tree.

There is an old saying: he who plants a tree loves others besides himself. Of course, the best time to plant a tree is 20 years ago. There is usually someplace on your estate to plant a tree next spring.

(Thanks to Niall Edworthy, an English gardener, for some of this information.)

What Is the True Cost of Incorrect Tree Planting?

Three researchers at the University of Minnesota did some research on the cost of planting a tree too deep. The three, Gary Johnson, Jeff Gillman and Chad Giblin, looked at two *Autumn Blaze* maple trees planted at the same time. Tree 1 was planted at the soil line it was in in the pot. However, Tree 2 had the dirt knocked off before planting. The few encircling roots were caught before planting and dealt with, probably by either pulling them straight before planting or removing the circling ends. It was then planted with the top roots only an inch or so under the soil line.

Ten years later, Tree 1 had a diameter of 4 inches and it is 25 feet tall. Tree 2, planted at the proper depth and with encircling roots removed or redirected, has a trunk diameter of 8 inches and is 35 feet tall. The leaves on Tree 1 dropped early and it looks anemic next to its sister tree. It may not live much longer. What happened? Because it was planted too deeply the roots began circling the stem, in effect strangling the tree. The true cost of this poor planting is time. If Tree 1 does die and needs to be replaced, it will be 11 or 12 years behind Tree 2. Even if it does live, it is essentially half the size of trees planted at the same time. This is most important if you have a group or line of trees. You want them to all be about the same size.

Another thing to take into consideration if you are planting a group of trees is the soil. If the soil under one of them is better or worse than the others, it will never be the same size or shape.

A third consideration is the tree itself. Is it zone hardy? If you planted a *Granny Smith* apple tree that lived for three years in mild winters then succumbed in a regular winter, what have you gained? Granny is a zone 5 tree, and will never live long enough here to produce apples. If you had planted a *Zestar*, it would have begun producing apples the 4th or 5th year after it was planted and would continue to live and produce if properly cared for.

The moral of this story: dig a wide hole for your tree, not a deep one. Dump the potted tree out of the pot and take a good look at the roots before you plant it, removing or redirecting any circling roots. Treat it right and it will reward you with shade or fruit and leaves to mulch with in the fall.

Updating Your Landscape

It can be difficult to find trees and shrubs that don't overwhelm a one-story house, especially if it is on a small lot. Too often the cute arborvitae planted by the corner of the house has now grown so tall it towers over the house. The maples and ash trees planted for a little bit of shade have grown to the point that there is no longer any grass, just moss growing in the dank, dark lawn.

Bunkey loves moss—it never needs mowing and stays green all summer, even as the grass turns brown and crisp from drought. Not everybody, however, is as entranced with moss as he is.

Moss grows in the shade on poor soil, as does creeping charlie. The cure: either limb up the tree to let more sun in, or remove the offending trees entirely and replace them with smaller ones. Trees have a finite life: they get old and ugly, and start throwing dead branches at you with every strong wind. That tree needs to be removed before it sends you to the hospital with a concussion or makes a nasty hole in your roof.

If you need to remove a tree, think of it as a chance to redesign your landscape.

Planning Windbreaks and Wildlife Cover

The guys were having their daily coffee klatch at the Pretty Good Café last week. The main topic of discussion was how easy the winter had been. "The worst was the wind," said Pete. They all agreed that the wind had been stronger than usual that winter. The snow cover, they agreed, was less than normal. That led to a discussion of windbreaks. Most farms in earlier times planted windbreaks as a common practice. "These kids don't know how much trees help keep the buildings warmer by slowing down the wind," remarked Tork. That led to an argument about what trees did best in various soils. While there are no hard and fast rules about which trees to plant where, here are a few guidelines from the experts.

If you have a driveway that fills up with snow in the winter, a line of trees and shrubs planted parallel to it will work like a snow fence, piling up the snow before it falls or blows on the drive.

On sandier soil, red and white pine generally are the preferred trees. They grow fast and can easily reach 35 feet. They are an attractive tree and can be cut for lumber. They are also a great protection for our songbirds in bad weather. Crows in particular seem to prefer conifers for their nurseries. One deterrent, if you have a musical ear, is having to listen to the fledglings attempting to learn crow. It is anything but music. Their elders have a peculiar sense of humor. They love to hide in the pines and laugh (or maybe swear) at humans. Conifers are the best windbreak as they don't get naked in the fall like the leaf bearers. Their bulk really slows down the wind.

In heavier soils that have more moisture and nutrient content, plant red and white oaks. Our native burr oak seems to do well in these conditions too. Oaks aren't as slow growing as is commonly thought. The trick is to remove grass around them and feed them while they are small. Grass is the most significant competitor to seedling trees. Oaks have nice extra value as the acorns feed wildlife. Deer, wood ducks and turkeys all love acorns.

If you want a tree that grows a bit faster, a shagbark hickory might be your choice. While deciduous trees aren't the best wind stoppers, they do slow it down.

If you want to conserve soil or prevent erosion and feed wildlife at the same time, look to shrubs. Highbush cranberry, hazelnut and red osier dogwood are good for food and protection of wildlife. All are very attractive shrubs in bloom, shape and size and could easily fit into a bird-friendly landscape.

Even birches will feed birds—they eat the catkins. Birches like damp feet and have some health problems, mainly birch leaf minor disease. Another tree for wet areas is the tamarack. It's a lousy windbreak tree—it drops all its needles in the fall—but it is very attractive, sort of light and airy-looking.

Even if you don't have a problem area, plant a tree or shrub anyhow. It adds value to your home and you probably need the exercise after sitting on your duff eating chocolates all winter.

Crimes Against Horticulture

Drive down any street and you will see landscaping goofs. The biggest one is planting too close to a building. That cute little spruce tree you planted 10 feet from the front door 10 years ago is now covering most of the door and all of the window next to it. And how about that apple tree? It now takes up a good part of the side yard. Yes, apples are good for you, but a 30-foot tall tree? Next time, pick a dwarf or semi-dwarf apple tree, or switch to a plum. They are much smaller and you still eat healthy.

Another goof is discovering your house is getting darker, or the only thing you see outside the window is leaves. Here in the wilds of Minnesota, where we spend months looking out the window waiting for the opportunity to get out and garden, one thing we don't need is a tree covering the view. Keep the conifers away from windows. They are just as dense in winter as summer. Instead, choose a leaf dropper to shade the south and west sides of the house. Those leaves are important in the fall. You need them for mulch or to till into the vegetable garden to add humus to the soil.

Plant your trees and shrubs in the right environment. Most need full sun to look their best. Of course, there are exceptions. Yew, juneberries and some dogwoods like a bit of shade.

Another crime is improper pruning. Cutting the bottom branches off a conifer so you can mow under it may look good to you, but the tree hates it. Those low branches protect the feeder roots from drying out or becoming too warm on a hot summer day. If there are weeds bugging you, simply put a heavy bark or other mulch under there. No weeds and the tree is happy. To keep a conifer from outgrowing its place, candle it. That is, nip a bit of the new candles as they pop out in the spring. Be aware that any branch removed from a conifer will not grow back. Never prune a normally triangle-shaped tree into a ball shape. They never look good and don't do well.

Last, while most people look at their house from the street to see how it looks, that is not where you live. It must look good from the inside, too. After all, needing to have all the lights on in the middle of the day to see to read because that juniper is now covering the window is not a good thing. Cut the monster down. You and your house will be happier.

Don't Do That!

If you have trees, you know that they will eventually need pruning. The trick is to know when to prune which tree. Apple trees, for instance, are pruned in February and March. This is so the wounds are healed before the tree starts to bloom. Even then, it is best to do this on days when the temperatures are in the 20s—above, that is. Too cold and the branches can split or snap off, leaving a mess.

Some trees must be pruned in warm weather. Maples, birches, cherries, and plums are pruned after they are fully leafed out, otherwise they "bleed." Of course, it is not actually blood, but sap—the lifeblood of a tree—and when you make a wound in one, the sap will run. It can actually suck the life out of a branch or tree if done in the spring. Not only that, the sap attracts birds, insects and possibly bears. Bugs can carry pathogens that can lead to diseases. When the sap starts to dry, it has a tendency to mold, opening the door to other diseases.

Then there are the trees and shrubs that have a squishy core. They need to be pruned in the spring as that soft center leads to excessive desiccation. While this won't kill the plant, it will make an ugly-looking canker. A few we need to prune in spring are the elders, honey locusts, pea shrubs (*caragana*), smoke bushes, sumacs and the various viburnums.

Never prune anything during hot, dry weather. The plant is already stressed. If it looks terrible, keep your shorts on and wait for cooler weather. You don't need to fry either.

There used to be a theory that when you transplanted a tree or shrub, you needed do some root pruning and then thin the braches so the tree didn't have so much to heal. Well, if the sap is the tree's blood, the roots are the muscle and fat. All the energy, starch and sugars are stored there. At planting time, the plant is already stressed and needs all its energy to become established in its new home.

There are times the gardener will need to prune a few roots. If they are growing in a circle and you can't pull them apart, you may have to cut some off. Don't, however, take any branches or leaves off to compensate. The poor baby needs all of them to feed herself. And never fertilize a tree or shrub the first year its planted. It is working hard enough to grow in its new home.

Choosing the Right Wood Mulch

Bunkey is having his usual hissy fit—this time about wood mulch. His friend George keeps harping on why mulching trees is so important, and his wife Petunia keeps hitting the newly-planted trees when she mows the grass. The idea of mulch is to protect the trees from Petunia and the lawn mower, and to help keep the soil moist and cool under them. Bunkey's problem is what kind of mulch he should use.

Wood-based mulches are derived from two main sources: materials harvested specifically for lumber production and materials harvested from land clearing or storm damage. Lumber mills debark trees in the process of squaring off the tree. The bark and excess slabs are shredded to produce mulch. This is usually a mix of local hardwoods. This shredded bark mulch has the shortest life span, about 1 to 2 years, and is the least expensive. Since it rots quite quickly, it is ideal for a spot that needs humus. Adding nitrogen to the bark will hasten this process.

Pine bark mulch is more interesting as the pieces have a layered look. This also lasts longer, two to three years.

The more exotic mulches—shredded cypress or cedar bark—will last up to 4 years and hold its color longer, but costs more as it needs to be shipped here. It also smells nice—for a while, anyway.

So what about all those colored wood mulches? They are often made of shredded slab wood that can be dyed. Bark can't. They have a 2 to 3 year life span, but can add a lot to a landscape as they can complement your house or make a dead area pop out with a contrasting color. A light-colored mulch around a tree in a deeply shaded area will make the spot look lighter.

If you are mulching to prevent erosion, don't use wood chips as they will float away with the rain. Instead use the fibrous bark. It has a tendency to stick together and stay in place.

Check to see if one of the electric companies is having trees trimmed in your area. The tree trimmers will happily dump a pile of trimmings on your lot. In the summer, this will include leaves.

Leafy mulch will rot quite quickly since it is almost a pre-made compost pile. Let this sit for a year to work and cool off. It will heat. Just the opposite of what you want a mulch to do. Stick with leaves or grass for your flowers. Wood takes up too much of the nitrogen in the soil as it rots. You will need to add nitrogen to any mulched area to replace what the mulch uses.

Be positive. Mulching season is coming—eventually.

Protect Young Trees

Bunkey is having tree problems. Last year he gave his wife an ornamental apple tree for her birthday. Being a little bit lazy, he didn't get mulch around it for a couple of weeks. In the meantime, he mowed the grass. Cutting too close to the tree, he bumped the trunk, leaving a nasty scar. The weed whip made the next ding. The rabbits and mice feasted on the nice tender bark all winter. Bunkey dug up a dead birthday tree this spring.

So, how do you protect young trees? First, do mulch out to the dripline of your new tree. This not only keeps the nasty machines from damaging the bark, it also keeps water from evaporating as quickly, keeps the roots cool and eventually feeds the tree as the mulch rots. Trees have a thin layer of cells called the *cambium* that is just below the bark. This layer transports water and nutrients to and from the roots and leaves. Anything that damages this *cambium* not only weakens a tree but make them more vulnerable to disease and insects. In the summer, the ring of mulch will protect the tree.

In the winter you will need to use some type of tree guard, something that protects the trunk from animals and weather. The protection should have ventilation holes to allow the trunk to breathe. Moisture build-up can cause the bark to split, which is why most guards should be removed in the summer. Tree guards should extend several inches below the soil and be high enough to be above the snow.

Here are some guards that the Ontario Ministry of Natural Resources has studied.

- *Arborgard®*—These are plastic forms that have ventilation holes. They are 23 centimeters (9 inches) tall and fit around a trunk up to 10 centimeters (4 inches) in diameter. (All measurements are in centimeters. It's Canada, after all.)
- *Texguard.* This a bright blue plastic mesh sheet. Their ads say they are easy to see. Visualize a row of bright blue trees against the white snow—great look for Easter. These will not have to be removed as they break down in sunlight in a few years.

- *Other Wraps—Paper* wrap will protect your tree trunk from weather, but not from animal damage. *Burlap* does the same thing. *Hardware cloth* keeps the beavers and rodents from lunching, but is no protection from sunscald. If you're desperate, you can cut the tops and bottoms from liter *pop bottles.* Cut them up the sides and stack them four high with each one on the outside of the bottle below. Do take them off in the spring when the weather settles. They look pretty ugly.

Trees are a long-term investment. Plant them properly. Give them proper protection and pruning and you will add thousands of dollars of value to your property. They are also nice to sit under with a drink on a hot day and watch your neighbors mow grass when you are done mowing yours.

How to Kill a Tree

When Bunkey moved into his house about 15 years ago, one of the things that sold him on the place was a huge elm tree that shaded the house from the south. Had he been more aware of how a tree should look, he would have noticed that instead of having a single trunk, the elm had a whole bouquet of them. The tree had been topped, either by man or a windstorm, sometime in the past. Five years went by and one spring, one side of the tree was full of dead branches. It had been attacked by Dutch elm disease and had to come down.

This left a big empty spot that just ached to be filled. So, Bunkey went to the nursery that fall and ordered the largest balled and burlapped tree they had on the lot. It was cheaper if he dug the hole it was going into, so he dug a nice deep one. The soil didn't appear to be very good, so he bought several large bags of garden soil and 4 of potting soil to put in the hole. The tree came and was planted and the hole was filled. But some of the top roots were exposed, so Bunkey added more soil, covering them to about a foot. Then, to keep down the weeds, he laid a foot of mulch on top of the soil, being careful to get it right up to the trunk of the tree to prevent moisture from escaping. He had put a handful of fertilizer and hormone root starter in the hole, so now he put a hose at the edge of the hole and let it run all night. He kept the tree well watered all summer, even though there was an inch of rain a week all summer and very good fall rains.

The next spring some of the lower branches kept hitting him in the head as he mowed, so he cut them off. He didn't want to get snagged on branch stubs, so he cut the branches flush to the trunk, and then, to keep them from bleeding, painted the stubs with some stuff he got from a big box store.

He kept fertilizing the tree that summer and kept it very well watered. He also backed into it with his pickup and left a nasty gash in the trunk that "healed up" nicely.

The 4th year of the tree, Petunia decided they needed an addition to the house on the south side. The bulldozers didn't hit the tree, but they piled dirt up against it most of the summer—and of course drove within 2 feet of it digging the foundation. The addition was up and nicely shaded by the tree that summer. In fact, it was fuller than usual.

The next summer the branches close to the addition didn't leaf out, so Bunkey had his friend Oscar (who had a bucket truck) come over and cut the dead stuff off. Oscar suggested that they thin the interior of the tree to give it more sun while he was up there. That was the final straw for this poor over-stressed tree. The next strong wind blew it down right on top of the addition.

What did Bunkey do wrong? Everything. Exposé to follow.

First of all, Bunkey bought a big balled-and-burlapped (B&B) tree—and in the fall. A large tree can weigh up to 400 pounds with the very compacted soil and the metal cage to hold it. A tree that has been dug by a tree spade can have from 75% to 90% of its roots removed when it's dug. Then, it was planted in the fall. It had no time to recover from the shock. Spring would have been better.

Even better, a potted tree has most of its roots intact. It will start growing almost right away. A B&B tree may take as long as three years to start growing, and the severed roots may start circling the trunk. If the soil is mostly removed from a potted tree, the roots can be seen and pulled away if they are circling the stem.

Next, Bunkey covered the roots with about a foot of soil. He also threw a handful of fertilizer and rooting hormone in the hole. Trees do not need fertilizer for the first year; then, if you fertilize your grass, the tree will get all the food it needs. The top roots of the tree should be no more than an inch below the surface of the soil. In the wild, roots are often above the soil—as homeowners of naturally-planted trees can attest to. They need air and water.

Another mistake Bunkey made was amending the soil around his tree. The pore sizes were different in the added soil than in the native soil the tree would be growing in for the rest of its life. Water has difficulty moving through soil of different pore sizes. Also, potting soil has no actual soil in it. It is compost (a pore opener) and maybe peat.

Overwatering his new tree was the next mistake. It will need extra the first five years, but an inch of rain a week is quite enough. Water in the fall if the weather is dry.

Next, the mulch. Yes, mulch your trees, but with only a few inches of mulch. It rots adding soil. Eventually, the soil gets too deep and the tree can't get enough air. Fungus and bacteria can attack the tree at the higher soil line, not a good thing. Do not put plastic or weed barrier under the mulch. Neither water nor air can easily get to the roots with that stuff on the soil.

It is fine to prune low-hanging, broken or crossing branches from your tree. Before you cut, look for the swelling where the branch meets the tree trunk. Cut several inches away from that branch collar, leaving a short (2 to 3 inch) stub. Don't paint it. A small wound will heal more quickly than a huge slice.

The wound from the truck bumper compressed the vascular structure where it struck. The tree could no longer pump water and food through that area, so the branches it fed, died.

Then came the bulldozers. They not only compacted the soil above the roots of the tree but piled dirt on top of its roots, compressing the soil more and cutting off needed air.

Oscar's trim was the last straw (Oscar owned the bucket truck). Cutting off dead branches was a good idea; thinning the middle of the tree wasn't. This left the branches with leaves only on the tips of them. This let the wind get a good whack at the top of the tree, and down it came.

Bunkey knows better now.

Arbor Day Tips

Here is a new word for the gardener's vocabulary: *mast.* Mast refers to the fruit, nuts and seeds of woody plants that are eaten by wildlife. While all trees and many shrubs produce mast, there are only a few that are a highly-valued food source.

Oaks are one of the most important mast producers. Acorns are eaten by turkeys, ruffed grouse, wood ducks, deer, blue jays, bears, squirrels and raccoons. Many of them use acorns to put on fat before winter, for the energy for migration or for food in the winter.

Oaks need full sun. Unfortunately, in the woods natural regeneration favors more shade-tolerant species, meaning our oaks are in decline. There are several ways to increase our oaks. You can purchase a tree from a nursery, dig up a sapling that is growing in the shade, or plant acorns. The trick is to plant at least two species of the tree. White oaks have acorns every year, while the acorns on red oaks mature on the tree during the second year. Planting both insures that a late frost won't kill the whole crop.

Planting acorns is quite easy. Simply poke a hole in the soil, drop the acorn in and step on the hole. If you are planting in grass, stick a shovel in the sod and drop the acorn in the resulting hole. White oak acorns need to be planted in the fall as they sprout shortly after falling from the tree. If you plan to plant red oak acorns and can't get at it in the fall, put them in the fridge and keep them moist until spring.

If you are more interested in feeding birds, plant a mulberry tree. This is a very interesting small tree. Each spring, you will be positive it has died because it leafs out so late. It gets leaves and flowers at the same time. You will know when the berries erupt as the tree will be full of birds. The berries look like long, black raspberries and have one drawback for the home owner: berried bird poop stains. You will find purple spots on anything left under any tree the birds perch in.

Two other bird-feeding trees are Mountain ash and its cousin, crabapple. The fruit that hangs on the trees is used by the spring migrators. It is often the only food available at that time. Deer, bears, grouse and turkeys love apples too. Nothing gets your attention like seeing a turkey on the topmost branches of your crabapple tree. Petunia gave Bunkey particular heck last winter for throwing a black plastic bag into the apple tree with his snow blower. Looking a bit closer, she discovered it was a turkey having breakfast.

Black cherry trees provide a valuable food for the young-of-the-year animals. The leftover pits are food the next year. The various dogwoods produce beautiful flowers, followed by bird-loved berries. The berries hardly have time to get ripe before the shrub is stripped of them.

Other mast trees are maple, ash, elm, basswood and hackberry. Red and silver maples produce their mast in the spring, while the sugar maple mast is released in the fall.

Mast can be messy; in the case of oaks, dangerous to walk on. Mulberries stain your lawn chairs, maple seeds clog the gutters, and pine cones plug up the lawn mower. But what the heck, watching the birds is worth a bit of hassle. And really, purple polka dots on a lawn chair just adds to its character.

Planting a "Safe" Tree

Bunkey lost a nice littleleaf linden one windy week. It snapped off just below the soil line. It had been planted by the previous owner of his house. While Bunkey was surveying the damage (it hit the house roof), his neighbor George the Master Gardener came over. It took only one look at the base of the tree to see what had happened. The tree had been planted too deeply and the roots had not been straightened out. One of those roots had circled the stem, compressing it.

The University of Minnesota Department of Forest Resources continues to stress proper tree planting. The concern is that ten years after you have planted a tree the wrong way, a strong wind will knock it over and smuck your car. The problem with improper planting is stem-girdling roots. The roots actually slowly kill a tree. Littleleaf lindens seem to be the most prone to this injury. Gary Johnson, Forest Resources, describes the problem: "Imagine blowing up a long skinny balloon. Now squeeze the middle of the balloon. Note that the diameter above and below is significantly larger than the area that is being squeezed, a.k.a. "girdled." In a windstorm, this compressed point is quite literally the "weakest link in the chain" and is the point where the tree will break off under the loading pressure of the wind.

The University of Minnesota conducted studies from 1994 to 1996 in urban tree decline. Of the 220 declining and dying trees that were diagnosed, 80% had stem-girdling roots (SGRs), and were the "only causal agents isolated from the 'patients.'" These trees had been planted from 12 to 20 years earlier and had more than 50% of stem compression. In all these cases, the SGRs were well below ground, from 4 to 14 inches in the soil. Later studies demonstrated that the deeper the tree stems were in the soil or mulch, the more likely they were to have multiple layers of the killing roots. Most people were not too impressed with the idea that a tree died after 12 to 20 years, as many felt that 30 years is a normal life span for a tree. Actually, urban landscape trees, whether planted in a sidewalk pit or in a landscaped yard, live only 7 to 35 years. The normal life for a boxelder, cousin of the maples, is about 100 years. Many of our native trees should live well into their 90s.

So, how often do trees die from strangulation of their roots? Who knows. When a tree falls during a windstorm, we don't as a rule dig up the roots for a look. However, the University did just that. The *Tree Failure in Wind Storms* research did 1,500 "tree autopsies" from 1995 through 2005. These weren't trees that fell during tornadoes or severe straight-line winds, but winds during thunderstorms or winds at the edges of severe wind events.

Does this mean you should not plant lindens? No, it just means you need to be careful when you plant a tree or shrub that the roots do not circle the tree. You may have to cut some roots off if the tree has been in a pot for a long time. They must circle as there is no other place to go in a pot.

So how do you, the homeowner, prevent trees from taking out your car or roof? When you get a potted tree, dump it out of the pot and shake the soil off the roots. Cut off any circling roots, then plant the tree with the top root only 1 to 2 inches below the soil. Mulch, but keep the mulch at least 2 to 3 inches from the trunk of the tree. Now you should have a tree that will outlive you, so be sure you put it in the right spot the first time. Remember, it will not only get taller, but wider, too.

An Exotic Replacement Tree

Bunkey will have to replace a boxelder tree next spring. As with most of its kind, it has been a fall pain-in-the-backside. It is a female, thus attracts the boxelder bugs that plaster the south side of his light colored house. He suggested painting the house dark green, brown or maroon, but Petunia wouldn't agree. She likes the combination of cream with aqua trim. "Just get rid of that blasted boxelder," she demanded. Since it shades the east side of the house, it must be replaced. After hitting every nursery and tree farm in western Minnesota, the two of them finally decided on a Kentucky coffee tree. While ideally it likes moist rich soil, the tree is a tough one. It will tolerate pollution, drought, high pH and road salt. It will need a bit more water than one usually gives yard trees, but is worth it.

The Kentucky coffee tree is a medium-sized tree, an excellent size for most yards. It's shape is oval to irregular, with an open spreading crown. The leaves are unbelievable. Up to 3 feet long, doubly compound and a bluish green. A nice contrast from our usual common green-leaved trees. In late spring it blooms greenish white. The flowers are very attractive to pollinating insects. That fact alone makes it a must-have. The blooms are not very fragrant. Nice if you don't tolerate strong-smelling flowers. Only the female tree blooms. Female trees develop 6 to 10 inch flat pods that are quite attractive in the fall, as is the deeply furrowed bark. The bare branches are quite architectural. Unfortunately, the pods are a bear to mow, so it is best to get a male tree. The fall color is nothing to write home about, but it can occasionally turn a dark yellow.

Since the leaves are so large, one would think the tree would provide dense shade. Actually, the shade is filtered or dappled so Petunia can plant grass or shade-loving plants under it. It gets its leaves quite late in the spring so it is perfect for a bed of daffodils or tulips either right under it or nearby. And it drops its leaves soon after the first frost, making it a good choice where you want sunlight spring and fall. Not only is it disease and insect free, it also has the ability to fix nitrogen in the soil.

This tree is a bit difficult to transplant because of a branching taproot. It is best to plant it in the spring. It is not a fast grower, so give it a bit of fertilizer the second year. It will also need watering during dry periods for a few years.

The seed pods have been roasted and used as a bitter, caffeine-free coffee substitute, thus the name. However, the raw seeds contain a poisonous acid, so keep them away from the kids—or better yet, get a male tree. Look for *Stately Manor*, a seedless male. It is more upright and has a narrower crown. *Espresso* is another with an upright growth habit and a vase like shape. *Prairie Titan* is an upright spreading male with interesting winter architecture. All are cultivars developed by the University of Minnesota (our money at work).

Let's Go Nuts

If you have the room and need a shade tree with benefits, think nuts. Some nut trees like walnut and hickory can be enormous, up to 100 feet tall in the wild. They need to be at least 30 feet from any structure or driveway because of the large invasive roots. They can buckle a drive, damage your foundation, and raise heck with sewer pipes. That's the bad news. The good news is that they are very long-lived, excellent shade trees and provide an excellent snack in the fall.

Walnuts are *allopathic*—meaning the roots exude a chemical that poisons most plants that attempt to grow under them. The husks stain anything they fall on and they are very difficult to crack. One neat way to do it is to build 2 troughs just slightly wider than the tires on your car. Put the nuts to be shelled in the troughs and drive over them. Crazy, but it works.

The Jung Seed Company catalog says that hazelnuts are a zone 5 shrub. Funny, they grow quite well here. It is a small tree or tall shrub, 10 to 12 feet tall. They are relatively easy to crack. A taller tree, 20 to 30 feet tall is the chestnut. There are at least 2 varieties available, the older Chinese chestnut and a hybrid called *Colossal*, a cross between the Japanese and European tree. The latter takes about 3 years to produce nuts described as bearing very large, high quality nuts. This tree needs a pollinator and the Chinese chestnut is recommended. She takes longer to bear, 5 to 7 years. The nuts are easy to peel and sweet. The chestnut is a cousin of the oak and can tolerate dry, lean soil. A drawback of the nuts is that the husks are covered in thorns. Tough on the pup's paws and barefoot kids.

Shagbark hickory is a triple threat tree. Tall, 50 to 80 feet, it is a good, long-lived shade tree. The bark peels off in strips, looking for all the world like it has a beard. A nice accent in the winter. The trees are quite slow growing and difficult to transplant because of a long tap root. The nuts are described as sweet and a culinary treat, Butternut hickory is pretty, with a smooth gray bark. The nuts are long and deeply furrowed. This is a Minnesota native growing at least as far north as Aitkin County. There is some discussion as to whether or not the nuts are edible. It depends on which book you're reading.

If you are adventurous and have a sheltered area, it might be fun to try a Ukrainian almond. They are listed as zone 5, but they come from Russia. Isn't it cold there? The shrub grows 15 to 20 feet high. They bloom late, so avoid early frosts. Even if you never get nuts from this shrub, it has lots of pinkish-white blooms in the spring.

All these trees and shrubs need a pollinator tree or shrub. If your estate is large enough, give one or more of them a try. If nothing else, you will have every squirrel in the township visiting in the fall, shelling and burying nuts, and leaving the husks and holes in the grass for you to deal with.

Fruit Trees

Bunkey is planning to plant some fruit trees this spring, but is concerned—he has heard that many fruit trees bear only every other year. To find out if this is just an old wives' tale, Bunkey went to have coffee and a talk with his neighbor, George, who seems to know everything about anything that grows.

Here is what Bunkey learned:

- All fruit trees need full sun, that means sun during business hours, 8 to 5. Often what happens is that another tree has grown taller shading your tree during the most important times of the day.
- Your tree didn't get pollinated. Apple trees, for one, require a different variety of apple to set fruit. To complicate matters, the two trees need to bloom at the same time. They do not need to be side by side. A bee will fly 1/4 mile from tree to tree, so if your neighbor has a crabapple that blooms at the same time as your Honeycrisp, you should get apples.
- The tree has "wet feet." It is in heavy clay soil in a hollow that has poor drainage.
- The tree is too young. Some trees take as long as seven years before bearing.
- They need pruning. If the branches are so thick that many of them don't get the full complement of sun, you need to prune. Do not take any more than one-fourth of the branches in any one year.
- The tree is not zone hardy. It blooms too soon or our Siberian-like winter temperatures have killed the flower buds. This is why it is so hard to get peaches and apricots to bear in Minnesota. Anything lower than -20 degrees will kill their flower buds. Fruit trees set buds for next year's crop in late summer. This is also why you need to thin the fruit in July. An apple tree has only five spots to set its fruit. If all those spots are filled with this year's apples, it has no place to set buds for next year's crop.

Forget about planting sweet cherries. They just can't take our winters. However, pie cherries, the kind that one bite will make you pucker for 20 minutes, do well.

Be very picky when you plant a fruit tree—it will be there for many years. Plan ahead. Pear trees, for instance, are fairly easy to grow and can live for a long time. And we have all seen ancient apple trees on old farmsteads. A major pruning can often bring these antiques back to bearing. The only problem will be that you have no idea what variety it is.

Fruit trees need pruning to do well. Get your pruners sharpened up—your fruit trees need to know who's boss.

The fruit that can grow at the highest attitudes is apples. Apple trees need almost 1,000 hours of cold fall and winter air to produce flowers. The seeds of apples, almonds, apricots, cherries, peaches and nectarines all contain cyanide. You would have to eat pounds of apple seeds before you had a problem. The pits of apricots, nectarines and peaches have potentially large amounts of the chemical—good thing most people have more sense than to chew or attempt to swallow those pits!

The average person eats a bushel of apples a year—not all at once, of course. The U.S. and China produce the most apples. A good thing as apples make up 50% of the world's deciduous fruit. A healthy, mature apple tree will produce between 220 to 440 pounds of apples each year. That is, if you thin your apples in the spring. If not, expect a crop every other year.

If you want bird-free tree fruit, trick them. String invisible fishing line back and forth through the branches. Birds can't see the line, and when they encounter it are afraid of getting trapped. Or a few old CD's tied to branches may scare them off. In England, they plant lavender or climbing nasturtiums around the bottoms of their apple trees. If the wasps are helping themselves to your fruit, hang a pop bottle ¼ full of fruit pop or jelly and water mixed with a few drops of liquid soap in your tree. They will crawl in for a drink and drown.

Pruning Apple Trees

It's early March, and Bunkey is feeling pretty smug this week. He just got all three of his apple trees pruned and his neighbor George, the Master Gardener, told him he did it just right.

So, you ask, *what exactly did Bunkey do?* First, he cut off all the dead branches. He knew they were dead—he scraped the bark with his fingernail before he cut. If he saw green in the wound, the branch was alive; if brown, the branch was dead and needed to come off.

Next, he cut off all the suckers coming from the bottom of the tree. They only take food and water away from the tree. Then he cut off all branches that were pointing down, or straight up. There were several spots in the trees where branches were crossing each other. The weakest of those had to come off.

Then he stepped back, and fell over a snowbank and lost his saw. Once upright, he looked at the tree. A good shape for an apple tree is a triangle. He had not cut 1/4 of the tree off, so he was able to do a bit of shaping.

The main branches growing from the trunk of the tree are called the scaffolding branches. Ideally, they should leave the trunk at an angle slightly higher than parallel to the ground. This allows the tree to bear the weight of ripe apples without breaking off, as they might do if the angle is too sharp. These scaffolding branches should be evenly spaced along the trunk and get shorter as they grow higher on the tree. This allows all the apples to get sun. If you look closely at your apple and see a green area, that is caused by shade. A leaf shading the fruit will cause a green spot the size of the leaf. To shape a tree, make your cuts about 1/4 of an inch above an outward-facing bud. This will cause the resulting branch to grow away from the trunk.

Get your woolies on, grab your hand saw, pole saw, loppers, hand pruners and stepladder and have at it. Your apple tree will be very happy.

"Plant Turkeys"

Turkey Day is in November, but gardeners need to be aware of plant turkeys all year. One that looks great for small yards is the 5-in-1 apple tree. It has five different apples grafted onto the same tree. Why is it a turkey? Most of the cultivars on this tree trunk aren't reliably hardy here. After a few years, the whole tree may be dead, or one or two will take over the tree—the one best suited for our zone. Instead, plant dwarf apple trees hardy for here. Not only do they bear sooner than a large tree, they are much easier to prune and bag. Also, beware of buying an apple tree from one of the "Marts" because it has the name of an apple you usually buy at the grocery store, like Granny Smith. Although it is a very good apple, it is only hardy as far north as zone 5, not our cold zone 3B.

You have probably seen ads for a tree tomato. It actually is a *tamarillo,* part of the tomato family. You must take it in each fall and it will be several years before it blooms. While they may look like a tomato, they don't taste anything like one. They are quite popular in New Zealand.

Another turkey is any tree advertised in a magazine as "fast growing." It is more than likely not hardy, or if it is, it is probably a weed tree. Remember buckthorn? It was sold as a good hedge plant. Yup. Now it is pushing out native trees.

Bunkey is discouraged. It seems as though every tree in his yard is subject to some killer disease. Maples die if they have a dry summer before an "open" winter. Their roots are quite close to the surface of the soil, so they are subject to drying and then freeze-drying. Ashes now have the ash borer, elms have the elm borer, and oaks are at risk from the oak wilt and two-lined chestnut borer. Oak wilt can kill red and pin oaks in a few short weeks, while with burr and white oaks it can take a bit longer.

Now Bunkey will have another group of trees to be pruned in the winter. Apple trees should be pruned in February or March, Oaks in late fall or winter. Bunkey is really looking forward to hauling a six-footstepladder through the snow drifts to prune trees in February! He lost two pruners last winter and unfortunately found them with the lawn mower this spring.

Sad Trees

People either love weeping trees or they hate them. Bunkey sees them as deformed, although he does have a weeping willow down by his lake. That is a natural tree, not an "engineered one," is his rationale.

There are several types of weepers. The weeping willow is a classic weeping plant—it develops its habit without any training. Next are broadly-weeper trees—these grow upright but have droopy branch tips. An example would be the old weeping crabapple or the conifers that have a strong leader trunk but all the branches weep, giving the tree a narrow profile.

Then there are the grafted weepers—created by grafting a cascading shrub onto a related, upright root stock. An example of this type is the willow, *Salix repens nitida*, grafted on a willow stem.

Strongly-weeping plants only become trees with training. No, the trainers don't go out with a whip and tell the plant to, "Weep, or else!" The shrub is grafted high on the root stock or staked up so it can weep. This type makes the best specimen trees as their size can vary depending on growing conditions and training.

So, you are thinking you could use an exclamation/dramatic accent in your rather dull yard. If so, there are quite a few to choose from. For instance, if you want blooms, pick a weeping crabapple. *Louisa* has pink flowers, green leaves and has good disease resistance. *Ruby Tears* has early reddish leaves before it blooms.

Weeping mulberries are zone 4 hardy. *Pendula* has fruit, a bird magnet; *Chaparral* is sterile—look for cutting-grown rather than grafted.

If you are looking for a conifer to act as winter accent, there is a weeping hemlock cultivar, *Sargentii*—while not fully hardy, it does well in acid soil in a winter shady spot. A juniper to look for is *Tolleson's weeping*. It likes well-drained soil and full sun. *Pendula* (the namers must like this descriptive word) is larger and hardy to zone 4.

While the native weeping willow is reserved for a large area, there are smaller specimens. There are two pussy willows—the male tree is *Kilmarnock*, the female, *Weeping Sally*. They too, can be marketed as *Pendula*. If you want more color, look for the purple osier willow (*Salix purpurea Pendula*). It has fine-textured blue-green leaves, making it a nice contrast to the bolder foliage plants.

If you like the tamarack (American larch), there are two to look for. *Varied Directions* not only weeps, it spreads. *Pendula* is a weeping form of Japanese larch. Both of these are zone 3 trees. Pines have their weepers too. The jack pine cultivar *Uncle Fogy* not only weeps, it is also contorted. The white pine contributions are *Pendula* (see, no imagination), a strong weeper with the silver-blue needles white pine is famous for. A newer cultivar is *Angel Falls*. If you prefer spruce, all four spruces—white, black, Serbian and Norway—have weeping forms. Look for *Formanek*, and again, *Pendula*. The Serbian selection is *Pendula Bruns*. It has bicolored needles the Serbians are noted for.

The developers are always looking for more exotic tree and shrub shapes, probably to name them *Pendula* too. Remember, these trees often touch the ground—plant them so they cascade over a slope or water feature. You don't want to try mowing under them—it leads to too much blue air.

Risky Trees

Trees have a finite life, like all plants. With enough wind, any tree, old or young, can fall over. Some trees are more apt to shed branches in high winds—willows, silver maples and boxelders, for instance. The first two because they have weak wood. Boxelders are risky because of the way they grow—rather fast and usually twisty.

Since Bunkey doesn't have the capability to look at a tree and determine how apt it is to end on top of his house in a windstorm, he needs to look for red flags. Depending on the severity and number of them, he can at least, make a wild guess how likely a tree is to fail.

- *Dead Branches*—These easy-to-spot widow makers don't even need a strong wind to fall. Take them down as soon as you spot them. Look for dead or dying branch tips on your trees and smaller than normal leaves, especially if they are pale or browning. This is a sure sign of a dying tree and it should be removed as soon as you can grab a chain saw.
- *Vertical Cracks*—These are normal, but not cracks that are beginning to open or are spreading. These can be on the trunk or on branches and are danger signs.
- *Internal Decay*—This is one of the hardest structural weaknesses to spot. Some decay can be normal, so don't get the saw out yet. However, a sure sign of decay is if the tree has mushrooms or conks growing around the base of the tree or on the trunk. Another sign is sunken or dark areas on the trunk or branches or oozing sap. This can be canker disease and can increase decay and weakness in the tree. Carpenter ants feed on dead wood, so a bad sign is if you see a trail of them diving into your tree.
- Included Bark— This is where two branches have bark sandwiched between them, making a very weak union. The branches are pushing against each other as they grow and have few if any interconnected fibers holding them together.

Petunia heard Bunkey yelling and discovered him stuck in a tree. She got a ladder and, then called an arborist. His assessment assured them that their trees were safe, for now anyhow—as was Bunkey, also for now.

Lightning-Struck Trees

During a recent thunderstorm, lightning struck a tree right outside Bunkey's house. "It sounded like a bomb went off." The tree looked like that had happened. The damage is thought to be caused by the electrical charge of up to 100 million volts at thousands of amperes that vaporizes the water inside the tree, creating super-heated steam that explodes when it exceeds the structural strength of the wood.

How can you tell if your tree has been hit by lightning, other than the boom that flips you out of bed? A common indicator is a vertical stripping where the bark, and sometimes the wood underneath, is torn from the truck or a major scaffold limb. It can be most of the way up the tree or hit and miss, straight up or spiral around the tree like a stripe in a candy cane. In some cases, the bark can be violently blown off the tree in sections or completely around the whole trunk.

A sneakier strike may not show any damage, but has fried the roots. Since sap is a better conductor then wood, damage is usually related to how much moisture there is in and around the tree. If it is between the bark and the wood, the lighting will follow a channel and blow the bark off the tree. A tree with a wet center may be totally blown apart. Or, the lightning could flow around the outside of a wet tree and flow into the ground.

So, what should Bunkey do next? First of all, stay inside until the storm is over. Then, if there are broken limbs, they can be cut off. If the tree has landed on the roof, get a professional to do the removing. Don't immediately cut down a lightning-struck tree, unless it has been blown apart. Take a wait-and-see attitude. If it leafs out next spring, it will probably live another 50 years.

Hazardous Trees

There comes a time in every tree's life when it is time to take it down. Removing a tree can be traumatic for many people. We become attached to them for several reasons. Maybe Grampa planted it. Or you planted it when a favorite dog died. Or maybe it is hiding your redneck neighbor's collection of used car parts covering his front yard. It could be an apple tree whose apples make the best pie. If possible, you would like to save those special trees. Now you need to decide if you can or should save that tree.

To start with, ask yourself these questions.

1. *Is the tree healthy?* If you can stand under the tree in full summer and see no sky, it is probably healthy, depending on the variety of tree. If it is a honey locust, you should be able to see blue between the branches as it is a rather "loose" tree. Not so an oak or maple. Any healthy tree should have a crown of at least 60% the size of the tree. If there are a lot of dead branches or abnormally small leaves, or it defoliates before others of its race because of insects or drought, it's unhealthy.
2. *Is it stable?* Will it remain so, or is it apt to fall down in the next big windstorm? Have some of the roots been cut off? Has the street been widened or buried utilities been dug close to the trunk? If it has roots cut within a few feet of a large tree on two or more sides, don't hesitate. Take it down, as it will fall on your house or utility wires or whatever else it is near. If the tree has extensive decay, it should come down. Look for cavity in the trunk. You may have to have an arborist look at it and determine if the decay is greater than 33%. If it is, murder it. If it is tipping, can it be stabilized? Is the tree large and squeezed in a small area? Danger. Take a very

good look at the base of the tree. Are there roots wrapped around it? They can strangle a tree, making it more apt to fall.

3. *How important is the tree to you and what can your budget handle?* What is the tree's value? This is harder. Are you willing to pay quite a bit to stabilize a tree that may not live much longer, even with proper care? Or does it just need some proper and judicious pruning?

Trees to get rid of without any head-scratching:

- Crabapple trees that get scab every year—there are scab-resistant varieties.
- A tree under power lines that has been repeatedly topped to the point it looks like a mop on a tree trunk. It is likely full of decay and there are many small trees that won't need to have a yearly haircut.
- A silver maple that has had construction activity within four to five feet. That tree is just looking for a chance to fall down.

Most people hate to murder a tree, but sometimes it's the tree or the house. Cut 'er down.

Protecting Your Trees During Construction

Any kind of construction, no matter how small, can adversely affect your trees and consequently, the value of your property. A wooded lot can cost 20% more than a bare lot, so it pays to take special care when working around trees.

If you have a large stand of trees that have matured together, take special care when removing any of them. This type of stand works together as a unit—the trees inside the group have been protected from weather such as strong wind and excess sunlight. Taking down the outermost trees and suddenly exposing the protected trees can cause them to die, or at the very least, be shocked to the point of stunting.

Some obvious damage caused during construction includes torn branches, wounds to trunks and torn bark. However, the most lasting damage may be what you don't see: root damage.

Unlike carrots, trees don't have a tap root. If you have ever seen a tree tipped out of the soil by a storm, you will see several large structural roots, then millions of small feeder roots. These small roots extend about 1/3 times the height of the tree and go down about 16 to 18 inches. This is why you don't water a tree at the trunk but at or beyond the drip line, as that is where it is able to absorb the water.

Cutting a structural root also cuts many of the small feeder roots. Now the tree is less able to absorb water and nutrients and may become structurally unsound—in other words, a lot more apt to take out your garage in a high wind. If you need to have underground lines installed, try to get the installer to go under the tree rather than trenching over the tree's roots.

Another tree killer is soil compaction. This can happen if a truck or any heavy machine drives under or even near a large tree. Piling building material under a tree may protect it from the sun, but it also compacts the soil. All plants need pore space—space filled with water and air so the roots can grow and feed. Compacting the soil reduces the pore spaces. Heavy weights can even crush some roots.

Another no-no is adding soil over the tree's roots. As little as two to six inches of added soil over a mature tree's root system can suffocate the roots it covers. The roots no longer are able to absorb water easily.

It is quite simple, although work, to prevent tree damage during construction. Fence the tree right out to the drip line. Do not let your contractor store material inside the fence or, even worse, pour the rinse from the cement trunk there. You have to write a contract with steep fines for violating those rules.

A mature tree can add up to $3,000 to the value of your lot, and two trees can lead to a hammock.

Yews, arborvitae and junipers tend to outgrow their spaces and get really ugly and misshapen as they age, especially those planted originally as foundation plantings. If this is the case in your yard, don't feel bad about removing them. They are probably overgrowing the driveway or the sidewalk anyway. You have grown used to the way the place looks, but really take a good look at it. Is the shrub a nice shape? Is it too big for its space or shading a flowerbed or encouraging moss to grow in a space you don't want moss? Dig the thing out!

Don't put another shrub back in the same place. Instead, plant starting at the lot line. Design from front of the house to the back. Plan gently-curving paths that lead to the backyard. Use small ornamental trees, dwarf evergreens, upright perennials and groundcovers to fill the area that used to be grass. Many of them will do well in light shade, like that cast by a large tree half of the day.

Even newer-home landscapes need a bit of tweaking, and older ones occasionally need a bulldozer. It's time to give your house a new setting. Just don't get run over as you stand in the middle of the street to get a real good look at your landscape. If you want to find exactly what your zone is , there is an interactive feature to the USDA map that lets you put in your zip code to pinpoint your personal zone.

Is My Tree OK?

Bunkey was showing a friend from the big city around his yard and bragging about his gardening prowess. He showed him his vegetable garden, all ready for the winter. "But, there are dead plants in it," the friend remarked, "and if that is your flowerbed, it's a real mess."

Bunkey had to explain that even though the gardens looked messy, in this case messy was a good thing. Bunkey had pulled up and removed all the vines but left the corn stalks, the flowers and lettuce and radishes that had gone to seed. He explained that what is left will hold any leaves that blow in—and snow, if we get any. The leaves, radish, lettuce and any other plant material will be tilled in next spring. Seeds from the radishes and lettuce will sprout long before he would be able to get into the garden to plant. Holding snow on the soil will prevent it from drying out and blowing away in the strong winter and spring winds. Another plus is that the birds will harvest any seeds left in the both the flowerbed and the vegetable garden.

The critical guest then brought Bunkey's attention to one of his trees. "That tree must be dying. It's got all that funny stuff on the bark."

That funny stuff, Bunkey told him is *lichen*. It can be orange, black, gray or green and look crusty or sort of leafy. It is a symbiotic association of a fungus and an algae. The fungus provides the body and the algae supplies the sugars for food for both of them. They don't hurt the tree as they are growing on bark, the dead surface cells on a tree. Lichens can grow on soil, rocks and logs. They do help in the decomposition of dead wood. Actually, lichen growth means that the air is clean—they will not grow in polluted air.

"Oh, how beautiful. Did you plant that vine in all your pine trees? Those red leaves against the green boughs are really spectacular."

Bunkey hadn't the heart to tell his friend that as soon as he could, he would be cutting that vine off at the base and brushing the stump with brush killer. The vine was Virginia creeper and was damaging the tree. The vine's leaves shade the tree's needles, reducing photosyn-thesis. Some vines can actually strangle a tree by twining around it and cutting into the branches and trunk. And, some vines can get up to 3 inches in diameter. Riverbank grape and oriental bittersweet, a very invasive plant, can also do nasty things to trees. If they get heavy enough, they can actually break branches. The Minnesota Dept. of Agriculture would like people to report any sites where the oriental bittersweet is growing as they want it destroyed.

There was one oddity that Bunkey brought to his friends' attention. Several of his oak trees had smooth spots on the bark, as though it has been stripped off. This is caused by a little white cup fungus that lives on the bark and changes the growth of the bark. It looks strange but is entirely benign, he explained.

"Boy, you sure have learned a lot living out here in the boonies. Guess you don't miss that apartment in Minneapolis."

Mentally blessing the Extension office and neighbor George, Bunkey agreed he had learned a lot and didn't miss the city at all.

How Do Trees Know It's Fall?

Bunkey is babysitting his five-year-old nephew, Wylie, also known as the "why kid." He always wants to know why, or how come. Now, he wants to know how the trees know it's fall and why they are no longer green. Here are those answers (with some help from Chris Curry, a University of Minnesota grad student, and Charlie Rohwer, a scientist from the University).

Longer nights indicate dropping temperatures and signal plants to begin preparing for winter. *Photo-periodic response* is the technical term for shortening length of day. It not only tells plants it is going to get colder, in the spring it plays a role in breaking dormancy and flowering for many species.

Shorter days tell our trees—red maple, sumac, Canadian hemlock and many of the flowering trees—that now is the time to get ready for that long, cold sleep. Of course, cooler weather also gets the trees prepared. If we had a nice warm November then suddenly it dropped to 10 degrees, many usually hardy trees and plants would be killed. Gradually decreasing temps enables plants to acclimate, and that increases their cold hardiness. Plant membranes adjust their composition to maintain fluidity at low temps.

Sap is another important part of tree winterizing. The dissolved sugars in the watery sap lower the freezing point below plain water. When ice is formed in plant cells, it pulls water from the cell, concentrating it and that lowers the freezing point, better protecting the cell.

The tree must also protect next year's leaves that are being formed now as buds. The buds are protected by bud scales. They will keep the tissues warm, prevent oxygen from reaching the buds and keep them from drying out in the low humidity and winds.

Trees must get rid of this year's leaves now. Simple aging of the leaf allows the tree to hold onto nitrogen in the form of chlorophyll, a very valuable resource. The tree moves it from the leaves to the stem, thereby removing the green coloring from the leaves. What is left are the pigments the tree makes from scratch each year. Two pigments are *anthocyanins* (which also make blueberries blue), and *carotenoids* (the pigment that turns carrots orange). Enjoy the colors as the next step the tree takes is to push the pretty colored leaves off. Another fancy term, *abscission*, causes this. Simply put, cell walls between the leaf and stem break down and the leaf falls off. Gardeners rejoice—right after they curse the job of picking them all up. Leaf mulch is great, and it's free—except for the energy used picking them up and piling them on the garden.

So, what did Bunkey tell Wylie? Long nights and cold days tell the tree to color up and get ready for winter. Enough information for a five year old.

Spruce Up Your Winter Landscape

After the snow covered his yard, Bunkey took a walk around it and discovered it was boring. There was no color other than the tree bark. "We need to get some color in this place," he told Petunia.

Luckily, there is a lot he could do next spring to improve the situation. The first thing that comes to mind is conifers. A green tree in a white landscape is a treat to the eye. However, do consider how big that tree will get. A 50-foot-tall white pine makes a ranch house look like it is cowering under it. There are a number of conifers that stay compact if you have a small yard or a small house. Trees that are tall and scraggly need to be removed, even if you do have a large house.

Another tree to consider is a crabapple. Many of them hold on to their apples until the birds eat them. The red, orange or yellow apples are a bright spot in the winter landscape. Mountain Ash is a smaller tree that not only has large blossoms in the spring but bright orange/red clumps of berries in late summer. Cedar waxwings and robins will flock to the tree when the berries are ripe. Watching a row of waxwings, passing a berry bird to bird is reward enough to plant this tree.

River birch with its peeling orange bark is a standout against the white snow. If you are looking for texture, our native burr oak has a strong, thick, rather horizontal-branching habit. Another sculptural tree is the Pagoda dogwood. It bears blue berries that seldom last a week after ripening. Its branches are very horizontal. Unfortunately, it can be quite short-lived. Another tree that is underutilized is the *Amur* chokecherry. The bark on this beauty is an almost metallic copper color.

There are other plants that hold their fruit if you don't have room for another tree. Rugosa roses, if not deadheaded in the late summer, develop hips, a red/orange fruit that is actually the ovary of the flower. We have a holly (*Ilex Verticillata*), better known as winter berry, whose stems are nearly obscured by small, brilliant scarlet berries. This is another bird-friendly shrub—they love the berries. Highbush cranberry bears clusters of red fruit that hang on most of the winter. Don't forget bittersweet. There is a new cultivar that doesn't need a mate. The older vines required you to get a male and female. Usually you got 3 vines, hoping at least one was of the opposite sex. If they were all the same sex, no berries. That IS the berries.

Don't live with a boring landscape. Do some winter planning and spring planting. As someone once said, "Gardening is better than therapy, and you get tomatoes."

Big Conifers

We have dealt with the suburban yard, now we will address the "estate-size" yard. Forget the Black Hills spruce, look for something different. Start with the Douglas fir. This is an open, pyramidal-shaped tree with shiny, dark green needles. He gets 40 to 45 feet tall and 15 to 20 feet wide. Plant in full sun or part shade.

If you must have a juniper, look for *Wichita Blue*. This is a fuller tree, broad, pyramidal, with bright blue foliage that holds its color in winter. What a beautiful accent against white snow, or planted well in front of a white or light-colored house! This tree gets only 14 feet tall, but 6 feet wide. That means don't plant it closer than 8 feet from a building. Plant in full sun.

There are 4 pines to consider. *Arnold Sentinel* an accent tree. It is 25 feet tall and narrow, only 6 to 8 feet wide, with dark green needles. A full sun lover. *Austrian pine* is a fast-growing tree that reaches 60 feet high and 30 to 40 feet wide. It will tolerate city living if you have a big enough sunny space. *Norway pine* is also a big boy. He gets 60 to 80 feet tall and will grow in full sun in a sandy soil. *Scotch pine* is a bit shorter, only 40 to 60 feet tall. It is quite sculptural as it matures at 30 to 40 feet wide. The needles are blue green when young. If you want a weeping conifer, look for *Siberian Weeping Spruce*. It gets 30 feet high, 15 feet wide and is very graceful with blue-green needles and red spring cones. There is also a weeping hemlock that needs to have damp feet to do well.

None of these trees is a foundation plant—they need to be well away from buildings. Even a two-story house is not 50 feet tall. A tree that tall in directly in front of a rambler will completely overpower the house in a very short time.

Evergreen is actually a misnomer. Conifers come in light, medium and dark green; blue, blue green, silver blue, reddish blue, yellow, gold and plum. Many have striking cones that range in color from pink through red to purple.

Get some excitement in your large yard with one of these beautiful conifers. They can be planted in spring through late summer. Do remember that a newly-planted tree needs to be babied. It will need watering for the next 5 years if there isn't at least 1 inch of rain a week. Mulching helps keep the soil cool and damp and keeps the dreaded lawn-mower and weed whip away from the easily damaged bark. A badly-damaged trunk will at least slow the growth of the tree is it doesn't outright kill it.

Smart Conifers

Winter is tough on trees. The ground freezes so they can't get a drink, and the winds zip around drying up what little moisture there is. Also, snow can be heavy. That's why deciduous trees shed their leaves. We have all seen pictures on TV where trees that still have their leaves, fall and break during snow and ice storms. You seldom see any conifers with broken branches after a storm. The reason is the shape of the tree and the shape of their leaves. They have a better way of dealing with heavy snow.

Coniferous forests grow in areas with low winter temperatures and high snowfalls, like Minnesota. That being the case, they need a way to shed snow and hold on to water. Conifers are conical. They have a single leader and branches are spaced out in horizontal tiers. As the upper branches droop down with a snow load, they touch the tier below. Each subsequent tier supports the one above it, preventing the full load from breaking off branches. The tree assumes an umbrella shape so much of the snow just slides off and branches bounce right back. Conifer leaves (needles) also have some unique skills to cope with our weather. The narrow shape doesn't allow much *transpiration* (water loss). With the soil frozen, the tree can't pull moisture up so it needs to keep all that it has. The needles have a tough, weatherproof wax coating on them called the *cuticle* that reduces transpiration.

Coniferous forests typically grow in poor soils and dry conditions during the growing season. Deciduous trees have to produce a new set of leaves each spring, so they need wetter conditions and better soil to grow and thrive. Conifers keep most of their leaves, a great energy saver. And with our shorter growing season they are ready to start photosynthesizing as soon as spring arrives, getting the jump on the leaf bearers.

The small evergreens we like to plant close to our homes can often get the whole roof full of snow as it falls off. Also, they are more apt to get "winter burn," caused by strong, drying winds. A simple tripod of boards set over the smaller shrubs will protect them from snow dump. If they get winter burn (brown and dead on one side from the wind sailing around a house corner), give them a winter sweater. Do not wrap with anything plastic. Just wrap a burlap bag, an old blanket or something similar around the shrub. They will keep the dry wind off—but may also heat up, causing the tree to think it is spring and starting to grow. Not a good thing in January.

If you do get winter burn on your conifers, don't be in a hurry to cut the affected branches off. They may recover. If the plant gets too ugly from constant winter weather and your attempts to repair it, dig it up and throw it on the compost pile. Lesson learned. A conifer won't do well in that location. Plant something else. House corners are death on most plants unless they have a windbreak. If your house's corners are so ugly you need to cover them up, you have another problem altogether.

Lighting Winter Evergreens

Bunkey found out the hard way (doesn't he always?) that Christmas lights, the old-fashioned ones, are not a good thing on a small evergreen. He has several small spruce trees in his yard and last winter decided to put lights on them. This spring he discovered that the weight of the lights had broken some of the branches. Not only that, the heat of the lights had damaged some of the needles. Lights can heat needles, buds and bark. When shut off, the cold air rapidly cools the sap/water in the cells below freezing, causing ice crystals to form before the cell's natural protective mechanisms can kick in. The tree doesn't have time to recover before it freezes again.

In younger, just-getting-established trees, new growth is very brittle in the low temperatures we get in the winter here in the frozen north. Putting lights on, and later taking them off, can cause the brittle branches to break off. Even though the tree is still growing in the winter, it is much slower than in the warm months, so healing is retarded. A broken terminal branch leader will make the tree grow lopsided. Broken branches in winter won't heal until summer, making the tree more at risk for disease and more tissue damage from the cold.

So what is Bunkey to do? He wants to compete with the neighbors for the most lights in the block. First, he should light a mature tree. Or if he must light a six-footer, put only LED lights on it. They don't heat like regular lights. Wait to put them on until the new growth has hardened in the late fall and before it gets so cold that you need a snowmobile suit to work outside. Take them off the first warm day in the winter. Better yet, hire a tree service or your neighbor with a man lift to light that 40-footer. If you light a deciduous tree, take care not to break any branches on it either. On any tree, keep the light bulbs from touching any part of your tree. Trees can't heal in the winter. If your lights don't light, blame the squirrels. They removed 2 inches of Bunkey's light string last week. Chewed it right off!

The 4-Season Shrub

You know about the Coffee tree, now let's talk about shrubs. Many *viburnums* are hardy in zones 2 and 3. They are truly a 4-season shrub. In the spring they bloom with clusters of frothy hydrangea-like blooms. The blossoms of the highbush cranberry look like a white pinwheel with a fuzzy middle. The flowers morph into red fruit and later red leaves. Other indigenous viburnums are arrowwood, wayfaring tree and nannyberry. Since they are natives, they can get wild and ugly if not kept pruned. Because they are so hardy, developers are working on more well-behaved varieties.

Bailey's in Minneapolis has bred *Bailey's Compact*, a hedge form of highbush cranberry. It has the trident leaf and the stunning fall color of its wilder cousins. A compact cultivar of the wayfaring tree is *Mohican*. This shrub has the red berries of the cranberry, but the leaves are a deeper red-purple. It also comes with a variegated leaf that does not change color in the fall. *Arrowwood* has a bright blue berry in the fall. All of these shrubs will feed overwintering birds and the ones that migrate through fall and spring. A slightly taller shrub or small tree—it gets 6 to 12 feet tall and 8 feet wide—is the *Pagoda dogwood*. This is also a native, and likes the understory or dappled shade of bigger trees. It does not like the hot afternoon sun. It also blooms with white flowers followed by blue berries. The birds strip those off as fast as they ripen.

If you have planted seedling trees, like the ones available from your local Soil and Water District office, you know how small they are and how easy it is to mow them down when planted in grasses. Here's a tip to help prevent murdering those tiny trees. Buy a bunch of Christmas tinsel. A few strings of that wrapped into the top of the small tree, catches your eye as you mow, preventing mow-overs. The only problem is that the birds like the stuff for nesting material, so you may have to re-tinsel them several times.

Pruning Panic

Petunia is a "yard proud" gal. She wants her landscape to look like it has been professionally planted. Unfortunately, Bunkey is her gardener. She has been nagging him to get out and prune the shrubs and trees. They have looked okay up to now, but the "estate" is looking a bit shaggy.

There are many reasons to prune your shrubs. Proper pruning of flowering shrubs, done at the right time of the year, promotes healthy growth, keeps the shrub a manageable size and promotes more and better blooms.

Since the terms *old wood* and *new wood* leave Bunkey in a coma, here is what he needs to know to do a proper job of it.

- Prune spring-flowering shrubs (lilac, viburnum, chokeberry, weigela, mock orange, flowering cherry) right after flowering—the buds for next year's flowers form on this summer's wood.
- Prune summer flowerers (smoke bush, snowberry, smooth hydrangea, potentilla, Japanese spirea) in late winter or early spring. The flower buds from these shrubs form on new growth this year.

If you mess up and prune at the wrong time you won't kill the shrub, but you may sacrifice blooms for that season. Never prune in late summer as that stimulates new growth. The shrub won't have time to harden off before the cold sets in and you have winter kill.

Now, how to go about the job. Start with a sharp pruning lopper. If you don't recognize the description, it looks like a scissors. Make the cut at a slight angle, close to the wood. Just don't cut into the main stem. The angled cut sheds water, and heals faster. Cut 1/4 inch above where there is a bud. You want a bud that is facing to the outside of the shrub—this will direct it to grow outward. Cut any broken branches back to healthy wood. Dead branches should be trimmed back to the base of the plant. If a branch is crossing another, remove one of them. The constant rubbing can cause an open wound.

If the shrub is totally out of control, you can cut it back to the first bud—anywhere from 4 to 10 inches from the ground. This is best for the summer bloomers like *Annabelle* hydrangea, Japanese spireas and overgrown lilacs. All plants need good air circulation, shrubs being no exception. If you have one with suckers, whack them off first. Next, remove up to 1/4 of the oldest stems. Take them right down to soil level. If the shrub is really shaggy, you may need to do this for several years to get it back in proper shape.

If the shrub is slapping you in the face as you walk by it, covering the window or just looking wild and woolly, you can give it a "haircut." Cut the offending branches back to a larger branch or bud. When done, you want the plant to look neat but not pruned. The cuts should be hidden inside the plant. Again, never remove more than 1/4of the shrub in a year.

Now, sharpen your lopper, or saw if the branches have really been ignored, and go to it.

Grass

Learn to love dandelions and crabgrass.

Talking Lawns

One only needs to walk by Bunkey's yard to see that he is not "lawn proud." There are all kinds of weeds in his grass. Most of us deal with some weeds in our lawn. Weeds are messengers. They can pretty accurately tell us what type of soil we have. If your lawn is more weeds than grass, this is because that is what that soil is predisposed to grow. Disgusting but true. You can spray them until you are blue in the face and out of chemical, but until you modify the soil, not much will change.

Thistle, plantain and quackgrass tell you that your soil is compacted in that area. Clover, trefoil or wood sorrel is an indication that the soil is short of nitrogen. Acidic soil will grow violets, knotweed and hawkweed very nicely. The hated dandelion is a bio-accumulator. It pulls calcium to the surface with its deep taproot. Adding calcium to the soil will reduce the bright flush of yellow dandelions spring and fall. Wood ash is a good organic way to do this.

Aeration will help reduce the plantain. Quackgrass needs more drastic measures. Bunkey has seriously considered dynamite, not really a good option, but understandable. The thistles need not only a pre-emergence like corn gluten meal (CGM), but also either physical or chemical removable so they don't re-seed. They are a bi-annual, growing a rosette the first year, then the tall seed-bearing stalk the second. If you absolutely must rid your lawn of clover, adding blood meal, feather meal or fish fertilizer will at least reduce the load. Reasons to leave the clover: it is an excellent bee attractant (think *clover honey*), a sturdy groundcover that can be walked on, and best of all it's pretty, spotting the green grass with white bubbles of bloom.

There are organic weed killers other than corn gluten meal. Some with naturally-occurring sodium or iron hold great promise for instant and environmentally-safe weed control.

To optimize what grass you have, keep the mower at 3 inches. Taller grass shades out weed seeds, and the soil doesn't dry out as quickly. Taller grass always looks thicker, even if it's not, and no, you won't have to mow any more often. That is an old husbands' tale. Keep your mower blades sharpened. Sharp blades mean sharp cuts. Dull blades just tear the leaf blades, leading to a gray-looking, unhealthy lawn. For the last two or three cuttings of the season, gradually lower the blades to about 2 to 2 1/2 inches. This not only helps prevent snow mold, it also makes it easier to remove leaves.

Water if you don't get at least an inch of water a week and water deeply. A sprinkle is worse than no water at all as it leads to shallow-rooted grass, more apt to scorch and die in hot dry weather. Keep watering through the fall to help sustain the active growth that allows the plants to make and store food to survive our winters. Weeds are also growing and storing food for the winter now—that's why fall is the best time of the year to kill them. The poison goes right to the roots. Most broadleaf weed killers work best between the temperatures of 50 and 80 degrees. You may not see instant results, but come spring you will see fewer of the nasties.

Early spring is not the time to rake. Wait until you can sit or kneel on the lawn and not get wet cheeks or knees. Raking a wet lawn can open up the soil to more weed growth and can actually tear out the grass you have been babying. Listen to your lawn and it will tell you what it needs. Yes, this is a "touchy feely" thing, but it works.

Fall is the best time to over-seed a lawn and apply soil amendments for best results in the spring. A soil sample in the fall will tell you what you need to add. Getting a sample in the spring is not a dumb idea either. If you have bare spots, rough them up with a rake, then seed. A light cover of straw or even grass clippings will keep the seed in place when you water. Keep the spot damp, not soggy, to ensure proper germination.

Preventing Lawn Problems

Bunkey had snow mold in every color this spring. It was especially bad in a low spot and in a corner of the lawn that is partly shaded where the grass is very lush. He is determined not to have the problem next spring. He has a mulching lawn mower and thought that mulching the leaves would prevent the problem. It probably would have, had he done it properly.

When he was done mowing last fall, there was a layer of chopped leaves at least an inch thick visible on the surface of the grass. He should not have been able to see any leaves if he had done it right.

His second mistake was not cutting the grass as long as it was growing. He had winterized his mower before the weather got cold.

The third mistake was not cutting the grass short enough. He had the mower set for 3 inches all summer and forgot to reset it to 2 1/2 for fall. Long grass holds leaves and snow, usually leading to problems. If you have had snow mold in your lawn, cut the grass short for as long as it is growing, remove any visible leaves and don't fertilize grass after Labor Day and you should have no problems.

Pain In the Grass

Bunkey is not a grass fanatic, but he does like his lawn to look nice. He just discovered patches of dead grass with a few green leaves here and there. Bunkey thought, *Now what? I just got through cleaning up the dog spots on the grass.* (By the way, this entails flooding the dead patch with water, then a flush of 1 part vinegar to 10 parts water.) Dig a bit, enough to rough up the soil, then plant grass and water well until it comes up.

Bunkey got down on his belly and really looked at the sick grass. He discovered that the tip of each affected grass leaf had black stuff on it. What he has is *ascochyta blight*. This disease is associated with underlying stress (poor soil conditions, compaction, dull mower blades that tear rather than cut, and most of all, weather conditions). The black stuff on the grass tips is fungus spores released by water and mowing. This is why you should never mow your lawn when it is wet.

To repair the lawn, cut the sick grass down to get rid of as much of it as possible. You may need to cut it with a hand clipper. Remove the clippings and rake the surface well, exposing the surface. Loosen the soil and re-seed with a resistant cultivar.

We leave Bunkey on his hands and knees, clipping grass with Petunia's good scissors. His excuse was that his hand clippers weren't as sharp as her scissors. Boy, is he going to be in trouble.

Bunkey's Lawn Problems

Bunkey was loading up his spreader when his neighbor George noticed what he was doing. "What are you going to do now?" he asked.

"I'm going to get ahead of the crabgrass this year," Bunkey answered. "I had it all over this area last year, but not this year."

"Well," said George, "if you spread it now, you'll have the same problem this year."

"But the bag says to spread it in April," responded Bunkey.

"Neither crabgrass nor the bag can read, Bunkey. Crabgrass is an annual and won't sprout until the soil is the right temperature. Spread your pre-emergence the first time when the daffodils start to show color, and the second time when the lilac buds start to color up. You will have a lot more success killing the seeds as they start to sprout. You are using corn gluten meal, aren't you? Not that chemical stuff?"

"Yup, I'm going all green this year," Bunkey replied. "Now if I could just get rid of the grubs, I'd probably have a pretty decent lawn."

George said nothing. He just handed him a flyer from the University of Minnesota showing the life cycle of grub worms. The U now recommends treating grub-infested grass for three years running. This not only gets rid of the grubs, it also reduces the number of night crawlers, a big problem for some lawns. If your lawn is full of miniature dirt volcanoes, you have night crawlers.

Do a Bunkey and wait for the right time to take care of your lawn problems. It will save you money and later hair tearing.

Brown Grass

Bunkey had spots of brown grass last fall, but, since they weren't too extensive, he just ignored them. This spring, the spots have enlarged. Now they are all over the yard. He tried the "grab and pull" to determine if the spots were grubs, but instead of a patch of dead turf, he came up with a handful of brown leaves. So, not grubs. What now?

Most, if not all, brown patchy grass has some kind of fungus killing it. Whatever the type, the treatment is the same. Rake all the dead stuff off, then treat the area with a fungicide for grasses. Next, overseed with a variety of fescue, not the usually recommended blue grass. The fescues are more resistant to fungi than the blues. Cover the area with straw or burlap. Remove as soon as you see a green blade. Keep the area watered until the grass is well established.

Safe Lawns

While Bunkey doesn't have grandkids yet, he does have 2 dogs. His neighbor down the street has 3 little yappers and 4 grandkids who are absolute terrors. His dogs have higher vet bills than people with chronic diseases. He also has the most beautiful lawn on the block, not a weed or bare spot to be seen. His total lawn care is mowing it at least once a week and having a professional lawn service spray it on a regular basis. He never connects the dogs' illnesses on all the chemicals sprayed on his grass.

Even if you don't have kids or pets that play on your grass, you should probably ask yourself if having a perfect lawn is worth spraying it with who knows what. Bunkey's lawn is organic—no chemicals to sicken dogs or future grandkids. The grass is still thick, but there is white clover, dandelions, an odd patch of plantain and several species of grasses in the lawn. And best of all, the bees are busy pollinating his flowers and feeding on the "weeds"—clover and dandelions.

There are a few steps to getting an organic lawn. First, of course, is a soil test. This will tell you the nutrients available in your soil, the pH and the percentage of organic matter in the soil. Note on the test that it is for a lawn and designate methods of growing on the soil test form.

Using a mulching mower adds organic material to the soil. This is food for worms and other beneficial soil dwellers. A season worth of clippings is equal to 1/4 of a lawn's need for fertilizer. Shredded leaves in the fall add more food and help protect the soil over the winter. Top dressing with as little as ¼ inch of compost in the spring brings the soil back to life. Compost adds humic acid. This improves the structure of the soil and its ability to hold water.

If you listen to TV ads, you will be convinced that you need to fertilize your grass at least 4 times a year. All a healthy lawn really needs is fertilizing in the spring with a slow-release organic fertilizer and again in the fall. As the health of your grass improves, you will eventually be able to forget the spring application.

Never fertilize in warm, dry weather. It causes more harm than good. If you want the grass to look particularly good for your annual lawn party, feed it with a light foliar feed using a hose end sprayer filled with an organic mix like a combo of fish emulsion and kelp. Do this in the morning and never if the temperature is more than 85 degrees.

Your guests will note that faint aroma of walleye, but the grass will look great.

Petunia's Pride

"Bunkey, you get out there and water that grass. What will the neighbors think when the only green in our lawn is weeds? I don't care if it does raise our water bill."

Bunkey is tighter than skin on a grape when it comes to watering grass. His philosophy: let it turn brown, it will get green when we get rain. Petunia doesn't agree. "Just look at that lawn down the block. It's lush and green as velvet."

"He has built-in sprinklers, a lawn service, more money than Romney and I've seen him trimming around his trees with a scissors," was Bunkey's answer. "We don't have any of those things." But to keep peace in the house, he did get the sprinkler going, then went next door to George's for coffee and some watering tips.

This is what he learned. Maintaining a typical Kentucky bluegrass lawn in an actively green and growing state during the hot and dry months of July and August will require 1 to 1 ½ inches of water a week, including rain. If you can tolerate some browning, that can be cut to ½ to ¾ inches every 7 to 10 days. This is just enough moisture to permit the spreading stems and growing points of grass to be able to resprout and start growing again when the conditions moderate. Yes, you can let it go completely brown, giving it an inch of water every 2 to 3 weeks. This should help keep just enough water in the plant so that it can start growing later in the summer.

However, if it stays hot and dry, this little bit of water can push even well-prepared grass over the edge and result in some permanent die back. To keep your lawn alive, you may need to water more often than usual to keep the grass alive. Try to keep traffic off stressed lawns. They are much more vulnerable to serious injury and die back from normal wear and tear under water and heat stress conditions. Whatever you do, don't fertilize your lawn when it is stressed. It will only stress it more and probably burn up what little green is showing. Save your money for the water bill.

For Love of Grass

Petunia thought she had to plant flowers to attract wildlife and insects. Then she read an article about native grasses. Not only do native grasses provide shelter, they also provide food for many of our grassland-dwelling birds. Grasses are critical for some butterfly larvae. Skippers, satyrs, pearly eyes, wood nymphs and brown butterflies must have grasses and sedges as larval food for survival.

Most people don't have enough acreage for a grassland prairie, so they will need to take a more restrained route. Grouping 2 to 4 kinds of native grasses and using multiples of 3 or 5 of each will add diversity to your garden. It will look more interesting and will attract a wider variety of birds and bugs—good bugs.

If you are a bit artistic, you could try a stylized prairie by grouping the grasses in drifts similar to a traditional flower border. Leaving the grasses standing through the winter will provide shelter for the insects you are hoping to attract. The seed heads will provide a nice snack for some of our hardy winter birds.

Unfortunately, this type of garden will also attract a few less-desirable critters. Mice, mosquitoes, ticks and snakes live in grasslands. So let's discuss that problem. Snakes are one addition that freaks out Petunia. They do eat small rodents, like the mice she hates with a passion; however, that doesn't make them any more welcome in her gardens. Ticks are another problem. They sit on the tips of grasses and leaves and get on people and animals as they brush by. Wearing long sleeves and tucking your pants into your socks will leave them less skin to grab onto. Wearing a spray of DEET and leaving the perfume for that hot date night will make the skeeters look for a better food supply. There is also a small handheld device that runs on thermacell gas cylinders that will repel insects. The gas heats a pad infused with repellent. This results in an invisible shield around the gardener. No ticks, no mosquitoes, pick your strawberries in comfort.

Why, with this drawback, should any gardener want a grass garden? Because gardeners need pollinators, usually enjoy wildlife and are willing to put up with a few weeds in the roses, so to speak.

Our native grasslands have lost 1,000s of acres to development and farming, resulting in drastic declines in grassland birds. Of the 37 species of birds the North American Breeding Bird Survey monitors, 32 are in some form of decline, largely due to habitat loss. Only 5 species have had some increase. While a small patch of grass will not help the birds much, it will help our pollinators. Pollinators are usually insects, and birds eat insects. It's a win-win situation.

Check your house for cracks where mice, ladybugs and boxelder bugs can infiltrate. Wear protective clothing when outside. And Petunia's scream when she encounters a garter snake will scare off every snake in a two-block area. If you see a herd of snakes heading for cover, you will know Petunia has been out in her grass garden.

Accent Plants

Bunkey has never been of the school that plants accent grasses. His philosophy is that grass belongs in the lawn and not in the flowerbeds. Last week, Petunia dragged him on a garden tour that featured grasses and sedges. He had to admit that they did add texture to the landscape. If you decide to add this type of accent, you need to know the difference between sedges and grasses. It is as easy as reading the labels. Grasses have *miscanthus* in their name while sedges have *carex* in theirs.

Here are a few sedges for the adventurous gardener to add to the landscape. Do be aware that sedges have edges—they need to be handled with leather gloves to prevent "grass cuts" on the gardener.

If you have a dry, sandy spot, and many lakeshore gardeners do, *Plains Oval sedge* may be just the foliage you are looking for. It gets up to 2 feet tall and 18 inches wide. Another is *Penn sedge*—it likes dry shade. Described as "easy to grow and having a soft textural look, fine textured, arching and semi evergreen," it is shorter, 8 to 12 inches tall, but 2 feet wide. These sedges want moist or even mucky soil. Brome-like sedge makes a bright green clump 18 to 24 inches tall. It will grow in either full sun or part shade. It looks great with the blue-green leaves of hostas. The two are a study in foliage color, texture and shape.

If you like the look of clumps, *Bristle-leaved sedge* is the one for you. It forms a clump described as porcupine-like, 6 to 10 inches tall and wide. It likes moist alkaline soil the best, but will grow in drier soil and even rock crevices. It spreads slowly by rhizomes, but can naturalize into a large colony if left unattended. You may need to keep close watch on this one or you may end up with a lumpy looking estate.

If you want a bluish groundcover, *Blue sedge* may be your answer. It likes full to part shade and a moist soil, but will tolerate drier soil once established. The soft, narrow blue-tinged leaves grow 6 to 10 inches tall. It spreads by rhizomes and looks great in a naturalized area that features ferns and hostas.

If you have a rain garden, take a look at *palm sedge*. As the name implies, it looks like small palm fronds. It may need extra water in full sun. Mixed with *Purple Smoke Baptista*, the 2 quickly smother weeds. That description suggests an extremely aggressive combination to Bunkey. Most sedges bloom in the spring, then the new foliage starts to grow. Leave them for accent through the winter, then mow in early spring and you are done. Note that Bunkey is not dashing out to purchase any of these plants. He still is not convinced that they are just grass in disguise and thus don't belong in his gardens.

Berries

If you want to grow blueberries,
move up north.

It's the Berries

Petunia has a love affair with canning, especially jams and jellies. She puts fancy lids on her produce, making for a special gift. If you are a friend of hers, you're likely to get a gift of a jar or two on your birthday, anniversary, birth of a baby or just because. Because of this habit of hers, Bunkey has had to find room for some different berry producers. He planted 2 Juneberry trees at the edge of the tree line. He has to put bird nets over them or Petunia won't get any fruit.

Juneberry trees are quite attractive. (It's not even a berry, being a cousin of the apple.) Plant her on a slope with good drainage and air circulation to prevent frosted blooms. They have white blooms that look like popcorn on her stems in the early spring and blue berries at the end of June. These are a native tree and are often called Saskatoon berries in catalogs. They tend to sucker, so they make a great candidate for an edible windbreak. You may need to cover the tree to get berries as the birds love them. This small, upright tree will do quite well on the edge of a tree line as she likes part shade.

Chokeberries, not to be confused with choke cherries, are a self-fertile plant, easy to grow in most any soil. They need full sun, but can even tolerate wet feet. They are relatively free of diseases and insect pests, but need winter protection from rabbits who love their bark. A spring show of white blooms is followed in late summer by glossy black, bitter astringent fruit. They need sugar and are good mixed with other fruit. Fall foliage is a brilliant red. If you don't use the fruit, the birds will, and this shrub is a very attractive addition to the landscape.

Honeyberry is getting quite popular in our climate. It is hardy to zone 2. This is actually an edible honeysuckle. The fruit is some shade of blue and has double the antioxidants of blueberries, plus it doesn't need the acid soil blueberries do. The plants live up to 50 years. They will tolerate part shade but prefer full sun. A mulch will greatly increase their production.

If you want a fruiting shrub the deer won't touch, plant gooseberries. They have sharp spines that hurt their hungry little deer mouths. Of course, it also makes it a bit challenging to pick the fruit. They like a loamy soil, average to moist. They need mulching to protect their shallow, fibrous roots. Gooseberries look like dime-sized, slightly transparent little beach balls. The green variety are quite tart. *Hinnomaki*, a red variety is described as having a plumy or apricot flavor can be eaten raw or in a fruit salad. *Pixwell* is more compact, nearly thornless plant and ripens to a pretty purple.

Some of these shrubs and small trees are available in local nurseries. Others, you may have to order from a northern seed catalog next spring. Even if you don't follow Petunia's lead and make jelly and jam, the fruit will attract birds and add 3-season interest to your yard. Bunkey is debating a hedge of gooseberries around his vegetable garden. Perhaps if he tops the berries with a fence of invisible fish line he may be able to have a deer-less garden next summer.

Growing Blueberries

Yes, you can grow blueberries in Otter Tail County, but it's not easy. Our soil is alkaline with a pH of 7.5 and up. Alkaline soil is found where evaporation exceeds precipitation (a real dumbed-down explanation, but explicit enough for now). Blueberries need an acid soil with a pH of 4 to 5. They are a member of the heath family, and as such have no root hairs. In nature, highbush blueberries grow in wet forested areas as understory shrubs. They don't sit in water but on top of mounds of decomposing or decomposed organic material matter with a pH of 4 to 5. These mounds not only wick up moisture but slurp up rain water like a sponge. To grow the berries, you need to attempt similar soil conditions.

Start by digging a hole 6 feet wide and 2 feet deep by whatever length you need. Add equal amounts of soil, peat moss and sand or perlite. In light soil, you will need ¾ pound of sulfur per 100 square feet to acidify the soil. In heavy soil, as much as 3 times that much. The sulfur should also be spread beyond the planting hole, as far as you expect the roots to go. Put the plant in at the same depth it was in the pot. Water them in and keep the soil moist. It will take 1 to 3 gallons per plant per week. Mulch heavily, to a depth of about 3 inches, with wood shaving, leaves or pine straw. You need to add soil sulfur every year to keep the area acid.

This is one place you don't want to use compost. It is too rich in nutrients. Instead, spread 1 pound per square foot of defatted, ground soybean meal in the fall. It is insoluble so it won't wash out and adds just the right amount of nitrogen.

You still aren't done. You need to monitor your plants each year. If growth is poor or odd, or the youngest leaves are yellowing, you need to add more sulfur. The new growth should be 18 to 24 inches and bright green.

Is it really worth all this work? You not only have to keep the soil acid, you have to pick the darn things on your hands and knees. Hint. The grocery store has blueberries already picked.

Strawberry News

The University of Minnesota is at it again. A U graduate student, Andy Petran, has been researching ways for growers to grow more berries.

As any strawberry grower knows, there are three types of strawberries: June bearing, everbearing, and day-neutral.

June bearing, as their name implies, bear from mid-May through June (providing the weather cooperates), then they are done for the year. This is great if you want to freeze or make strawberry jelly. If you want berries again later in the summer, plant everbearing. A misleading name if there ever was one. They actually don't bear continually, but have a crop at the beginning of summer then another later after a rest.

Day-neutral strawberries don't care how long the day is, as do the other two types. They have the potential to flower and bear all summer. However nice as this sounds, they haven't done well here in the frozen north.

Mr. Petran was picking some day-neutral berries in October last year. He did this by planting improved plants in a low tunnel (probably not too practical for the average gardener). However, mulching the plants with straw or plastic mulch with drip irrigation under it can extend the season.

He has a few tips for the home grower. The day-neutrals will try to flower right after they "wake up." Don't let them. If they flower and set fruit too early, they don't have enough energy left to develop strong roots and leaves to feed themselves. Remove the flowers for the first month. Since the plants will be flowering and fruiting for a long period, he recommends fertilizing once or twice a week all season. Pick all the ripe berries as any left to rot can spread diseases. He treats his plants as annuals, but the home gardener will probably not go that far. The patch should be good for 3 years before needing to be replaced. Then move the patch to a new area for better soil fertility.

Rhonda Flemming Hayes, a writer for the *Northern Gardener* magazine (published by the Minnesota Arboretum), has had luck growing strawberries in a container, specifically an 18-inch-square box. She filled the box with compost, potting soil and granular fertilizer and watered the container with compost tea. The box was planted with three *Tribute* berry plants. She got hundreds of berries from the planting. Having the container on the deck kept the rabbits and other four-footed critters from sharing the bounty.

Strawberry plants are as attractive as a lot of other container plants and the bonus of fresh berries for breakfast make it a no brainer. And for those who find the ground too far away, they are a heck of a lot easier to pick.

A strawberry is not strictly a fruit. Its 200 seeds are the actual fruit and the sweet part is the enlarged receptacle at the end of the flower. A cut strawberry rubbed on teeth will whiten them—just use a fluoride toothpaste right after to reduce the acid in the berry. Straw is the usual mulch for strawberries, but pine needles are said to improve taste and growth. If you don't have pine trees, you can purchase bundles of pine straw next spring.

Lingonberries: A Norwegian Treat

In the olden days, 60 to 70 years ago, you always knew Christmas was coming by the smell when you went into the corner grocery store. There would be a big wooden barrel filled with slabs of soaking lutefisk and next to it another barrel full of lingonberries. Most of the younger populations know lingonberries from restaurants like IKEA that sells lingonberry syrup for their waffles. This berry has been a Swedish staple for centuries. Countries in northern Europe produce about 80 million pounds commercially a year. Lingonberries can be dried or made into jams, jellies, pickles and preserves. They are quite tart (similar to cranberries) and need to be sweetened.

Here in the U.S., lingonberries grow in northern parts of Minnesota, Wisconsin, Michigan and New England. The plant tolerates harsh growing conditions, cold temperatures and poor soil, making it an ideal plant for us here in the frozen north.

It's a pretty groundcover, only growing 18 inches tall. It spreads slowly by underground rhizomes, forming dense mats about 3 feet wide. In the spring, glossy red-tinted buds appear. They mature into leathery oblong leaves. The undersides are matte and covered with small black dots. These leaves are semi-evergreen, turning purple in colder months. They need snow cover to do well, something we usually have no problem providing.

Pinkish-white bell-shaped blooms emerge on last year's growth. They are pollinated by honey bees and bumblebees. The small red berries are ready for harvest a few months later. Wild lingonberries flower only once a year, while the cultivated European varieties can flower twice, producing berries in August and again later in the fall. They taste best after a light touch of frost. If not picked, they will stay on the branches throughout the winter—unless the songbirds find them first.

Lingonberries are a superfruit, containing impressive amounts of vitamins A, B and C, and are high in antioxidants. The phytochemicals may have health benefits, including preventing urinary tract infections and lowering high blood pressure.

If you have a problem area with poor soil and shade, this may be your groundcover answer. However, don't hold your breath until you get a crop. If the summer temps are 80 to 90, the berries cook on the branches. Lingonberries are an understory plant. They like to be under birch, pine or spruce trees, and live happily beside reed grass and the sedges. They want an acid soil, with the pH of 4.5 and 5.5.

Lingonberries are low maintenance. They don't need pruning, and have few pest problems—that is other than rabbits, squirrels and birds eating the shoots.

Bunkey was quite interested in lingonberries as a groundcover for one of his problem areas until he discovered all the extra care they needed to get established. He opted for heavy bark mulch instead.

The Other Berries

It seems everybody wants to grow blueberries, but there are other berries that do well in our alkaline soil. Our native elderberry is a bit ugly, being gangly (10 to 12 feet wide and tall). It has beautiful white blooms in the spring, followed by dark purple berries. If you can beat the birds to them, cook them for pie, jam or wine. If you don't have room for that large a shrub, cut it back. It blooms on both old and new wood. It will grow in either full sun or part shade.

Black currants have not been available for 40 years due to being an alternate host to white pine blister, a fungal disease. There have been more resistant cultivars developed since then. However, there are both red and white varieties available that aren't hosts. Currants are a bit fussy, wanting a north-facing or winter-sheltered slope so the early blooms don't get frozen. They need quite a bit of nitrogen to do well.

Jostaberries are a hybrid cross between currants and gooseberries. They are also resistant to the white pine disease and have larger fruits.

So what if we can't grow blueberries without a lot of fuss. We have many neat alternatives. Try one. You may like it.

Flowers

Too much "Martha"
is not a good thing in a flowerbed.

Big Annuals

If you have a bare spot in your landscape and just can't afford a shrub just now, there is a cheaper solution: monster annuals.

Castor beans can easily top 6 feet. The leaves are large and resemble Japanese maple tree leaves. They are very easy to start if you can't find a started plant. The leaves can be either red or purple, with several colors of flowers and stems. One caveat: the seeds are a deadly poison—not a problem if you keep them picked or if you don't have small children or plant-eating dogs. If you don't promptly remove the seed heads, the plant will self-seed.

A plant that is a "twofer' is the *Mexican sunflower* (*Tithonia rotundifolia*). This bright orange daisy-like bloom will grow 4 to 6 feet tall. A definite landscape brightener. The twofer part is that butterflies love the flowers. This flower will grow in that hot dry spot that fries every other plant you attempt to grow there. *Sunflowers* have nice bright flowers, come in a multitude of colors, and can feed the birds when they are done blooming. One interesting way to use the 5- to 6-foot plant is to plant a circle of them, plant a climbing bean or other annual vine on the outside of the circle and you have a perfect play house for your smaller kids. What kid doesn't like a hiding place?

For a less dense planting, try *cleomes*, more commonly known as spider flowers. They will grow 4 to 5 feet tall with an explosion of large airy flowerheads of pink, white purple or rose. They make a pretty bouquet, but wear gloves when you pick them—the stems have sharp thorns on them. Some people object to the citrus odor of the plant when cut.

If you are a fan of *cockscomb*, you probably picture them as a nice 2- to 3-foot plant. Not *Cramer's Amazon*. This puppy gets 5 to 6 feet tall and 3 to 4 feet wide. That will fill a pretty big gap. One down-side is the color, an almost florescent magenta. Not a color that blends well with anything other than green or white.

If you are into grasses, *Purple Majesty millet* (*Pennisetum glaucum*) is an easy-to-grow ornamental annual grass. It grows up to 5 feet tall. The leaves and stalks are a bright purple—quite an accent.

One wild-looking annual is called *Kiss Me Over the Garden Gate*. The 5- to 6-foot plant has big heart-shaped leaves and a long drooping spike of pink flowers. It will give your visitors a giggle when you tell them what that odd-looking plant is. It can actually hang over the garden gate, if you are so inclined.

For a big flashy pot plant, check out *coleus*. A couple of the larger variety will fill a whiskey barrel quite easily. Add a sweet potato vine and you have a large, spectacular show piece. Because these plants are really extra large, people are bound to ask you what you are feeding them. A smart-alecky answer is "small children." That answer should keep the neighbor's brats out of your yard.

Flower Cages

Do you have floppy phlox? Are your dahlias droopy, mums lying down on the job? If so, here are a few hints to encourage your plants to become upstanding citizens.

For bushy plants like mums, peonies and the taller Oriental lilies, grow-through grids work well. They are simply a round grid on legs. The plants grow through the holes in the grids. They come in several diameters and heights. Don't bother to bring home the plastic ones. Being Scotch by both nature and nationality, I bought the cheaper plastic ones the first time—the legs break!!! You could probably McGyver new legs, but why bother—get metal to start with.

For smaller flowers like snapdragons, lisianthus and other small, tall floppy plants, try tomato cages. In the fall, you can often get the small ones for 50¢ or less. Cut the top ring off—it is too wide. Push the rings and the grids in far enough so at least half the plant sticks out the top of the support. These supports are surprisingly unobtrusive.

In a year or two, the rings get rusty and nearly disappear in the foliage of the plants. The rings are easy to store as they stack into a neat cone. The cut off rings can be used for the shorter, wider plants like pinks. Unlike loops, the wind will not knock the plant out of the support. Delphiniums need the tallest cage you can find to prevent them from wind damage.

The rings and grids sure beat the old stick-and-string supports. They look much nicer, the garden is neater and the gardener doesn't have to spend hours after a windstorm redoing supports.

If your hanging baskets have a bit of incontinence after you water them, or just get too dry between waterings, put a layer of sphagnum moss in the bottom of the pot before planting. It can hold up to 20 times its weight in water. You can also use a cut-up diaper or an old wool sweater cut to fit the bottom of your pot.

Gardeners are invariably optimistic. "Next year I will pull weeds as they come up. Next year I will beat the rabbits to my peas. Next year, my flowerbeds will look like the pictures in the gardening magazines" Yup! Optimistic. If your flower garden is blah, with no excitement to it at all, maybe you need to "spike it up" by adding some vertical accents. If you have a backdrop to your flowerbed, a wall or a building, you have always been told to put all the tall plants in the back. For a bed seen all the way around, the rule is the tall stuff goes in the middle. Hey, it's your flowerbed. Are the flower police going to arrest you if you bend the rules? To heck with the rules, add some excitement! Put an odd number of taller or spiky plants toward the front of the bed, or scatter them here and there in the bed.

Bulbs–The Easiest Perennials

Too many gardeners, Bunkey included, think bulbs are too much work to plant, too fussy and too expensive. Actually, bulbs are easy. Just dig a hole and drop them in. Well, not quite, but almost that simple.

Take daffodils, for instance. If they are planted too close to the surface of the soil to suit them, they will actually put themselves down to the depth they like. All parts of the plant are poisonous, so deer won't eat them and squirrels and chipmunks won't dig them up. They multiply each spring and disappear by July so you can plant a mum next to them and have both spring and fall color in the same spot.

Then there are the lilies, spectacular flowers for very little work. *Asiatic lilies* bloom in June, *Oriental lilies* in July and August. *Trumpet lilies* need room—they often grow to 6 feet tall—making a stunning accent in the middle of the flowerbed. *Martigon lilies* may grow to 4 feet tall, with as many as 50 flowers on a single stem.

For the first color in the spring plant the small bulbs, collectively called *minor bulbs*. Many of them are blue or purple, colors difficult to find the rest of the year. Blue squill flowing around a clump of bright yellow daffs make quite a show. Hyacinths perfume the air for many feet. They actually look like bright exclamation points. While they may never be as full as the potted plants, they add great color and texture to the spring garden.

Planting bulbs is easy. Dig a hole and drop it in. The broader side should be down. Some bulbs give you hints, as they have a few dry roots on the bottom of the bulb. However, if you do happen to plant them upside down, don't fret. They will figure out which way is up and bloom anyway. If you are planting a clump of bulbs, tulips for instance, dig a wide hole, plant them with the flat side to the outside of the hole. That will keep them in a neat clump.

No bulb likes wet feet. Do plant all bulbs in a well-drained spot. They originally came from an arid area. The bulb stores water, and if it gets too wet during the year it can rot. This is often the reason tulips disappear from your garden. Some of them just aren't hardy here, but planting them deep—6 to 8 inches from the top of the bulb—will often ensure a repeat bloom.

Clay soil is death to bulbs. If that is your problem, dig a wider and deeper hole. Add about 6 inches of sand to the bottom and fill the rest of the hole with good soil. A bed with a slight slope is perfect for any bulb. Like any good perennial, bulbs multiply. You can leave them or dig them up to share with your neighbor in the fall or spring, whenever you have the most time. Replant the largest bulbs, throwing a little bulb booster into the bottom of the hole.

For the beginning gardener, bulbs are almost goof proof. Bunkey did goof, however. He planted several trumpet lilies near the front of his flowerbed. Last fall, he had a 6-foot hedge of blooms hiding the rest of the garden. Read the package!!

Better Luck Next Year

Two years ago, Bunkey decided he needed more spring color in his flower gardens, so he ordered 100 tulip bulbs, 100 daffodil bulbs, and an assortment of 100 minor bulbs. Unfortunately, he didn't do his homework on the catalog company. When he hadn't gotten his order by October, he called the company. That was when he discovered that they didn't expect to get their order from Holland for another month. They wouldn't cancel his order, so he put huge piles of leaves on the areas he planned to plant. When his order finally came in November, Bunkey had to use a pick ax to plant. Needless to say, many of the daffodils never came up and only a few of the late tulips made it. The deer ate the few that did come up.

Last year Bunkey called before he ordered and found a company that shipped the end of September. This spring his garden was a symphony of yellow, peach and blue. No red. What tulip bulbs the squirrels and chipmunks hadn't eaten last fall, the rabbits and deer cleaned up this spring. Since daffodils are poisonous in every part, nothing eats them. Tulips, however, are top-of-the-line salad.

So this year, Bunkey is going to try again. He put 2 inches of chicken grit on top of each tulip as he planted them 8 to 10 inches deep. The grit will usually stop diggers. Also, they don't usually dig that deep. He also laid a piece of hardware cloth on top of the ground where he planted the tulip bulbs, and was very careful not to leave any of the papery coating shed from the bulbs on the grounds. The smell of those dry tunics is a call to lunch for critters.

Next spring, Bunkey plans to put up an electric fence around the flowerbeds with disposable foil pie plates folded over the wire. A bit of peanut butter for bait on the plates will entice Bambi to put her wet nose on the plate for a smell. The next view of the deer will be her backside going over the hill. Let's hope Bunkey has better luck with his spring garden next year.

If you got a pot of mixed spring flowers (daffodils, hyacinths, etc.) and you want to enjoy them next spring—ignore the information that comes with them. It tells you to cut the plants down after blooming. If you do, compost the whole thing—you won't get another flower. The leaves need to keep feeding the bulbs until they turn yellow and are easily pulled off. Then stop watering the pot and put it in a cool, dry place until you can get in the flowerbed. Plant the bulbs 3 times their diameter. You will probably get hyacinths and daffodils. Some of the other bulbs may or may not bloom, but you are only out a little effort planting them.

Petunia will have to wait to move her tulips and daffodils until all the leaves have turned brown. The leaves look terrible, but they continue to feed the bulb for next year's blooms. They should only be moved in the fall. The problem is that in the fall, you can't find them as all the leaves have died and left no forwarding address. Again, Master Gardener George has the answer. Plant an annual right beside your dying bulb. Say a marigold. In the fall, all you will have to do is dig up the marigold and there will be your ripe, ready-to-be-replanted bulbs. Your flowerbed may look a little odd, but you won't have to dig the whole plot up to find a tulip.

Petunia had another problem in the garden this spring—alliums! She had planted 6 allium bulbs three years ago. The next spring they bloomed. She loved the way they looked, tall stems with a ball of purple on top. They reminded Bunkey of fireworks. This year, alliums popped up in the middle of a mum, crowding a clump of lilies, and a couple of them had the audacity to come up in the lawn. Alliums are part of the onion family. They look much like a chive on steroids. They spread by seeds. Petunia had left the seed heads standing because they were so attractive. The hundreds of seeds in each head spread quite nicely. Now she has to dig each of the offenders up or her whole flower garden will be covered with balls of purple. The moral of this story: if you have alliums, cut the flowering head off as soon as it begins to fade and remove it far from the flowerbed.

How to Care for an Amaryllis

Petunia got an amaryllis, the giraffe of flowers, for a Christmas gift. Petunia has a well-known brown thumb. Her plants are either looking for a life raft or hanging over the edge of the pot with their tongues hanging out. Since neither condition bodes well for her new amaryllis, it's lucky that directions came with the plant. Petunia loves the amaryllis flower, and would like to have the plant re-flower again next year.

The first rule is to keep it out of direct sunlight while it is in bloom. If you got a potted amaryllis that is about to bloom, put it in a warm sunny spot until the bud shows color, then move it. The cooler temperatures in lower light will prolong blooming time. Be sure you don't go the other route and put them near a cold blast from the door opening or next to a leaky window. They are very sensitive to cold.

Now, to keep the plant for next year cut off the dead blooms. Leave the flower stalk, ugly as it is, as it will make food for the plant as long as it is green. When it yellows, cut if off. Put the plant in your brightest window for the winter, remembering to keep it warm.

Keep it watered, but only when the soil becomes rather dry. Too much water will rot the bulb. This is why tulips often don't return. A wet fall or summer rots the bulbs. If you have other houseplants, hide the amaryllis in the middle of them—it is a pretty ugly plant without its flowers. Fertilize with half-strength fertilizer as you do the other plants, once a month. In the spring, when you put your other houseplants out under the trees for a summer vacation, move the amaryllis out, too. Slowly move it until it is in full sun, then sink the pot in the garden.

Amaryllis like to be pot-bound, so you will probably need to repot it only every 3 or 4 years. In the fall, bring all your plants in. Put the amaryllis in a dark closet and don't water it. As the leaves shrivel and brown, gently pull them off. Check the pot after about two months. You should see a new green shoot. Bring it into the bright light, full sun, and begin watering it again. Even if you don't see green, do this. It should trigger new growth. If you don't see a flower stalk, you goofed. The bulb didn't store enough food after the last blooming period. They need full sun just before and after blooming. Don't despair. Just go through the routine again. Or you could pitch it in the compost and buy another one next Christmas.

Pruning Clematis

Every spring, the Extension office gets calls from people wondering how or if to prune clematis. The problem is, there are three different types of vines: groups A, B and C. If you kept your plant tag, it will tell you which group you have.

Forget about group A—it's not hardy here.

Group B (like *Nellie Moser*) usually flowers in mid-spring on last year's stems. Later in the season, they have blooms on this year's stems. The flowers are all over the plant. If you have a double flowering clematis, the odds are it is in this group.

As soon as you see leaf buds starting to swell in early spring, remove all the dead leaves so you can see what you are doing. Cut off any broken or dead branches. These will be the branches with no buds on them. Now you need your artistic side. Stand back and take a good look at the vine. Is it filling the trellis? If not, trim back some of the long stems that are sticking out. If it is thin, bend these stems back on to the trellis. You may have to tie them there. If it is too thick, you can either cut it off the trellis to thin it or just thin out some of the branches. You will have to tie it back on the trellis if you pull it away. Do train new growth back into the trellis.

Then there is group C. This group flowers mostly on new growth. They are later to bloom than group B, in late spring or early summer. If they haven't been properly pruned, they will have naked stems and a full head of blooms and leaves, not the prettiest look. These are easy to prune. As soon as you see new sprouts starting to swell (about the time the tulips are blooming), cut the whole vine down to about a foot. Now they will bloom their full length. If however, you want them to cover a tall wall or your pergola, fasten the long, bare stems to the structure and cut only the top half to one-third. They will only bloom on the top this way.

All clematis wants warm heads and cold feet. With group C, you may need to plant quite a tall perennial or annual at its feet to shade them. With group B, the covering plant will not need to be quite as tall, but do provide shade of some type for her.

Petunia is cutting the taller seed heads of the columbine. This not only makes the gardens look neater, it ensures blooms next year. Growing and ripening seeds takes a lot of energy from a plant. We want blooms not seed-heads. Leave about half the seed heads on the columbines. Goldfinches love the seeds and spread them as they feed, ensuring more flowers next spring with no effort on Petunia's part.

Saving Geraniums

Petunia bought a boat load of geraniums this spring, making for a spectacular flowerbed in the front of her house. Now she would like to keep a few special ones for next year. There are several ways for her to do this. One way is to pot them up, put them in a dark, slightly damp area and water them just enough so the soil doesn't totally dry out.

Or she could take a cutting. Cut off the very top, most tender stem of the plant. Don't attempt to root it in water. While this works, the roots are not very strong. Instead, make a rooting pot. Start with a large plastic pot with a saucer that fits its bottom. Fill the pot about ½ full of vermiculite or soil starter. Set a smaller clay pot with the drain hold plugged in the middle of the plastic pot. Add more medium until it is up to the edge of the clay pot. Dampen the medium, then fill the small clay pot with water. It will seep out and keep the potting medium just damp enough to get the plants started. You can tell if the cutting has rooted by giving it a little tug. If it resists, it has roots. Pot it up and set it in a sunny window.

You don't want a window full of pots? If you have a root cellar, you can use Gramma's trick. Dig the geraniums just before frost. Shake the soil off the roots and lay the plant in a shady spot to dry. The object is to have all the leaves dried up and fallen off. Store the dry plants root side up in a cardboard box with the top closed. The temps should be between 50 and 60 degrees. Check them often for mold. If the stems dry up and shrivel up, its' too dry and that plant is dead. Chuck it out. You can attempt to rehydrate it by soaking it in warm water, then put it back in the box. Black mildew can be simply cut off. Two months before the last frost pot the leftovers up. Bury the stem deep. It should have two leaf nodes below soil line. Trim the stem back to healthy green growth. Since geraniums are a semi-tropical plant, wait to put them out until it is 50 degrees or warmer at night.

Lots of luck with this method. Most of our basements are much too warm and dry for this to work. Let the moths out of your wallet and just buy new ones in the spring. It not only is easier, there are apt to be some new varieties even prettier than last year's. Besides, what gardener doesn't love to wander through the greenhouses in the spring and drool over all those beautiful blooms.

Hostas—Small Wonders

Verna had retired and moved into a small house with a very small yard. It was well shaded with large maple trees limiting the plants she could put in her new surroundings. After some research (and several trips to 3 or 4 nurseries and 3 garden tours), she decided she had just enough room for the smallest of the hostas. They come in small (defined as those with a leaf blade bigger than 10 inches but less than 2), mini (they have a leaf blade no larger than 6 inches), and very small (everything tinier than a mini). Since they are so small, they get lost in a regular flower or hosta bed. Like Greta Garbo, they "vant to be alone." They are great as an edging, in a bed with a dwarf conifer or with a few other very small shade plants. Hostas love the dappled shade cast by maple trees.

Verna decided on a rock garden on a slight slope on one side of the house and a fairy garden behind it. Like their larger cousins, the mini hostas seem to call for rocks for accents; this and their size make them ideal for rock gardens. A hosta snuggled up to a rock just seems like it must have grown that way. The minis come in all the colors and shapes the big guys do, and they do well and are showier in raised beds.

The little ones are the perfect size for fairy gardens. You can let your imagination run loose with these gardens. A toy tire, hung from the branch of a dwarf tree is a swing. One small flowering annual can be a flowering shrub. Check your kid's toy box for "people" or other small things. If you want houses, check your local Salvation Army, Goodwill or the dollar stores—they will often have other bits and pieces to get your artistic juices flowing. Local nurseries have miniature trees that only grow an inch a year and are hardy enough, with good mulching, to live in a hosta bed. Or, if you want to try container gardening with hostas and the tiny trees, consider putting them in the garage with an old quilt covering them for the winter.

If you have more room, mass plantings of the small hostas really put on a show. Group them by color or leaf shape. Snake a dry riverbed through them or just use your imagination—it's your show after all. The small hostas do need extra T.L.C. They want a well-drained soil with lots of organic matter to keep their rather shallow roots moist. Mulch them with mulch that fits their size: coco bean shells, buckwheat hulls, ground pine bark or finely shredded bark. Big chunks of bark will overpower the look you are attempting. Have fun with these tiny wonders. Your gardener friends with sunny gardens will envy you.

Hostas are tougher than woodpecker lips—you can transplant them almost any time during the growing season.

The Hydrangea Blues

Bunkey bought an *Endless Summer* hydrangea as a birthday present for Petunia last spring. She planted it on the north side of the house and watered it every day, even though we had a very wet summer. Needless to say, the plant didn't survive. What should she have done? First of all, the new hydrangeas need at least 6 hours of full sun with dappled shade in the hot of the afternoon. The east side of a building, but not right up against it would be ideal. The south side, again not too close to the building, where trees would shade it after noon would work well. Then the water. Hydrangeas do require more water than most shrubs, but they can be overwatered. An inch a week should so it unless we have very hot days, then they would need an extra drink mid-day.

Fertilizer—If you want blue blooms, don't use aluminum sulfate. It can easily make the soil toxic. Instead, use elemental sulfur to acidify the soil. Use sulfur for the other acid lovers too, such as blueberries and azaleas. Do feed your shrubs, but use a 10-30-10 fertilizer. You need to do this only once with a slow-release fertilizer, either in the spring or early summer. If the plant is still in a pot, you may need to give it some liquid fertilizer during the growing season. If you overfeed, you will have the most beautiful dark green leaves and a dearth of flowers. In other words, follow the directions and use a light hand.

Pruning—*Annabelle* can be cut right to the ground and bloom heavily. Not the endless series. While they bloom on new wood, they also bloom on old wood. The shrub will have fewer flowers and bloom later if you give it an *Annabelle* cut. Besides, the old blooms add winter interest to the yard.

Winter Cover—Hydrangea buds emerge early in the spring. Early in zone 3 b can bring some pretty cold, nasty weather. Your babies need protection for the first few years. Cover the crown of the shrub with mulch, leaves or straw and don't uncover until the weather has settled down in the spring, usually late May here in the frozen north.

Moral for the day. Don't poison the soil. Enjoy *Endless Summer* as a pink bloomer, just plant her in a place where she will flourish.

All About Irises

Bunkey's irises were beautiful this year. Every one bloomed. However, he can see some problems with them. Several have turned into St. Bernards. They have attempted to take over the whole flowerbed. Worse yet, they are only blooming at the edges of the clump. Another clump is showing the brown stripes on its leaves, an indication of iris borer. Even worse, there is a copper-colored clump that somehow got next to a dark purple clump. The color combination makes Bunkey's teeth hurt. All these things mean some major iris digging.

He needs to cut the flower stems off as the blooms fade. This prevents the plant from forming seeds that reduce the energy needed for next year's flowers. He needs to mark the clumps as to color if they clash and need moving by writing on the leaves with a permanent marker. Bunkey will need a big trash bag, a shears and a potato fork. He should dig up the WHOLE clump and knock as much of the soil off as possible, then trim the leaves down to about 4 inches, break off any rhizomes that don't have a healthy fan of leaves and discard them.

Now Bunkey can divide the clumps left into those with flower stems and those without. Keep 5 to 7 of the flower-stemmed clumps to replant. Share the rest. To plant iris, make a mound and space the clumps around it, "toes" pointing out. Cover the roots and just enough of the rhizomes to stabilize the clump. Don't mulch them—iris rhizomes like to sunbathe.

If you see evidence of iris borer (brown streaks on leaves), dig that clump up. Often you will find some of the rhizome has rotted, and boy can that stink. The borer wounds the rhizome, letting soil bacteria in to do the rotting. Cut the bad parts off, then replant. One way to at least reduce the number of borers is to cut the iris leaves down to about 2 inches in the fall. Never put diseased iris on a compost pile. It will only encourage the worm. Do not cut iris leaves any other times except when moving them or in the fall. They need all those leaves to feed the roots for next year's blooms. Yes, they are messy and take up a lot of room, but live with it. No flowerbed is perfect all the time, except maybe Martha's and she has gardeners. Here it's just us and Bunkey.

Lilies—Easy Color

July is the time of year to shop for lilies. They are not only easy to grow, but make a spectacular show in the garden. Be aware that we are not discussing daylilies as they aren't really a lily at all. True lilies have a bulb that looks like a gigantic onion. It is usually white and has scales similar to an onion. Daylilies have a fibrous root.

Lilies come in all heights, from the trumpets that get 4 to 6 feet tall to the short 14 to 16 inch Asiatic, bred for the border. There are five types. *Trumpet lilies* are the tallest. The bloom is, as you would expect, is trumpet-shaped and faces down. They need a strong support as the blooms come in a bunch on top of a tall stem. They bloom in July and some may be fragrant.

Asiatic lilies bloom in June and July. They range in height from 2 to 5 feet tall and usually don't need much support. They can be one, two or three colors. The tips of the flower can be one color and the base another, they can have splotches, or petals that have one color on the throat and another on the tips. They are excellent cut flowers. Again, the blooms are in a clump on top of a stem.

Oriental lilies bloom in July and August and have a wonderful fragrance. Smell them before bringing them in as a cut flower as the fragrance can be so strong as to bring on nausea in the delicate. They are also 2 to 5 feet tall, and like the Asiatics have flowers that face out. They are colored differently from the Asiatics. The white flower may have a pale pink stripe leading to a pink petal tip or a yellow throat, while the dark red could have a narrow white stripe edge on the petal. One white has a dark red freckled throat.

Tiger lilies face down and the petals are covered in freckles. They are 3 to 4 feet tall and bloom from July to September. A warning: unless you enjoy lilies coming up all over the flowerbed, in the middle of iris, crowding out the mums and attempting to strangle the shorter flowers, do not plant the common tiger lily. Go with the hybrid. The common tiger is orange only. The hybrids can be yellow, white, peach and two shades of orange. They are much less aggressive.

Orienpet lilies are a hybrid cross of the trumpet and the oriental lily. They reach medium height, 3 to 4 feet. The flowers are huge and can be solid color, striped or have ruffled edges. They usually need staking and do best in a partly-shaded area.

All of these lilies come in red, pink, peach, yellow and white. So far, there are no lilies with any blue/purple blooms.

Lilies can be moved in the spring as soon as you see them, or later in the summer after they have bloomed and rested for 2 or 3 weeks to recover from the hard work of blossoming. All need feeding each year and dividing about every 3 to 4 years. Plant these beauties in a well-drained area. Wet feet will kill them—the bulb rots. They will tolerate light or dappled shade. The trumpets are the only types that aren't good cut flowers. They look at their feet instead of the sun. The only other care is staking, deadheading and being sure they have good air circulation. A great, easy-care, spectacular disease-free beauty. Go get some for your estate.

Think you'll plant this year's Easter lily in your garden? Well, DON'T! According to the University of Minnesota, almost all Easter lily bulbs are produced by about 9 growers, all located in California and southern Oregon. There is one predominant cultivar, *Nellie White*, named for the woman who first grew them. Apparently, it is the hardiest and is resistant to leaf scorch. The problem: all the bulbs have a symptomless virus. It makes the plant shorter, which is OK, but it also takes longer to bloom. This virus can infect other lilies, so don't plant the Easter lily in your garden! The others, such as *Stargazer* or the various colored lilies are safe.

All mints have square stems and are very invasive, but not all square-stemmed plants are mints.

Growing Orchids

Bunkey gave Petunia an orchid for Christmas. There were no instructions with it, probably because he got it at the last minute at the local drug store. Well. It is the thought that counts. Actually, *Phalaenopisis orchids*, commonly called moth orchids, are not that difficult to grow. They need the same thing as other plants: light, water and food—but with a bit of a twist.

Moth orchids are *epiphytic* plants—in their native, tropical environment they live in trees, clinging to branches for support and getting their water from the wet bark. Since most of our houses don't have room for a growing tree, we need to do some MacGyvering.

Start with a special potting mix especially made for orchids. This will be a mix of bark chunks, *osmunda* (a fiber from tropical tree ferns) and sometimes a bit of sphagnum peat moss. The first time Petunia watered her plant, she nearly had a fit as the water ran right through the pot. It is supposed to. The roots grab what water they need as it flies by. This means she will probably need to water every few days in warmer weather. Ideal temps are 75 to 80 during the day and 65 at night. If the house is kept cool all the time—mid to high 60's, once a week is probably enough. She will have to be sure to empty the saucer as the roots are thick and fleshy and will rot if left standing in water. Most of our houses are quite dry in the winter, so to get the most out of the orchids they should be set on a pebble filled tray with water in it. Just don't let the roots touch the water.

Since these orchids live in trees in their native habitat, they get filtered light. Even so, they will not do well in a north window. Petunia grows African violets and gets huge blooms from them. Her orchid needs just a bit less light than her violets. She could also grow them under fluorescent lights, but the lights need to be on for 12 to 14 hours a day for best results. Petunia's orchid was a young one and had 4 flowers on it. They should last about 2 to 3 months. As the plant ages, she will get more blooms, up to a dozen at a time.

Phalaenopsis orchids don't have a distinct rest period, so they need year-round feeding. (There are special foods sold just for orchids.) They need a weak fertilizer solution every other watering, less in the dead of winter. Under lights they will need feeding all the time.

Petunia was thrilled with her orchid, thinking Bunkey had really put a lot of thought into her gift. Little does she know. Guys, if you are in a panic, buy your lady an orchid post-Christmas. Be aware, however. This may get her hooked on them—by next Christmas, she may not have room for a Christmas tree. The room will be full of orchids.

All About Lady's Slippers

Petunia was at the regular weekly coffee klatch at the Pretty Good Café when the subject of the state flower came up. "You don't need a permit to dig lady's slippers in this county," said one of the "girls."

"That can't be right. Who told you that?"

"I called the DNR and they said they weren't protected."

Comments came from every side of the table. "I will call and find out for sure," said Petunia. She called the DNR and talked to a gal in Ecological and Water Resources to get information from an expert. This is what she discovered.

The lady's slipper is protected statewide; however, you can dig them up for your personal garden. To do so, first you must determine if the plant is on private or public land. If it is on private land, you must get written permission from the landowner to enter the property and dig it. If the plant is dug to be sold, the person digging it up must get a permit from the Minnesota Department of Agriculture. This department has the responsibility for administering the statutes (Minnesota Statutes 2010, chapter 18H.18 pertaining to collection and sale of native orchids, trilliums, gentians, lilies, lotus coneflowers, may apple, bloodroot and trailing arbutus, so there).

If the plant is in a county ditch, you need to get written permission from the county to move the plant. For township ditches, contact the township for written permission. The county needs a letter as detailed as possible noting where the plants are, how many and where they will be moved.

The Department of Transportation considers the lady's slipper an asset and attempts to move any that are likely to be damaged by roadwork. They prefer to use their own crews—it can be dangerous working around heavy equipment. The *Showy Lady's Slipper* (the pink one) is given first priority, followed by the two varieties of yellow lady's slipper. If the road work permits, DOT prefers to mark the plants, then dig them in the fall after they have faded and are dormant. They transplant them the same day.

Transplanting this plant may be easy, but it will seldom be successful. She is a very fussy lady and wants very acidic soil, especially the duff that is under conifers and oaks. The plant has thick curly roots. As with other plants and trees dug in the wild, take as much of the soil surrounding the plant as you can. It contains the specific fungus that plants need to do well. Unlike most plants that symbiotically pair with soil fungi, orchids enter into a one-sided relationship with their fungi.

They steal energy and nutrients while giving very little back. When times get tough for the plant, it retreats underground and sponges off the fungi until the situation improves. The gardener may think she has successfully transplanted her lady, only to discover she has disappeared the next year. She may have died from rot and pestilence in your good, rich garden soil. Then again she may just hide for up to 10 years, then pop up again. It takes up to 25 years from seed for many of our wild orchids to bloom, so if you can save them, do so. Just get the proper permission. If you haven't transplanted one of these beauties, ask an expert before you dig.

Peonies are tougher than woodpecker lips. They can bloom in the same place for 100 years, but only if they are in their happy place. They will pout and even die if you plant these beauties in a damp place, in heavy soil or where they don't get good air circulation. That doesn't mean you should put them on the top of a breezy hill, however. They are a bit of a snot. They don't want to have to rub shoulders with any other plant, including other peonies. Too often they are planted in a row, nearly touching each other—this is just asking for trouble. Peonies come in a wide array of colors and color combinations. You can even find peach and yellow. Hit your favorite nursery this spring to see the new and improved varieties. There are some real honeys out there.

Easy Roses

Petunia loves roses—she thinks it's because her middle name is Rose. (What was her mother thinking?) That being the case, Bunkey would buy her a rose bush every spring. Come late summer and all that was left was a leafless stick, or if there were a few leaves they were spotted with diseases.

This year, Bunkey will buy *rugosa roses* rather than the *tea roses* he was used to buying. This type of rose gets its name from the heavily-textured or *rugose* leaves that are typical *Rosa rugosa* hybrids. Tea roses, in contrast, have smooth shiny leaves. Here in the frozen north, they are also annuals. The rugosas are perennials.

The heavily-textured leaves are impervious to almost all the ailments that affect roses. In the fall, they change colors to match our fiery maples. You can find golden yellow, burgundy, burnt orange, russet or even a combination of colors on the leaves, an uncommon trait among roses.

Many of the rugosas have decorative hips (seed pods) in the fall. Hips can be deep cherry through tomato red, yellow or even apricot. These should be removed, deadheaded, until late summer. If you let the blooms go to hips earlier, you sacrifice blooms.

Rugosas are not the polite plant the tea rose is. They are a shrub with thick prickly stems. Some even sucker, growing into an impenetrable colony. They have even been used for a pig-proof fence. They are a great deterrent to thieves if planted under your windows. Some of these great roses even have colorful canes that show up after the leaves have fallen.

These tough plants aren't particular about soil conditions. Just give them a spot with 6 to 8 hours of sun, an inch of water a week and maybe a shot of organic fertilizer just before the big flush of blooms in June and they will reward you with beautiful blooms.

Forget the sprays. They will actually cause rugosas to drop their leaves. They don't get black spot or other foliar diseases like the princesses, the tea roses.

And they are hardy! The *Rosa rugosa* is native to cold coastal areas of China, Japan and Manchuria. Many of the hybrids, including some bred in Canada, are safe in zone 2. The toughest are those with white, pink or red blooms. The yellows and peaches, not as much. Don't let the fancy French names fool you either. They are as hardy as the Canadians.

If you have never grown roses because of all the fussing they need, rugosas are for you. They are not the classic tea rose shape, but they smell like roses and, like peonies, are tougher than woodpecker lips!

It's Dividing Time

Bunkey will sleep well this week. Last fall, he made a note that some of his perennials had died in the middle or just weren't performing up to their potential. That means that they will have to be dug up and divided. Hard sweaty work, but well worth it in the long run.

It was pretty easy deciding on which plants needed redoing. They were either dead in the middle, too big for their spot or in the wrong place. Often a sunny area will become shaded as trees mature, leading to poor performance of a sunny plant.

Here is a list of plants that need dividing or thinning every one to three years—depending on the soil, the gardener's preference, and either willing neighbors looking to fill their beds or an upcoming garden sale. Achillea, fall aster, penstemon, monarda, dianthus, oenothera, coral bells, delphinium, fern leaf bleeding heart, mums, painted and Shasta daisy, phlox and coreopsis. Monarda can become invasive, running through the garden just under the soil—she may need to be reined in more often than the others.

In another two years, Bunkey will have to be checking another group of perennials that need thinning or moving (every five years, that is). These include: astilbe, campanula, gaillardia, coneflower, liatris, loosestrife, Jacob's ladder, meadow rue, meadow sweet, heliopsis and Siberian iris. Some of those, like the Siberian iris, will need an ax to divide. The roots are very fibrous and thick.

Of course, if any of these plants are attempting to smother their neighbors, they can be attacked earlier, and often, with some perennials. "Attacked" is the proper word—they get so dense and deep-rooted they take a long-bladed shovel and lots of sweat to do the job.

Wait until fall to thin or move iris, Asiatic lilies and peonies. Peonies really don't like to be moved and will happily bloom in the same spot for 100 years if they are cut down in the fall and given a bit of fertilizer early in the spring. While they are quite deep-rooted, when transplanted the roots should be only 2 to 3 inches below the soil line. They will grow if planted deeper, but not bloom. Hostas can be divided at any time.

The rule of thumb for dividing plants: if it blooms in the spring, divide in the fall; if it blooms in the fall, divide in the spring. There is a good reason for this. A blooming flower is, in effect, pregnant. After it blooms, it wants to set seed. These activities take a lot of energy from the plant. It needs from 6 weeks to 2 months to recover its strength. Move it before that time and it will take much longer to recover and bloom well.

A few plants should never be divided. They just don't like it. They are baby's breath (very deep-rooted), balloon flower, butterfly weed, clematis, flax, lupine, monkshood and Russian sage. Be very careful where you plant these—you may be working around them for years. If they end up in a really terrible place in the flowerbed, you can, of course, murder them and buy a new one.

Houseplants

A spider plant can clean the air
and entertain the cat at the same time.

Clean Your Air With Plants

NASA discovered what gardeners have known for years: houseplants make for a healthier house. They did a study in conjunction with Associated Landscape Contractors of America to determine that the astronauts breathe cleaner air with fewer chemicals when they have plants in space with them. Houseplants remove chemicals that can foul our air—including formaldehyde (found in wood paneling and new carpets) and benzene, both known carcinogens.

But, you say, I kill plants. Most houseplants are killed with kindness rather than neglect. They are over-fertilized, over-watered and fried. When you buy a houseplant, it will fill the pot—usually because there are several plants in the pot. Separate the plants and repot in smaller containers. Do not, under any circumstances, use garden soil. It not only is full of bacteria, but funguses and who knows what else. Also, it is too dense for an indoor plant. Get potting soil—it's cheap insurance. You can fertilize with a slow-release fertilizer, or if you are more the Martha type, feed them monthly with a water soluble fertilizer made just for houseplants. Keep an eye out for diseases.

Now to watering. Let the soil dry out before you water again, then give it enough water that the container under it gets water in it. Let it sit an hour then dump out any remaining water. Leave it longer and the roots start to rot or you get fungus gnats. They love wet soil. The two exceptions to this are African violets and poinsettias. They both like constantly moist soil. To determine if the plant needs water, stick your finger in the soil up to the first joint. If the tip of your finger feels dry, water. Or make a schedule. Water every Saturday, for instance. It will at least keep the plant alive.

Many houseplants don't do well in full sun; they need it filtered. If the only window you have to put plants in is a south-facing one, hang a sheer curtain in front of it or put your geranium and hibiscus there. Stick the rubber plant in a corner.

When you bring a new plant into the house, give it a good shower and quarantine it for several weeks to prevent bringing in any problems. If you touch your plant and stick to it, you have a sucking-type bug to deal with. Aphids will be on the underside of the leaf. Spider mites leave webs. Scale looks like brown spots, mostly on the leaves. *Schefflera* is particularly susceptible to scale. A good treatment for all these stinkers is a good shower followed by a shot of insecticide.

Plants that are easiest to grow are spider plant and Boston fern, also dragon tree (*Marginata dracaena*), peace lily, golden pothos, English ivy, aloe vera, snake plant (also known as mother-in-law's tongue), Chinese evergreen and Areca palm. These plants can remove Xylene and small amounts of carbon monoxide, along with the formaldehyde and benzene.

Give them a vacation outdoors in the summer in a shady spot and you will have healthy air all winter—if you don't smoke, that is.

Let's Clear the Air

If you are like most people who live in snow country, you have houseplants. We need the green to remind us that winter doesn't really last 9 months. Another reason many people have houseplants is that they have heard that some houseplants clean the air. However, the "experts" don't always agree on which plants are best at this and are a bit vague about the science behind the claims. So, should you fill your house with indoor plants expecting them to clean the air of pollutants? Or should you just compost that good-for-nothing spider plant? Are your various vines, palms and geraniums just a waste of space? Actually, no. The plants do have a positive effect on indoor air in large enough numbers. The soil they are in may be even more active. Potting soil is full of microbes, bacteria and fungi. The microbes are capable of using pollutants as food, even down to amazingly low concentrations. Another good thing about houseplants that they improve your mood, accelerate the recovery of hospital patients, and can boost your creative performance. And as any gardener can tell you, they just make us happy.

To get the most out of your indoor forest, keep the leaves clean. They collect dust and cooking oils that reduce their ability to clean your air. (That is, if they actually do.) Do hose off any plants that have been vacationing outside this summer. Bacteria and microbes are O.K, but you probably don't want spiders, slugs and other wildlife to come in with your plants.

Flowers for Valentine's Day

Bunkey always buys Petunia red roses for Valentine's day, and she usually has to throw them out on the 18th. They droop and look terrible. This year he is planning to buy a flowering plant instead, and if possible, one she can put out in the summer for more lasting color.

Reiger begonias (also called tuberous begonia) look very like roses, but they come in many colors roses never dreamed of. Keep them in until the weather is nice and warm, then put them in a shady place on the deck for a full summer of blooms. Take them in before the first frost, winter them in a bright window, and next summer Petunia will have her Valentine's flowers again.

Another plant to consider is the *primula*, a very short plant with very bright-colored blooms. Again, she can be a porch flower next summer. A small zone-hardy *hydrangea* is another good flowering plant. Do read the hang tag carefully to be sure the plant is at least zone 4, but better zone 3. This shrub will be around for years, so care should be taken when planting it out to ensure it likes its new home. The new cultivars like full or part sun, a sheltered area and lots of mulch in the fall to prosper.

A *cyclamen* is a great houseplant. The blooms hover over the heart-shaped leaves like a cloud of butterflies. They come in red, white, pink and purple. While this is not a long-lasting plant in most homes, it is much more lasting than a $50 bunch of roses.

If your Valentine has no garden or room for another houseplant, do buy the more long-lasting flowers. Mini carnations and mums can look good for 2 weeks or more if given proper care. Iris, while they add blue to a bouquet, are very short-lived. If you are going to get cut flowers for Valentine's day, take an insulated bag or a pre-warmed cooler to bring them home in. Chilling will drastically shorten their lives. Pop the whole bouquet in warm water up to their necks, then cut the stems while underwater. Now you can put them in a hospital-clean vase with water and the packet of stuff that comes with them. Remove any leaves that would be under water, change the water every day (or when it gets cloudy) and keep the bouquet away from full sun or drafts. This will help keep your gift fresh and reminding her of you for much longer. A floriferous gift won't add inches to her middle as chocolates would. Of course, you could splurge and bring her both. Only old poops forget their sweeties on Valentine's Day.

Brown Thumbers' Plants

If you are blessed with a brown thumb, don't despair—you too can have a thriving planter full of interesting houseplants. Think *succulents.*

Succulents come from warm places like South Africa, South and central America and Australia where they have adapted to dry conditions by storing water in their leaves, thus earning the nick name, "camels of the plant world." This makes them almost carefree. They are water-wise, slow growing and very low maintenance—perfect for the person who likes to travel and leave her gardens to fend for themselves.

Succulents need good drainage, so look for a soil especially formulated for cactus or African violets. Mound the soil up in the middle and plant along the "slope." This ensures not only good drainage, but good circulation—and it shows off the plants, highlighting their interesting shapes. The object with this "lean" soil is to prevent fungal diseases and rot. Top dress the soil with pebbles or gravel to help keep the plants dry and accent their uniqueness.

Succulents seem to be made for containers because you can set them in the middle of your outdoor table, on a pedestal or on the deck rail. This makes up for their low-growing habit, as you can get them up close without peering through a thicket. You can use most anything for a container for succulents, depending on your style. They look good in an old shoe or a very modern stainless steel pot. Just be sure the container has good drainage.

Accent the reddish leaf edges of some succulents by putting them in colored containers—copper, bronze, or even purple or wine work well. Add a plant with the blue/green tint to make the combination spark. If you go for the quirky, mix them with billowing or softer annuals. Try ornamental grasses, geraniums, New Zealand flax strawflowers or a herb—lavender, thyme, oregano, rosemary and santolina, for example. You will need to either re-pot your succulent in the fall if you plan on overwintering it or if you add it to an annual pot. Most succulents are not winter hardy here. The exceptions are hen and chicks and the sedums.

There are many varieties of succulents. Remember that, other than the hen and chicks and sedums, these are actually houseplants. Of course, if you are hard-hearted enough, you can let them freeze and start new in the spring, but you can pretty much ignore them in the house too, watering them when they start to shrivel (or you remember to look at them), and they will do well until next summer.

Holiday Cacti

Petunia has always envied her mother-in-law's hand at growing both Thanksgiving and Christmas cactus. Not only are they huge, they bloom on time. She finally got up the courage to ask Alma (she is quite a formidable woman) if she could have a slip from her two cacti. Not only did she get her slips, she also got in a lesson in how to tell them apart and how to start and then grow the plants. Here's what Petunia learned.

The way to tell the two apart is to look at the segments, more properly called *phylloclades*. The Christmas cactus, as is fitting (think *pine trees*), has pointed lobes on the edges of the segments. The Thanksgiving segments are rounded, no sharp points. So why—since they are cousins—do they bloom at different times of the year, the Thanksgiving plant six weeks earlier than the Christmas one? Flowering is triggered by the length of day—how much light the plant gets. The Thanksgiving plant needs 12 hours of light during the late summer and early fall. The Christmas cactus has a shorter critical need for hours of light.

These cacti are native to Brazil, and in their native environment grow on trees like orchids and bromeliads. You would think then that they would require warm temperatures, until you hear that they grow at 3,200 to 5,500 feet up in the mountains. This is why they need house temps between 65 to 74 to do well. That is why Grandma was able to grow them so successfully. Her windows leaked!! And, she probably didn't stay up to watch Leno, so the 8 to 11 hours the plants require to flower were not a problem. If you are a Leno watcher, and want to ensure blooms in mid-September, put the plant in a room that has no lights turned on between sunup and sunset. Take them out in mid-April and they will bloom at the proper time. Another tip is to put the plant outside for the summer. Leave it there until the temps drop to 50. Then put it in an east or west window and try keep temperatures to about 57 or so.

Now to propagation. Start with a 4-inch pot full of damp soilless mix. Remove three or four mature segments that are least an inch long. Then, simply stick them about half their length into the medium and cover the pot with a plastic bag. When you see new growth, repot and begin to fertilize as you would any houseplant. To one gallon of water, add one teaspoon of 20-10-10 houseplant fertilizer during late fall and early spring. In the winter, cut the fertilizer to half that. Holiday cactus can be fertilized every watering, but use plain water once a month to flush out any salt build up.

Petunia is hoping to prove to her mother-in-law that she has just as good a green thumb.

Winter Houseplant Care

Jeff Hahn is our bug guy from the University of Minnesota (his real title is Extension Entomologist, but bug guy works for most of us). He reminds us that this is the time of the year we start to notice problems with our houseplants. Sometimes we brought the bug in when the outdoors vacationing plant came in for the winter. Or it may have snuck in through the screen of an open window. Worse yet, it may have hitch-hiked in on a plant from a friend or from a plant you bought. Even a live Christmas wreath could be the culprit. At any rate, you don't want a buggy plant. So what should you be looking for?

Discolored leaves, not all of them are infested. Poor light, too much or not enough water or just old age of the leaf can cause discoloration.

Webbing on the plant is a sign of spider mites. You will need a magnifying glass to see them. Or hold a sheet of white paper under a leaf, tap the leaf and see what falls off. Yellow sticky traps will capture whiteflies, thrips, fungus gnats and winged aphids. Unfortunately, Jeff doesn't tell us where to buy yellow sticky traps. Improvise.

So how do you get rid of those unwelcome house guests? Jeff suggests you wipe off the pests with a soft rag or paper towel dipped in rubbing alcohol. (Not for hairy leaves, however.) Or a solution of a dishwashing detergent, ½ teaspoon to a quart of water. Be very careful with that as it can also damage some plants. If these don't work or you have a heavy infestation, you can try insecticides. Check the labels for your bug.

A flying circus around your houseplants. You have fungus gnats. Here is a home remedy: for a small plant, dump out the soil, wash the roots clean and pull off any rotted roots. Scrub the pot with ½ teaspoon bleach to 1 quart of water. Repot in soilless mix. For a big pot, cover the soil well with 1 to 2 inches of pebbles. Colored aquarium rocks could even match your color scheme. Moral for this week: don't overwater, watch for bugs and get them while they're small.

If your houseplants don't seem to do well for you, look at the pots. Many gardeners think more is better when it comes to potting soil so their plants are in a pot that is much too big. Put the ailing plant in a pot not much larger than the plant's roots. Only transplant when roots start to stick out the bottom of the pot. Keep those plants cozy in a smaller pot and they will reward you with a fuller, healthier plant.

Did you get a flowering plant for Christmas? If you want to keep it blooming, there are a few things you must do. First, take that fancy wrapper off the pot. It holds water and will lead to root rot. Keep the plant away from drafts. Yes, it looks nice on the stand right beside the door but it hates the cold breeze that comes in every time you open the door. It will reward you by promptly giving up the ghost. Enjoy your blooming holiday plants, but treat them like annuals. Very few of them will continue to look presentable all winter.

Pot It!

Yes, there is a right way.

To Pot or Not To Pot

As you get older, you start to notice that the ground is further down than it used to be. And the way back up is even further. This seems to be the result of maturity in the gardener. Not only do you assess a garden tool for the proper function, but also for the ability to be a third leg in helping the agility-challenged to return to a standing position. This is just one of the coping mechanisms the aware gardener uses due to this ground-lowering trend. Since the option of raising the ground level to a more convenient height doesn't seem in the cards, the only option is having the ground meet the gardener halfway.

Raised beds are nice, but not every yard has room or a proper place for one. They tend to take up a lot of space and are not necessarily the most attractive addition to your estate. A better option is a container of some type.

Whiskey barrels are waist high and have lots of planting room. They don't need to be filled top to bottom with soil either. (The mature gardener is also a bit close with the dime.) Fill the bottom half with packing peanuts, the plastic 4 or 6 packs annuals come in, aluminum pop cans or even branches that seem to appear out of nowhere every spring. Now your barrel will need only 1 bag of good potting soil. It is easily renewed each spring. Simply remove about 1/4 of it, then add a fresh layer with a pelleted fertilizer mixed in and you are good to go for another year.

A stroll through a farm and feed store can lead an imaginative gardener to other large planters. In containers, big is beautiful. Not many plants like hot feet. A large container will have less temperature fluctuation, and it will not need to be watered as much either. To avoid having your yard looking like the town junkyard, find containers that go with the style and color of your house. Then have fun planting.

There is no reason vegetables and flowers can't be in the same pot. Think about a sun coleus surrounded by red and green lettuce, or a tomato with nasturtiums spilling over the edges. Herbs are often quite ornamental. Their leaf colors ranging from a bright green to a soft gray/green, even bluish. One with a bluish cast can complement yellow or orange flowers. The most attractive containers will have plants with a limited color palate. However, it's your pot. If you like orange, fuchsia and lavender together, do it. If the combination eventually makes your teeth hurt, the great thing about pots is that they are easy to replant as your taste or the seasons change.

If you are handy with tools, or can co-opt a carpenter, build your own containers. The best wood is cedar, but if your yard would look better with weathered barn boards, use that. If you do have a container that will eventually rot, you can line it with a plastic waste basket, a pail or anything waterproof. Just be sure there are drain holes in it. Sticking an open umbrella over an overflowing pot after a week of rain looks a bit strange. It will help, however, but drain holes are really a better idea.

To make an interesting hanging pot, you will need a fabric-lined basket. Soak it well, then cut X's in the sides about half-way down the basket. Fill with soilless mix to that level. Put a plastic bag over the roots of the plant you are going to put in the pot to protect it while you stick it into the cut. Pull the plastic off, fill the pot, then plant the pot. The plants in the side of the pot will cover the fabric, making for a ball of hanging flowers. Get out and get your hands dirty. It won't be long before it's hotter than a fried frog out there.

How to Get the Most Out of Your Pots

Every year about this time Petunia used to dump her hanging basket of wave petunias on the compost heap.

They looked so bad that she couldn't stand them. Not this year. When she bought her baskets this spring, she asked the nursery worker why the flowers were so short lived.

"They actually aren't, if you take proper care of them."

Here is what Petunia was told to do. First, fertilize them with ¼ strength fertilizer once a week. Second, never let the pots get too dry. If the weather is really hot, she may have to water 2 or 3 times a day, depending on the size of the pot. Third, when they start to look ragged, cut them back. This works for most container plants. Even tomatoes in a planter can be thinned out for better fruiting. Just don't cut off any stem that has a blossom on it.

"Of course, you started planting right, didn't you?" Petunia learned she must replace about 1/3 of the old potting soil with new stuff and add a fertilizer like Osmacote to the mix. She had to buy healthy plants, not the Little Orphan Annie's that were water starved and root bound. With the proper start, most container plants will flourish, no matter the weather. They may need protection from the wind however.

Garden Recycling

Many of the local nurseries recycle the larger flower pots, and often the trays too. The small ones holding 4 or 6 plants are usually just thrown away—if they are not broken, offer these to a gardener with a home greenhouse. Or, if you start your own plants, scrub them up and sterilize them with 1 part bleach to 10 parts water.

There are several products for the home gardener who doesn't use the plastic pots. There are "cow pots" (pots made from compressed cow pies). They break down when planted in the garden. Peat pots are not as easy to use. They dry out quite rapidly. You almost need to put them in a plastic pot to retard this. Another drawback is that they are so dense you need to tear them apart before planting them in the garden. Otherwise, the plant's roots have a hard time pushing through the sides of the pot. Coir pots made from coconut fiber are a bit better, but both types damage tender roots when you do this.

Or you could make your own pots. Burpee's sells a wooden "pot maker" that forms pots from newspaper. This is great if you only have a few to make as it is time consuming. You plant pot and all—the paper deteriorates in damp soil.

If you have a pest digging up the plants in pots, buy a bag of chicken grit and sprinkle that on the surface of the pot. A one-inch layer should do it. It is made from ground granite and consists of very sharp small rocks. This may deter cats from using flowerbeds for a litter box, too. Large pine cones covering the soil will also send them running. The spines hurt their tender pads. It's not that gardeners hate small animals—we just hate the damage they do.

Veggies

If you won't eat it, don't plant it.

Gardening Saves Money

Everyone wants to save money in these hard times. If you haven't planted vegetables before, now is the time to get your fingers dirty. Here are some approximate savings.

- *Tomatoes*—Three tomato plants will cost you from \$2 to \$3, depending on where you buy them. Three tomato cages are about another \$6. In the store, one pint of grape tomatoes is \$2 to \$4. Grow your own and you will have that many every two or three days. Plant full-size tomatoes and you will eat fresh ones all summer.
- *Lettuce*—A packet of seed can cost as little as 75¢. Plant a short row at the edge of the flower garden. The red varieties are particularly colorful. You can cut it off right to the soil line and it will keep coming until the temperatures get into the 80's. As soon as the temps go down, replant and you can harvest until frost.
- *Peppers*—Why pay \$1 to \$3 for red, yellow, purple or even green peppers? Three plants will cost about \$2. Starting in July, you can harvest green peppers. If you let them get ripe, you can have the fancy colors and they are sweeter when they are ripe. It is the difference between ripe and green apples.
- Herbs—If you cook with herbs, you can buy small plants for as little as 50¢ each. Basil, for one, is a fast grower and may overwhelm you with leaves.

The upside of all these vegetables is that they can be grown in pots. They will not have to be sprayed with chemicals to kill bugs, hurry growth or preserve them for shipping. And you can pick when they are fully ripe for the best flavor.

Other vegetables that can be grown in pots are bush cucumbers, bush muskmelons, onions, carrots, and radishes. Plant a whiskey barrel with a growing salad. On one side, a cherry tomato surrounded by onions and radishes with a ruffle of lettuce around the front.

Gardening is good for the pocketbook, the soul and your health. And you can brag that you have the biggest tomato on the block.

Pre-planning Your Vegetable Garden

Bunkey read in a magazine that he has been planting his garden all wrong. He should be planting it so no soil is showing in between the rows. That brings up a few problems...

First, how are you going to get into the garden to harvest anything without stomping something down? Second, unless you have hundreds and hundreds of feet of soaker hose, you will have to water from above. This causes problems, especially for tomatoes. Since the author of the article doesn't mention mulch, water splashing soil on tomato leaves is a perfect way to introduce disease to your tomatoes. With plants so close together, there is little air circulation. This leads to fungus, disease, mildew, and mold.

Here are a few tips Bunkey learned.

Planting in blocks, 3 or 4 rows of plants in a square, does save some room in the garden. Just keep the blocks narrow enough to reach across to be able to harvest your crop. Of course, corn should always be planted in blocks for proper pollination.

Start a list of what you plan to plant. Check the seed packet or the catalog description to see how many days the plant takes to reach maturity. For instance, radishes have a harvest period of a few weeks, while indeterminate tomatoes produce for many weeks. Planting lettuce and spinach in the shade of corn will lengthen the time before they bolt (seed out). Planting beets on the other side of the row will also lengthen production as it shades the roots of the lettuce and spinach.

Another way to maximize your garden space is by succession planting. That is, planting a late crop after harvesting an early crop. If the weather is cool, start another crop of lettuce and spinach as you pull the bolted plants up and compost them. If it is too warm, cover the area with mulch until it cools and you can replant.

Another neat trick is to plant carrots and radishes in the same row. As you pull the radishes, you automatically thin the carrots. Since carrots are slow to sprout, it is also an indication as to where you planted them.

Do not plant a family member plant in the same place it grew the previous three years. Tomato, peppers, potato, eggplant, and tomatillos are all first cousins. Another family are the cabbages: broccoli, Brussels sprouts, kale, cauliflower. Keep a map of the garden from year to year to prevent planting problems.

If you want to freeze or can produce, plant a variety of concentrated harvest, like bush beans or determinate tomatoes. Pull the plants when they stop producing and replant something else for continuous harvest. For longer harvests, try pole beans and indeterminate tomatoes, cabbages and broccoli. The latter two will produce another crop if you cut the top and leave the root in the ground. Another trick is to buy plants of squash, cucumber and herbs and direct seed at the same time. The plants will produce first and the seed-planted crop will follow, making for a longer harvest.

Onion plants will produce larger onions and usually store well. Onion sets are great for using during the growing season. They will be smaller at maturity and often sprout sooner than onions from plants when stored.

If you have very sandy, light soil, start saving liter bottles. Poke holes in the bottom and cut out enough of the neck to make it easy to fill the bottle. Bury a bottle beside each individual plant; peppers, tomatoes, vines and so forth. Keep the bottle filled with water and a weekly dose of fertilizer at ¼ strength, then run! This will probably work for row crops as well, but the holes need to be in the sides of the bottles. You can also buy spiked tops for liter bottles. The bottles sit on top of the ground with the spike driven in next to the plant. A five-gallon pail with holes in the bottom can feed 3 tomato plants planted around it. The down side is finding critters drowned in the pail. They attempted to get a drink and fell in. Perhaps drowned mice could be dug in as fertilizer.

Bad Company

We've all heard of companion planting, but how about plants that hate each other? Here are a few combinations you should avoid. Don't plant beets with pole beans. The cabbage family hates basil, sage, radishes and grapes. Carrots dislike dill, caraway and tomatoes. Beans and peas can't abide chives, peppers, fennel and garlic. Lettuce doesn't want broccoli near it. Onions get upset with sage. Potatoes and squash just don't get along. Spuds can't abide sunflowers either. Most vegetables like marigolds. If you plant plants that dislike each other too closely together, you will know it by harvest time—one with not be doing very well.

Tomatoes are easy-going plants. They like beans, carrots, parsley, chives, sage, dill, marjoram, cabbages, peppers, marigolds, radishes, spinach and onions. Don't plant potatoes too close or where the tomatoes were in any of the last three years—they are cousins and can share soil borne diseases. You can pair them with cabbages, beans, corn, lettuce, onions, radishes and marigolds. Cucumbers and squash will readily climb up the south side of corn stalks. This saves space, but makes for a bit of difficulty picking the cucumbers, and make sure the squash are small ones.

There are other combinations that work quite well. If you have problems with getting carrots to grow, it may be that you forget where they were as they are very slow to germinate. Try planting carrots, radishes and leaf lettuce all together. As you pull the radishes, you thin the other 2 plants. The lettuce roots will help keep soil in place for the small carrot seeds and will be finished before you are ready to pull the carrots.

If you haven't tried heirloom tomatoes, you are missing out on the real tomato flavor. One drawback, however, is that most of them are not disease resistant. If you have had sick tomatoes, stick with hybrids in the garden. Look for lots of letters following the variety name of the hybrid tomato seeds. These letters are shorthand for the type of diseases the plant is resistant to. Plant your heirloom in a pot with sterile potting soil and you should have no problems.

Mimic Martha by putting your garden plan on paper before you plant. Most of the rest of the year, she's just wrong.

Listening to Mother Nature

Should you plant potatoes on Good Friday? SURE!! If you live in Ireland, that is. Try it in Minnesota most years and old Ma Nature will quickly let you know you made a mistake. Call it Mother Nature, or more scientifically *phenology* (a study of, among other things, soil temperature's effect on plants).

According to the University of Wisconsin Extension Service, you should plant spuds when the first dandelion blooms. Plant peas when the forsythia blooms, and beets, carrots, lettuce, spinach and cabbages when lilacs are in first leaf. Plant corn when the white oak leaves are the size of a squirrels ear. (They don't specify which squirrel, however—red, gray or fox. You're on your own there.) Plant bean, cucumber and squash seeds when lilacs are in full bloom. Tomatoes go in when the lily of the valley is in full bloom. Transplant eggplant, melons and peppers when the iris blooms. If you plant tomato, pepper, eggplant or cucumber plants when the soil temp is cooler than 55 degrees, they will just sit there and pout until the soil warms up.

You Can Grow Veggies In the Shade

Bunkey has been told many times that you can't grow vegetables in the shade. That is, until he read an article in *Northern Gardener* written by Meleah Meynard. There are some vegetables that actually do better in the shade. This doesn't include plants grown for their fruit, however. Tomatoes, peppers, cucumbers, squash and eggplant must have at least 6 hours of full sun and 8 hours is better. If you only have 3 hours of full sun, you can still grow beets, carrots, onions, turnips, radishes and the cole crops of cabbage, cauliflower and broccoli quite well.

No vegetable will grow in full, dark shade, so forget that spot under the oak tree. Shade in this case means dappled sun/shade, with at least 2 hours of full sun. So, what are these miracle plants? All the leafy veggies will grow in part shade—kale, lettuce, mustard greens, Swiss chard and, if you are a Martha fan, arugula. Sounds like you are gargling. Many shade-tolerant plants will be slower to bolt in the shade. Lettuce will stay edible longer, and shady areas don't dry out as quickly as do full sun areas. You will need to monitor the shady areas, especially if you planted in a building's overhang or near large trees. Trees are water suckers and will take all the food and water they can get, leaving little for the plants grown in the area of their roots.

Is It Done Yet?

Do you know when a fruit or vegetable is ready to be picked? Do you poke it or squeeze it or go by color or just make a wild guess? There are a few things you will need to know to get the best from all your summer's labor. Peppers, tomatoes and eggplant all taste better when ripe.

Take peppers, for instance. Green peppers are not ripe. They will change from green to red, yellow, orange or brown, depending on which variety you planted. There is a good reason to wait until this happens. Not only will they taste much better, a ripe pepper has three times as much vitamin C as an orange. Pick a tomato when it is at least 75% red. Chipmunks usually wait until a tomato is fully ripe. Then they suck out juice. Not only is this icky, but the tomato will rot if left in the garden. Eggplant should be picked when the skin is glossy and the *calyx* (that green cap on the bottom) is filled out. Overripe eggplant is dull, often cracked and the seeds are quite bitter. Feed those to the pigs or, lacking livestock, the compost pile. All three of these fruits love warm weather, so they can live for a short period of time on your counter top to finish ripening. Ripe peppers can be stored in the fridge, but below 55, tomatoes and eggplant will lose flavor. These triplets can get through a few light frosts if well covered.

Now for vegetables you can store for the winter, that is if you have a cool place for them—a temperature between 45 and 50 is best for most storables. This includes carrots, beets, turnips, parsnips, onions, garlic, sweet potatoes and regular potatoes. Harvest on a dry day. Remove leaves and stems, leaving about an inch of stem. Leaving the stem on is most important for the squashes. Brush, not wash, soil off and let the veggies dry (on screens if possible), in a well-ventilated space. Turn them over a few times so all of the vegetable is dry. Brush off any remaining soil. Don't even attempt to keep any vegetables that are bruised or have damages to the skin. Squash are an exception, but only if the damage is skin deep and healed. Deer will nibble squash as will squirrels, but they usually don't get very deep if the squash is ripe. You can determine if it is ripe by trying to stick your fingernail into the skin—if you can't, its ripe and ready to store.

Garlic and onions need a humidity of 50% to 60%. Store them hung up in mesh bags. If you were lucky enough to successfully grow sweet potatoes, keep the humidity at 60% to 70%. Squash like these conditions too. They can sit on a shelf in the dark for the winter. Potatoes also need dark to keep from sprouting and turning green.

Since most of us don't have root cellars, it is difficult to provide a cool damp area to keep our produce. Try large clay pots. If you have mice, plug the drain hole with steel wool, then cover the pot with a clay saucer or a piece of wood. Options for layering are sand (perfect for carrots), leaves, sawdust or wood shavings. A closet on an outside wall or under the bed in an unused cool room are a possibility. Check on your stored veggies regularly and remove any bad ones. That way, when aunt Agnes stays in that bedroom she won't be gassed by rotting spuds.

Asparagus needs a ditch 18 inches deep with the best soil and compost in it. Just barely cover the roots. As the plant grows, keep adding your very best soil/compost mix until eventually the tip of the asparagus reaches soil level. It needs at least a year to become established, and even then cut only stems that are larger than a pencil. Stop harvesting about the 4th of July. It needs the rest of the summer to recover. Don't worry about the negative, nosy neighbor when you dig a ditch in your garden. Let him think you are digging graves, or just moving dirt for the exercise. He will be the first one at the door with a bowl begging for handouts when he sees the result.

All About Beets

Heirloom or hybrid? You can save heirloom seeds and get the same vegetable you planted last year. Most heirlooms have been kept and replanted year after year because of taste first, then amount of crop. If it is disease resistant or repels bugs, that is a bonus. With hybrids you never know what will pop up—it's a combination of at least 2 plants, bred for specific traits: disease/insect resistance, ease of transporting, large crops and taste.

If you have never eaten beet greens and you like cooked spinach or Swiss chard, you are in for a treat. They are milder flavored than either of the other 2 greens. They can be eaten raw, like spinach, braised or stir-fried, and are loaded with *lutein* and *zeaxanthin*, nutrients that help keep your eyes healthy. No matter what the color—red, gold or striped—they are full of cancer-fighting nutrients.

If you are growing beets for its roots, plant in full sun. If you want tops, partial shade is fine. Since beets are a taproot, they do best in light sandy or loamy soil. If you have rocky or clay soil, either grow them in raised beds or expect a small, deformed root. They like cool weather, so plant them with the spinach, peas and radishes 2 weeks before the last expected frost. For a fall crop, plant 2 months before the expected fall frost. Here, your guess is as good as mine.

To prevent overly-strong flavor, keep the soil around them mulched. Hot soil equals bad beets. Harvest the tops when they are young and tender—be sure to leave enough leaves for the beets to develop enough sugars to sweeten the roots. If you have never grown or eaten beets, take a chance this year. Try them, you may like them. Petunia can't get Bunkey to choke the roots down, but he does like the tops in salads.

Cabbage—since Petunia is not fond of "supplemental protein," (worms) in her cabbage plants, Bunkey covers the new cabbage, broccoli and cauliflower plants with a floating row cover as soon as he plants and mulches them. The edges are anchored with metal "hairpins," a U-shape that is stuck in the edges of the row cover. Now the cabbage butterflies can't get at the plants to lay eggs, so no worms. The covers can be used for many years if they don't get torn.

Growing Carrots

Bunkey can't grow good carrots. They either split into multiple roots, taste like cardboard or don't bother to show up at all. Last year, after another spring failure, he swallowed his pride and asked his neighbor, George the Master Gardener, what he was doing wrong. George had a list of the things Bunkey needed to do to have success with carrots.

Bunkey's first problem was that he had heavy and rocky soil. Carrots prefer light, sandy soil with no rocks in it. A growing carrot that hits a rock will form legs to grow around the rock. While this doesn't affect the taste, it makes it a real stinker to clean. George's fix for Bunkey's problem was for Bunkey to build a wide mound of light sandy soil in the garden to plant the carrots in. It would be in full sun.

Next, he was to mix bone meal in the mound—phosphorus encourages root growth in the carrot. Since the seed is so small, Bunkey should invest in pelleted seed. This will help ensure more spacing between the plants and help keep them from blowing in the wind.

Another important step Bunkey usually missed was keeping the freshly-seeded row damp. George gave him 2 options: either lightly mist the row each morning or cover the row with burlap. With the latter, Bunkey will have to check under the burlap every day for signs of sprouting carrots. When the first seed sprouts, he will need to remove the burlap and continue to water daily until all the seeds sprout. This method will reduce weeds too, as they will sprout and be smothered well before the turtle-slow carrots decide to show their faces. Like many gardeners, Bunkey hates to thin plants. A neat trick is to plant radishes at the same time as the carrots. As he pulls radishes, he automatically thins the carrots. This method will not work with a covering of burlap, of course.

Since sandy soil is usually a bit on the lean side as to fertility, occasionally watering the crop with half-strength fish or seaweed emulsion will encourage growth. Like most other vegetables, don't overdo the nitrogen. Too much of a good thing here will result in a beautiful row of ferny carrot tops with little tiny roots. Nitrogen encourages top, leafy growth—as he discovered one year when his tomato plants were 10 feet tall, looked like a shrub and had tomatoes the size of peas instead of baseballs. We leave Bunkey contemplating the seed catalog and dreaming of his next carrot crop.

Growing Corn

Bunkey was complaining to his neighbor George about how seed catalogs exaggerate the height and production of corn in particular. It didn't take George long to discover what Bunkey's problem was. He was doing it all wrong.

First of all, there are now 4 types of sweet corn. There are 2 classes of sugary enhanced: regular, styled se and SE. They have very tender kernels but don't adapt well to stress. They do have better seed vigor, cheaper seed and need less isolation. Then there is normal corn. It can be planted earlier than the sugary enhanced but doesn't have the sweet taste. Start the water boiling before you pick this type as the taste deteriorates rapidly. The 3rd type is Super Sweet, sh2. This needs isolation from all other types or you lose the sweetness. The advantage of the newer varieties is that they keep their taste for up to a week if properly cooled.

Now, how to grow corn. If you plan to grow more than one type (for instance, popcorn and super sweet), they must be separated by at least 100 feet. If they cross pollinate, you will be left with starchy, not-sweet corn. Next, plant corn in blocks, not rows. Corn is pollinated by wind. Plant no fewer than 4 rows, 4 feet apart. Soil temps need to be 75 for untreated seed and 60 for treated. Too cool soil will result in rotted seed. When the seedlings emerge, side dress with bone meal. When they are knee high (depending on your height, but 15 to 18 inches), side dress again with a high-nitrogen fertilizer, alfalfa or soybean meal if you are an organic gardener. They will need another shot of this just before they form cobs.

Give them 1 to ½ inches of water a week. Keep weeds down. Weeds take nutrition from your plants. This is true of all plants. If you mulch, you will have many fewer weeds to deal with. Nice to know in July when the temps and humidity are in 3 digits. Check the plants every 2 to 3 days for insect damage or smut. Smut is the black glob growing where there should be a cob. Bag it and get it out of the garden.

It's best to harvest corn in the early morning while the cobs are still cool. The rate of sugar loss is 10 times greater at 70 degrees than at 32. Dunk them in ice water as soon as you get them in the house, shake off the water and refrigerate. They will be perfect for supper (or lunch, if you can't wait). With these tips, Bunkey's corn should be 10 feet tall and full of cobs this summer.

Garlic—If this is the first year you have planted garlic, you're probably wondering what the heck that funny curl is on the top of the plant. It's called a *scape* (flower stalk). Unless you are planning to share your garlic, cut them off to increase the size of the bulb. If you do induct a friend into the garlic grower's league, leave the scapes. While they may produce flowers (rarely), they will produce bulbils on the end of them. These small bulbils are actually small bulbs of garlic and can be planted to produce regular-sized bulbs next fall when it is time to harvest garlic.

Potatoes—Both Bunkey and Petunia love new potatoes, so as soon as the plants bloom she sends Bunkey to the garden to "tickle" the spuds. You have never heard of this trick? It's easy. Simply stick your fingers in the soft soil around the potato until you feel a spud. Dig out one or two from each plant until you have enough to eat. The plant will continue to grow new tubers and you can not only have new spuds all summer, you will still have a fall crop. Not as big perhaps, but you can enjoy treats all summer.

When you dug your potatoes, did they have scabs on the skin? While this looks pretty yukky, it really doesn't affect either the flavor or nutrition of the spud. If, however, you don't like scabby spuds, you can cure the problem by putting a couple of tablespoons of soil sulfur in the hole when you plant them. Potatoes want a slightly acid soil. Our soils here in Otter Tail County are alkaline, more so in some areas. Adding soil sulfur acidifies the soil. Of course, the very best thing to do is get a soil sample so you really know your soil.

Pumpkins & Squash

Is it a pumpkin or a squash? Most of them, the hard stemmed ones, are in the same family (*Cucurbita pepo*). These are the acorn, delicata and spaghetti types. Winter squash has a wider, softer, pulpy stem you can penetrate with your fingernail—this family is *Cucurbita maxima*. Canned pumpkins, usually butternut squash (*Cucurbita moschata*), are excellent for baking and pies. All are cousins and related to cucumbers.

Winter squash and pumpkins are easy to grow; however, they have a history of wanting the whole garden to sprawl in. Look for bush types, or cut down on the veggies you really don't like but grow just to brag about. Also, be aware that some squash are big enough to feed the whole neighborhood. Cooked, they do freeze well, or plan on inviting ALL your relatives for Thanksgiving and feeding them squash and "pumpkin" pie.

Several pumpkins are grown for their sweet flavor, but most people look to winter squash to cook. If you grew your own or got them at the store and you want to keep them for a while, you will need to take proper care of them to prevent rotting.

If you grew your own, start by wiping any dirt off the rind. Store at 80 to 85 degrees with 75% to 80% humidity for about ten days to cure the fruit. This will heal any wounds, enhance the color, help ripen any immature fruit and ensure a longer post-harvest life. There are a few squash that don't need curing: butternut, hubbard, and quality are three. Curing acorn types will make them rot more quickly. This type needs to be cooked within a month of harvest.

After you have cured your squash and pumpkins (or not), store them at 50 to 55 degrees. Immature fruit will not fully develop indoors, so chuck those. If you don't mind four-footed invasions, you can chop a hole in the unripe to feed the deer. Do be aware that action will be an invitation you may not want next spring, so don't feed them in the garden.

While all squash and pumpkins are edible, not all of them taste great. Some have more sugar and flavor. If the fruit is fully mature, it will stay firm and the flavor can actually improve for three to six months in storage. If you haven't cured it well, however, be prepared for a big glob of rot where your pumpkin or squash was.

All About Rhubarb

The reason rhubarb grows so well in the northern tier of states is that it originated in Siberia. It actually likes our cool summers and deep- freeze winters.

One thing many people don't know about rhubarb is that it is a very hungry plant. That said, if you are planning to transplant a hunk of it to a better spot, you need to plan for a lot of digging. Start with a spot in full sun (from 9 to 5). The plants should be 4 feet apart for best results. Dig a hole 18 inches deep. That's' right, 1½ feet deep. Throw all the good stuff you have been saving in the hole—compost, composted manure and ½ cup of organic fertilizer.

Even when you get the rhubarb planted and growing, you still have chores to do to keep it growing and healthy. Mulch it in the fall. In early spring, when you see those pink noses poking though, pull the mulch back and fertilize heavily. Keep the soil moist. Actually, if you have a low, damp spot in your yard, put your pie plant there.

You can transplant *stecklings* (the old-timer's word for the pieces), usually in April. Don't pull any stalks for the first year as the plant needs to get well established before you make pies from it.

Whether the stalks are red or green, if you cook them for any length of time the result is green. Add food color if you insist on red rhubarb sauce. Flower stalks should be pulled out—they take energy you want to go to the roots for bigger ribs.

Rhubarb is a plant that, like the apple needs a cold spell. The plant can be forced. To do this, they are grown in a totally dark, warm place. They race upward looking for light. They grow so fast in these conditions that the buds make a popping noise when they open.

Sprouts— A Winter Crop

If you like sprouts, why not grow your own? All you need is a sunny window sill, soilless mix (like seed starter), clean seed (preferably organic), jars for soaking, a shallow planting container with drain holes and a spray bottle.

Step 1. Soak larger seeds for 8 to 12 hours. Use this for pea, daikon radish, sunflower, kale and broccoli seeds. Drain and let them sit in the jar another day, then plant. The seeds will be starting to show roots and should be dry enough to handle easily. The smaller seeds, like bok choy, arugula, mustard, chard, basil and sorrel won't need this pretreatment.

Step 2. Planting. Dampen the soil just enough that you can form a ball when squeezed. Fill your containers to about an inch below the rim. To ensure you have no empty spaces in the soil, gently tap the container on a hard surface, then pat the soil smooth. You have to get your hands dirty or it's just not gardening. Now spread the seeds on TOP of the soil. Don't cover them. You want clean sprouts. Spray the seeds to wet them and help them settle into the soil. Now, cover the container with a cardboard box or anything you may have laying around to keep the container dark and keep the soil from drying out. Most roots need dark to get a good start.

Step 3. Check your container in 2 or 3 days. If the seeds have starting to root, put the container on bright window sill, avoiding direct sunlight. If you have a dark house, a fluorescent shop light hung about 6 inches above the green's leaves will do just fine. Irrigate by setting your container in a tray of water for about 20 minutes each day. After they have had their daily drink, set them back into a dry tray.

Step 4. Harvest. Most micro greens are ready to eat in 8 to 11 days or when they are 1 to 2 inches tall. Some herbs will take as much a month to reach eating height. You can eat your crops at any stage. Cut a few of the leaves off, leaving the stems and roots alone, or whack off the whole crop. Once the greens are the optimal size, you can pop the whole container in the fridge. It will stay fresh and edible for up to 2 weeks. After you have harvested a container, pull out the remaining stems and roots. If you planted some of the larger seeds, you will have very little leftover soil. Chuck what little is left into the compost pile. Now you are ready to start the next crop.

The Tomato (a.k.a. Lyopersicon Lyopersicum)

Even people with tan thumbs grow (or attempt to grow) tomatoes. However, not everybody knows the history of this interesting fruit. Yes, fruit.

Tomato plants were first discovered in the Andes more than 2,000 years ago. They were traded north and in about the 16th century got to the Aztecs. It took a while to get to Europe. Since it was a member of the nightshade family, easily discovered by looking at the flowers, Europeans decided it had to be poisonous. They grew it as an ornamental, called it a "love apple." Italians, apparently being more adventurous, tried it—thus, spaghetti sauce.

Tomatoes slowly spread to the more unadventurous countries and became an unstoppably popular fruit. Colonists, being bold people or they wouldn't have left their comfortable hearths, took the seeds to the new country. Thomas Jefferson grew them. The Italians and French, being the good cooks they were, took them all over the country.

Of course, there were a few doubters. A Colonel Robert Gibbon's doctor warned him that if he ate tomatoes, he would "foam at the mouth and die." The good Colonel gathered a crowd of 2,000, in Salem, New Jersey, in 1820, stood on the courthouse steps and ate a full basket of tomatoes as the crowd watched, believing he was about to commit "tomato suicide." The people remained skeptical. Of course. These were the same people who hung "witches." It took years for tomatoes to be accepted as not only safe, but good.

Here are a few tips that will help ensure you get the most out of your plants. One of the most important things tomatoes need is full sun (from 8 a.m. to 6 p.m.). The more sun, the better the tomato taste. If you plant in a container, it should be at least 18 to 14 inches deep and 15 to 20 inches wide per plant. If you insist on planting upside down tomatoes, stick to the cherry types. They are less apt to break off in the wind because they weigh less.

Check your soil if planting in a garden. It should drain well but hold moisture. Mulching will help retain what moisture it gets. To prevent tomato diseases, Bunkey mulches the new plants as soon as they are planted. He sticks a 3-pound coffee can with both ends cut out over all new plants for about 10 days (or until they are strongly rooted). This keeps them from being wind-whipped and dried out or broken before they get established.

Each plant should have about 2 gallons if water a week (not all in one dose). One inch of rain a week is an equivalent. If the weather is hot, they may need more. If you have heavy clay soil, be careful you don't drown the plant. Even watering will prevent cracking, cat facing and the dreaded blossom end rot. A liter pop bottle with the top cut off and holes punched in the bottom dug in next to the tomato will ensure the water gets down to the root. Try not to water from above as this can lead to diseases. Never let any plant go to sleep wet—wet leaves encourage mildew and mold.

Don't plant tomatoes until daytime temps are consistently 70. They will just pout. Plant 3 feet apart for good air circulation, and either lay them on their side or dig a deep hole and bury them so only a few top rows of leaves show. The stems will develop roots. The more roots, the more fruit.

There are two types of tomatoes, *determinate* and *indeterminate*. The first ripen early with smaller fruit. They grow to a determined size, produce their crop (usually over a month), then quit for the season. Indeterminate have larger fruit and keep growing until frost, producing fruit the whole time. They are usually later to ripen. Almost all heirloom tomatoes are this type.

Early season tomatoes ripen in 65 days or less from time you plant them. Late season varieties take 80 days or more. Tomatoes like wild swings in temps—days 77 to 86 and nights 60 to 68 are optimal. They won't set much if any fruit if temps are above 86 or below 59. If it gets to 100+ during the day or 75 at night, they go into a snit, say "the heck with it," refuse to set fruit and drop blossoms. They do recover when the temps become bearable for a shorts-wearing gardener. Guess plants can be divas, too.

Try a few of Bunkey's tricks to make your garden less work and a lot more enjoyable. Let's hope for a good 'mater' season.

Birds & Bees & Butterflies

Yes, birds poop on windows, bees sting, and who knows what butterflies do—but we want them around next year!

Birdwatching

Petunia has been feeding birds for years. Her feeders are right outside her dining room window so she can watch birds as she eats. The other morning, she was finishing her second cup of coffee while Bunkey was shaving. He nearly cut his throat when he heard her yell, "Bunkey, come here right now!"

"What the heck?"

"It's a cardinal, a real cardinal," she answered.

While some lucky bird watchers have cardinals at their feeders on a regular basis, others, without the proper evergreen trees for cover near the feeder, never see them. Cardinals were so named for the male's bright red color, the color of cardinals in the Catholic church. There are actually seven red birds called cardinals, but all the others live in South America. Ours are the only ones found in North America, hence the proper name northern cardinal. Odd that, as it is actually a southern bird. In the early 1900s it started moving north. Why did it take them so long to get to Minnesota? They are poor long distance fliers.

Roger Tory Peterson, who is the grandfather of bird books, once speculated that since the birds don't fly long distances, perhaps wide rivers like the Ohio kept them down south. Once the rivers had bridges, the birds could stop and rest part way across. Of course, people like Petunia who feed birds may have had something to do with it too.

Did you know that birdfeeding started after World War II? Only then did people have enough extra money to throw away on frivolities like bird feed. As people started to hang feeders in their yards, the cardinals had the slight advantage they needed to expand their range and slowly move north.

During the summer, the bird is very territorial. A pair will claim a territory about a half-acre and they will fight to keep their mate and hold their territory. In the winter, not so much as the hormones that cause this aggressiveness wane. They will group together at feeders and other food sources.

They won't eat from a tube type feeder. They want their food on a platter, that is a platform. Keep it close to the ground, full of black sun flower seeds and enjoy these flashy red birds.

Black sunny seeds in a tube feeder will attract chickadees, goldfinches, house finches, downy and hairy woodpeckers and nuthatches. The seed that falls on the ground will feed doves, turkeys and rabbits—whether you want them to or not.

Rake the fallen seed up and discard it during the winter to help prevent the messy spring cleanup. That stuff gets really yukky in the spring. Enjoy the birds. They keep the bug population down. If you left your flowerbed messy, they will clean that up too and spread a few plants in unexpected places, already fertilized.

Feeding the Birds

One of Bunkey's hobbies is birdwatching. To make that easier, he feeds them. He has planted bird-friendly shrubs and trees all around his yard. Some, like conifers, serve as shelter; others serve as lunch counters for the fruit eaters like the robins and cedar waxwings. Most hardy bird-favorite fruiting shrubs and small trees are double-duty plants. That is, they bloom in the spring, have pretty fruit in the fall and are attractive additions to the landscape all year round. The red twigged dogwood, a nice short shrub rarely getting 12 feet tall, is one. In spring it bursts out in white umbel flowers, followed in the fall by bird-loved berries. In winter, the red branches are an eye-catching red against the white snow. The gray dogwood has similar blooms and fruit, but is taller, with more subdued colored stems. The fruit eaters swarm crabapple trees. The trick with a bird-friendly crab is that the apples must be very small. If your tree produces the larger fruits, you may be visited by deer who will stand on their back legs to get to the fruit. They do the same thing to chokecherry bushes.

Bunkey has 2 crabapple trees with the larger fruit near his kitchen window. One winter day he happened to look out and yelled at Petunia that there was a black plastic bag stuck in the tree. He was muttering to himself about careless neighbors until the bag started moving. It was a wild turkey having breakfast in his tree. It was also breaking some of the smaller branches as it did so.

If you can find a mulberry tree, buy it. You will swear the tree is dead as it doesn't leaf out until all the other trees in the neighborhood do. It gets leaves, blooms and shortly thereafter, berries. The berries look like elongated raspberries and are small enough for most any bird to swallow. The tree looks like a strong wind is blowing as birds flock to eat the feast. It's a small tree, with an umbrella shape. The leaves are small, shiny and dark green.

Another bird feeder with a totally different shape is the native serviceberry, a.k.a. Juneberry. It is a medium-sized tree, rather narrow, that likes a bit of shade. Plant this one on the east side of your taller trees. The berries taste much like blueberries, but you will be lucky to get a taste before the birds strip it in mid-summer. For the fall fruit eaters, plant mountain ash. This tree can get quite tall, 20 to 30 feet. The blooms are umbel shaped, followed in fall by clumps of bright orange berries. The yellow bellied sapsucker loves this tree. He will peck holes all the way around the trunk to get sap in the spring. While this makes the trunk unsightly, it doesn't really hurt the tree.

Don't stop feeding the hummingbirds in September—they are plumping up for their trek south. Here's a tip Bunkey just heard. If the bees and hornets are frightening the hummers away from the feeder, wet a cotton ball with hornet spray. Wrap the wet ball in a thin cloth and tie it near the hummer's feeder. It will keep the hornets at a respectable distance so the birds can feed in peace. Even a dead hornet can sting, as Bunkey found to his dismay as he accidentally squished one when he removed it from the feeder. One thing Petunia could never figure out: how can a bird, flying level, poop on a vertical glass window? Is it deliberate?

Keep Feeding the Birds

Bunkey was sitting with his buddies at the "men's coffee table" at the Pretty Good Café yesterday. The talk was about signs of spring. One guy mentioned he had seen the wood ducks house hunting in his trees. Pete said he had seen some bluebills. Their tuxedo coloring is hard not to miss. Bunkey, a newcomer to Minnesota, popped up. "The goldfinches are back, too."

The crowd broke out laughing. George was kind enough to tell Bunkey why they were laughing. Goldfinches live here all year. You don't notice them in the winter because in the fall they turn a drab olive color. Now they are molting into their bright summer yellow, black and white.

Many of our summer birds are back and are they hungry! Most of the apples left on trees are too big for the robins and cedar waxwings to swallow whole. The finches have pulled all the seeds out of the flower heads we left standing for them. The woodpeckers and nuthatches are running out of the high-protein spider eggs and larvae that they have been digging out of the cracks in tree bark and your house. Even the blue jays and chickadees that squirrel food away are finding their pantries are getting bare.

The migrants are hitting the feeders to tide them over until the bugs and plants come back. The various finches are looking for nyjer seed, a good source of fat, carbs and protein. Robins, cardinals and chickadees will decimate the sunflower feeder in no time. The oil in black sunny seeds can be as high as 49%, a real high-energy food. If you can find the proper feeder, shelled peanuts are full of calories. The nuthatches, blue jays and woodpeckers are crazy about peanuts.

Don't forget the ground feeders. Wood ducks, juncos and even some cardinals will flock to a scattering of cracked corn on the ground.

Suet is always a treat for the woodpeckers and chickadees. Often you will see an adventurous finch try it. Keep your feeders filled year round and you will enjoy one of the best shows nature has to offer, especially when mama bird brings her brood and tries to teach them what a feeder is all about.

Keep the bird bath full. It is really fun seeing the different styles of bird bathing. Some, like the robins, believe in full-body immersion. Others enjoy a beak-flung shower.

Migrating birds build fat deposits on the center of their breasts so it doesn't interfere with their ability to fly. Experts have determined this by blowing the feathers apart on the bird's breast. How's that for an odd job? A bobolink's fat reserve is especially critical as it flies all the way to the southern tip of South America.

Did you know that naturalists call the blue jay "nature's foresters"? Squirrels carry away acorns, but bury them too deep for the nuts to germinate. Blue jays hide the nuts in the leaf litter or gently push them into the soil. They will search through a pile of acorns, most beginning to deteriorate or with worms in them, and 88% of the time the jay will pick up only the 10% that are viable. Not only that, one jay may hide or bury as many as 5,000 acorns every fall. Of course, being birdbrains, they never remember where they hid them all.

Blue jays are migratory birds, so why would they bury food for the winter? The wusses are the young birds. The older, wiser jays stay here, dig up some of the hidden acorns and attempt to dominate the feeder, terrifying the smaller birds. There are feeders that only allow the small birds to feed from them if you have this problem. Scattering sunny seeds and cracked corn on the ground will help keep these robbers out of the feeders—sometimes. Feed the birds in the winter and they will reward you by eating bugs and worms in the summer.

Spring Bird Chores

Our summer birds are back. The geese and the ducks are waltzing around looking at the housing situation. Wood ducks have already scoped out houses and holes in trees and are laying eggs. Robins are hunting wormsicles, bluebirds are back, looking for bugs with little luck. Why should gardeners care? Other than bats, who eat a lot of mosquitoes, birds are the next biggest bug reducer. They also keep us company in the garden—robins and cedar waxwings by eating the strawberries and raspberries, wrens when they chase them away, purple martins who dive bomb us if we get too close to their territory and geese who just love fresh garden greens.

If you have been feeding birds all winter, now is the time to do a little clean up. All the discarded stuff under the feeders is a real danger to our birds. It can carry diseases and kill birds that eat it. A barn broom works very well to push it up in a pile to discard. The resulting goop can be composted or bagged. Hose the area off well to finish the job. Next, wash out all feeders with soap, bleach and water. This should be done periodically all summer. Bake egg shells a few minutes at 350 degrees then crush and feed. This helps keep birds healthy during laying season. It takes a lot of energy for a bird to make a shell, which is why chicken people feed their birds oyster shells. Water and suet are as important in the summer as in winter. Robins need a mud puddle, not a problem some springs.

Clean out the bird houses and put a layer of aromatic cedar bedding in them. The cedar helps keep down the mites and ticks birds usually carry. If a mouse has rented the house for the winter, use a putty knife and scrape it out well. You may have to leave the house open for a few days, as mice wet the bed. Do leave out short hunks of string or yarn, dog or cat or people hair and grass for nesting materials. Feathers are always welcome. DO NOT put out dryer lint. Once it gets wet, it stays that way and the baby birds die of cold. Nesting material can be offered in a clean suet basket or draped on shrubs, depending if you are more Martha or Bunkey.

Enjoy the birds. They are a sign summer will really get here—eventually.

Hollywood Birds

Bunkey has been feeding birds for about five years. His feeders are on a hanger on his deck, so the birds feed only about 10 feet from the glass doors. About 2 years ago, he noticed a flock of what at first he thought were purple finches. They have been described as sparrows that have been dipped in raspberry juice. These birds, however, were the wrong color. They looked more strawberry colored.

When Bunkey started watching birds, he bought three different bird books. (He always goes to extremes with his hobbies. Just ask Petunia about his attempt to build wood duck houses. He bought piles of wood, two power saws, several different types of measuring devices, three boxes of screws—and that was just the things she knew about.)So when he started watching birds, he got the books, four different feeders and three different feeds (black oil sunflower seed, a finch mix and thistle seed). It only took days for the birds to find the feeders, but the unidentified finches just showed up 2 years ago.

He discovered they were actually house finches and a long way from their native area, the West Coast. Because of their exuberant, tumbling song, they were captured and sold as cage birds, a very illegal practice. A flock of them were sent to New York pet dealers in the early 1940s. When the federal inspectors came around, the finches were released to fend for themselves. And fend they did. They thrived. They had soon spread from the East Coast to the Mississippi River with a population in the hundreds of millions, becoming firmly established by the 1990s. No other native bird has colonized such a wide area in so short of time in such huge numbers. One factor in their survival may be their habit of congregating in large flocks. They are very social birds. They seem comfortable with people, often nesting in hanging baskets or wreaths hanging on doors. They nest two or three times a season here and turn out a large number of babies. They are also big fans of feeders, especially those filled with black sunflower seeds.

House finches are susceptible to a bacterial disease that causes their eyes to swell shut. This eventually leads to the death of the bird. It is caused by dirty feeders or contaminated feed on the ground. Many of our other birds are affected by this disease, so do keep the feeders clean and the poop-contaminated seed on the ground picked up.

So how do you identify these songsters? A boy house finch has red on his head and upper body, and if he has his tail toward you you'll see a red spot under his wings on his rump. His wife is a modest brown-and-white striped, plump lady.

Not long ago, no one had seen a house finch in the wild in our area; now they are one of the most abundant birds at the feeder. To keep them around, keep the sunflower feeders full, hang flower baskets in the trees for nests and just enjoy these little Hollywood birds.

Winter Birds

If you feed the birds in the winter, you probably have two black, white and red woodpeckers coming to your feeders. One is larger than the other, and no, the smaller one is not the female. They are two separate birds.

The larger one is called the hairy woodpecker, although the only hair is a few narrow feathers around his bill. The smaller bird is called the downy woodpecker, although it is not any downier than any other bird. Both have feet with 2 toes in front and 2 in the back with long sharp claws. Their tails have an abundance of melanin pigment and are strong enough to use as a prop when they land on a tree. When you see a woodpecker attack a tree you wonder why he doesn't get a raging headache. They have reinforced skulls, and their long barbed tongues extend to the top of their heads. Males of both species have red caps, no two being alike.

December is the time of year the hairy starts his territorial drumming, his smaller cousin starting not far behind. Both excavate new nesting cavities each year. Downies will return to the same tree year after year, while hairy will use a different tree each year. The babies of both are very noisy. You really don't want a nest of them close to your bedroom window.

So, why would you welcome a bird that digs hole in your trees and has loud, obnoxious babies? There are several reasons, actually—their nesting holes are adapted by other cavity nesting birds that aren't carpenters, and they feed on insects that are harmful to trees.

If you are superstitious, they are supposed to protect one from being hit by lightning, although why you would be out in a thunderstorm is another question.

A Beautiful Relationship

All gardeners know that hummingbirds are attracted to tubular flowers, preferably red ones. The unique beak and hovering ability our little flying jewel enable them to get the sweet nectar from specific plants. Most of these plants grow in the western hemisphere, especially in central and south America.

The largest of these are salvias. The flowers have developed a sneaky way to get pollinated by hummingbirds. In many salvias, the birds literally push a lever that brushes the stamens against their head as they feed on the nectar deep in the bloom. This deposits a crown of golden pollen on the bird's head that fertilizes the next flower she visits. The bird gets fed and the plant gets pollinated—a sort of marriage. If you would like to see this in action, try it out on the *salvia gurarанitca*, more commonly known as the anise-scented sage. Poke a toothpick into the corolla and watch what happens. Salvias have fine-tuned their flowers to fit the hummingbird's beak.

Oddly enough, hummingbirds have taste buds very like ours. They prefer sucrose, more specifically, the type found in cane sugar. They will use simpler sugars, but their physiology allows them to break down sucrose molecules for more energy than other sugars. They need every bit of that energy, considering that their wings beat 50 times a second and their heart beats at over 1,000 times a minute. Their acute sense of taste leads them to the most sucrose-rich flowers.

Bird vision sees reds, oranges and pinks as brighter and more attractive, while insect pollinators are attracted toward the blue and purple spectrum. Hummers will visit yellow and cream-colored salvias, but those plants have to rely on more subtle tactics to attract them. Actually, it's more about deterring insects. To that end, they are scentless and don't have the landing strip effect, known as nectar guides, that insects look for. Insects are attracted to the perfume in flowers, not necessarily their color. Plants want to make it easy for their preferred pollinators to do their job, and dissuade other creatures that might like to steal their nectar but are unlikely to transfer pollen successfully.

Hummers are very good at recognizing the sorts of flowers that have the rewards they want and they are very fast learners. They have become reliant on gardeners for survival. Their high rate of metabolism means that going without nectar for even a short time can mean the difference between life and death for these little beauties. Here in the frozen north, we have very few perennial salvias, so look for the annuals as hummer magnets.

That Darn Bird

People either love or hate blue jays. The haters because they have heard they eat other bird's eggs and nestlings. (A study done on the stomach contents of 292 blue jays during nesting season found no evidence of such predation.) They are a bit of a bully at the feeder, however, the red-bellied woodpecker will send them to the bushes to wait their turn.

The haters don't like their habit of picking up 10 to 20 sunflower seeds at a time. They aren't eating them, just carrying a throat-pouch of seeds to a cache site. Many of the caches are discovered by other birds, thus expanding the effective feeding range of your feeders. When they do eat sunny seeds, they take one at a time, pop it open with a peck or two, pry out the kernel and swallow it—just like the more favored chickadee. One trick a blue jay has is imitation. He will imitate a hawk's call to clear the feeder so he can eat.

Blue Jays are first cousins to the brainy crow. They are intelligent, but some of their behavior can evoke human disdain. Mark Twain claimed to be quoting a hermit when he wrote, "There's more to a blue jay than any other creature. He has more moods, and different kinds of feelings than any other creatures; and mind you, whatever a bluejay feels, he can put into language. A jay hasn't any more principle than a congressman. A jay will lie, a jay will steal, a jay will deceive, a jay will betray, and four out of five times, a jay will go back on his solemnest promise."

Both male and female are bright blue. They are a family bird traveling with both direct and distant relatives, when and if they go south. They migrate during the day and near the ground, unlike other birds. Here in Minnesota they are year-round residents, usually staying in a small area that features a feeder or other good food sources.

So, if you have been calling the jay a baby killer, hopefully you have changed your mind. He really does more good than bad, even though his theme song is *Oh Lord, It's Tough to be Humble.*

Christmas Hints

Still don't know what to get that favorite uncle for Christmas? Get him started birdwatching. He will need a squirrel-proof feeder or two, a suet feeder, a heated birdbath and seed. Black sunflower seeds, nyjer seed and suet will do it.

Nyjer seed and mixed finch seed spread on the deck rail or on an open feeder will attract the various finches. Woodpeckers are attracted to suet. You don't need to buy commercial suet cakes—birds are very happy to eat raw suet and it is much cheaper at your local meat store. You will need a feeder for it. Just hanging it from a tree will attract not only woodpeckers, but also cats.

These few things—a feeder, birdbath, suet container and seed—are all you need for Uncle Phil's gift. Next year, you can get him some good binoculars so he can watch distant birds, or maybe his neighbors.

What You Didn't Know About Bees

People used to think that large bee was the king bee—that is until someone caught the "king" laying eggs. The queen will live from 3 to 7 years and lay up to 2,000 eggs a day. She controls the workers with *pheromones*. Workers only live from 20 to 30 days. Its' no wonder they have such short lives—they do the construction, storage, guarding, caretaking, foraging and keeping the nursery. The drone has only one duty: to mate with a virgin queen, then die. He is the acrobat of bees, able to fly backward, rotate and flip. After all, he has to keep up with the queen in flight.

Bees fall into two categories: short-tongued and long-tongued. The bee's tongue length determines which flowers it will visit. Flowers with shallow reservoirs will feed the short-tongued types. These are miner bees, cellophane bees, metallic and sweat bees. Bumblebees, leaf cutter bees, honey bees and the oil collecting bees go for the same type of blooms the hummingbirds do—the tubular types. Even some of those blossoms are too long for the bumblebees' tongues, but they have figured out how to get to the nectar at the bottoms of them. They will crawl to the base of a flower, such as the blooms of the hostas, slice a hole in the base of the flower with their tongue, stick it in the hole and draw out the nectar. Ingenious.

In a single trip, a worker bee may visit up to 100 flowers and carry more than half its weight in pollen back to the hive. And after all that, it will produce about 1/12 of a teaspoon of honey during its life. To make 1 pound of honey, workers will fly 55,000 miles and visit 2,000,000 flowers.

Yes, they can and do sting, dying when it tears the stinger out of your hide. The venom has a unique mix of chemicals that may play a role in stopping the spread of HIV, which it has been shown to destroy.

Why should we really care about this marvelous creature? Because we depend on her to feed us. Bees pollinate 100% of almonds; 90% of apples, asparagus, avocados, broccoli, blueberries and onions; 80% of cherries, cucumbers and celery; and 65% of plums and watermelon.

Farm fields are a desert to a bee. They need flowers. The chemicals that kill other insects kill bees too. The moral for gardeners: don't use insecticides willy-nilly. Don't use systemic food for roses as the blooms have insecticide in them that will kill the bees.

Check your flower garden one morning. Bees will be on the old-fashioned flowers and not on the pretty new hybrids. There is no food for them in those fancy blooms. That doesn't mean you should only plant the old single flowers, but a row of them at the edge of the vegetable garden will attract the bees and other insects that will ensure your garden produce gets pollinated.

Bumblebees—A Native Pollinator

We all know that our European honey bees are dying off by the gobs and no one really can tell us why. Hives of them are shipped all over to pollinate commercial crops like almonds. We are lucky that we have a native pollinator: the fat, fuzzy bumblebee. If you spend any time in your gardens, you will see this chubby bee busy gathering pollen on the sacs on its legs while hunting for nectar. They are so big that they often bend the stalks of the more delicate plants as they hunt.

Bumblebees have smaller hives than the honey bee, usually about the size of a half a grapefruit underground in well-drained soil with only about 50 bees each. All but a few young, newly-fertilized queens die in the fall. These ladies burrow deeply into the soil and hibernate for the winter. In the spring, the young queen begins to gather nectar and pollen and builds a nest for a new hive. She builds a mound of pollen at the base of the nest, lays her eggs on it and sits on the mound until the eggs hatch. Once they do, she feeds them more pollen until they pupate. The newborn worker bees then become the nectar-pollen gathers while the queen stays in the hive laying more eggs and brooding them like a bird.

Bumblebees are among the few known insects that can control their body temperature. That is why they can work in lower temps than other bees or insects. During the first hard frost, the old queen and all her workers die. Only the newly-mated queens live to hibernate.

That bumblebee you see in your garden is pollinating your tomatoes, apples, flowers and other vegetables. You need to take steps to see that your crop of bees live to do their job. The first thing on that list is not to buy any nursery plant that was treated with *neonicotinoids*. Any pollinator that feeds on the nectar from a treated plant will either die, or at the very least become too sick to work. If you spray your apple trees at bud break, as recommended, you will kill off those young queens before they have a chance to enlarge their hive. Instead, wait until petal fall and spray at night when the bees and other pollinators have retired for the night.

Without our native bees, all flowers, apples, blueberries, strawberries, almonds, melons, peaches, pumpkins and CHOCOLATE would be in trouble as their flowers depend on insect pollination. Plant more native flowers and don't kill off the clover. (Think *clover honey.*) Bees love clover, as does your grass. Clover is a nitrogen-fixing plant, and it's nitrogen that makes the grass greener. Leave a few dandelions if you can possibly put up with them. They are nectar and pollen producers. Your neighbor (who has nothing but grass in his lawn) will probably call you a few interesting names, but you can shut him up. Just give him a nice juicy tomato, still warm from the garden and tell him that the clover and dandelions fed the bumblebees that pollinated it. It might work. Maybe.

Why is pollination important? No bugs, no tomatoes. *But*, you say, *I don't like bugs.* If there are no insects, including spiders and moths, we also lose amphibians, bats and rodents. Don't like bugs? Then you better learn to forego all vegetables and fruit. And meat. If there are no grasses or grains, what do you think your cows, pigs and chickens will eat? Hate even the thought of rodents? Like to watch that cute red fox hunting mice and voles in the snow? In the summer 25% of his food is insects.

Have You Inadvertently Killed Honey Bees?

Several years ago, 2,500 bumblebees died in a parking lot at a Target store in Oregon after a neonicotinoid called *dinotefuran* was sprayed on nearby trees. In Ontario, it was cornfields planted with seeds coated with the stuff that was responsible for killing 37 MILLION honey bees.

Neonicotinoids, more commonly called *neonics* (Roundup® and the like), are now the most commonly-used insecticide in the world. This, after only about 13 years on the market. Because they were tested as safe for humans and mammals, everybody started putting them in their products. They are listed on the containers as "user friendly," nothing is said about their effect on bees. After all, it is supposed to kill insects, right?

Neonics are systemic killers. The plants or treated seeds absorb the chemical into their tissue. It gets into the plants' stems, blooms, pollen roots, and even the surrounding soil. This makes for a very effective insecticide, killing all insects that feed on a plant, or even land on a pollen-laden bloom.

Not only is it used on most of the corn grown in the country, it's commonly used in the nursery and landscape trade. It is mixed in the soil of bedding plants. Research has discovered that the neonic load is much higher in bedding plants than in corn.

No gardener wants to kill either bees or other beneficial insects, so what are we to do? First of all, inspect any chemicals you may have to see if it has neonics in the mix. If it does, dispose of it in the hazardous waste. Instead, use insecticidal soap, Bt, or garlic and pepper sprays. Second, ask your nursery if their plants are organically grown. And third, grow your own.

It is up to us to protect our bees. After all, 2/3 of the world's crops depend on bees for pollination, and there are reports that from 30% to 90% of bee populations in some areas are dead.

If you like to eat, preserve your bees. Don't use neonics.

Monarch Butterflies

Monarch migration is an intricate journey. They spend the winter in the mountains west of Mexico City. Their resting area has gotten smaller and smaller due to removal of the trees they depend on. The now smaller cloud of butterflies starts north in early March with the first generation getting as far as Texas, where they lay eggs and die. The newly-hatched Monarchs get to the cornbelt states in May. Some of them head east to New England, others keep on going clear to Canada.

All of them depend on milkweed for food. Until recently, that weed—and other wildflowers that farmers view as competition for their crops—has been rapidly declining due to farmers' use of herbicide-tolerant crops.

The object of a new government program is to convince farmers to plant milkweed and other nectar-rich plants along field borders, around wetlands, next to buffer strips, in pastures or any other suitable location. The program hopes to encourage farmers and ranchers to increase milkweed populations while enhancing the health of their rangeland. The hope is to have a corridor of Monarch-rich milkweed along the migration route. This roughly follows I-35. There are small patches of milkweed on this route already, but the need is for large scale plantings.

The moral of the week: get your bloomers in a bunch and get growing a bug-friendly garden. And maybe nag your farmer-neighbor into leaving a strip of weeds along the edge of the field.

Going Native

Bunkey noticed that his oak tree had caterpillars, quite a few and more than one kind. He got his "bug book" out and identified 19 different species having lunch on his tree. Surprising enough, there didn't seem to be much damage to the tree. He started checking some of his other trees and shrubs and discovered that only the native trees and shrubs had insects and/or caterpillars on them.

At coffee later that day, he mentioned this odd discovery to his neighbor George. "Maybe I need to cut down that oak. It's full of bugs and crawlies."

George was aghast. "You would cut down a beautiful shade tree just because it has insects on it? That tree is feeding native birds and insects. Your foreign shrubs and trees like the burning bush are bug free just because they aren't native. Sure, they are prettier than our wild ones, but they are a desert for birds and pollinators."

This is the lecture Bunkey got: almost all native insects have a special relationship with native plants. Take the eastern red cedar. Most insects die if they eat the tissues of that tree; however, if you don't have that tree in your landscape, the juniper hairstreak butterfly would starve. Many people consider the native violet a weed in their lawn. It is the only host for the great fritillary butterfly.

Monarch butterflies need the native milkweed to live and reproduce. Farming has reduced this weed by planting weed-free fields, either by spraying or planting weed-resistant plants. The highway ditches are either sprayed or cut, further reducing native plants for our pollinators. Even the ugly tomato horn worm that can defoliate a tomato or potato plant in no time at all will turn into a sphinx moth. This moth pollinates a specific wildflower. No moths, no blooms. Even wasps, a real pest this time of year, are pollinators.

The Atala butterfly, a native of southern Florida, nearly died out when its host plant, a native evergreen, was harvested almost to extinction to make starch from its roots. Then, as the weather changed and got drier, landscapers rediscovered it, finding that it could take both drought and heat. As the tree started showing up in more and more landscapes, the butterfly returned and is flourishing.

Weeds, Invaders & Killers

Yard thugs.

What, Actually, Is a Weed?

The official definition of a weed: *a plant that is not valued where it is growing.* That can include that nice ground-cover that is now covering the sidewalk and headed for the nearest Interstate. That shrub rose that looks like it was hit by a bomb. The *cilia* (squill) that you planted in the grass and now cover all the available soil in the tulip garden each spring. In other words, it is not just dandelions and creeping charlie.

There are three types of weeds we need to deal with: annual, perennial and biannual. As the old saying goes, "Know your enemy." Annual weeds can be further divided into summer annuals and winter annuals.

Winter annuals germinate in the late summer or fall, overwinter, grow and flower in the summer and die. Chickweed, speedwell, knotweed, wild mustard, bedstraw, groundsel and henbit are winter annuals. Apply a pre-emergence herbicide before they sprout in the spring, then a herbicide in the fall for the sneakers that escaped.

Summer annuals germinate in the spring, grow, flower in the summer and die. They include: morning glory, crabgrass, ragweed, purslane, wood sorrel, spurge and sweet clover. Again, a pre-emergence herbicide will kill the emerging seeds. The escapees need to be sprayed with a post-emergence herbicide. Do this only when plants are actively growing, there is adequate soil moisture and the day is still, sunny and between 45 and 85 degrees. Dave Barry once said, "Crabgrass can grow on bowling balls in an airless room and there is no known way to kill it that doesn't involve nuclear weapons."

Biannual weeds need two years to mature. These include bull thistle, garlic mustard and wild carrot. The first year they are either just a clump of leaves or a rosette of them. Since they go to seed the second year, kill them as soon as you recognize the weed in fall or early spring.

Some perennial weeds reproduce from seed, such as dandelion, plantain, chicory and curly dock. If possible, kill them before they go to seed. This can be nearly impossible for dandelions, as they produce seed almost year round. Best to dig them up if possible.

Then there are the monsters—*perennial weeds* that reproduce *vegetatively*, a fancy word that means they spread from underground or above-ground stems, or from bulbs, corms and tubers. These include creeping bellflower, bindweed, creeping charlie and quackgrass. Bellflower was once a favored ornamental. It can still be found around the foundations of old farm houses. It not only spreads by roots, but also has a tuber as deep as six feet to deal with. These plants are best killed as seedlings, usually impossible as they are up and running by the time we see them. Kill them in the fall. Start spraying Labor Day and continue once a week until freeze up. This should at least slow them down.

The grasses can be killed with a herbicide made to kill just grasses. Yes, even in the middle of iris without damaging the iris. It takes several applications and you will still have to cut or pull the dead grass out. Unfortunately, unlike weeds, it doesn't just shrivel up and die. It just sits there and glares at you, dead and brown.

Weeds are the bane of gardeners everywhere. You have to admire their incredible guile. Weeds didn't get where they are today by letting the fancier plants in the garden walk all over them. Over the millennia, and without the slightest help or encouragement from man, they have evolved and adapted in a number of ways to ensure they can hold their own with their more sophisticated cousins. To start with, they tend to grow faster than other plants, either strangling or suffocating any plant in the vicinity. Or, they steal the light, moisture and food of their rivals. They make themselves unattractive to many insects and animals that might damage them. To add to the problem, they spawn an enormous family, prodigious amounts of seeds that they send into the world in a host of ingenious ways. To make matters even worse, the seeds are often so well protected that they can lay dormant for years, until the unfortunate gardener exposes them.

Bunkey hates hot humid days. All he wants to do on those kinds of days is sit in his air conditioned house with a good book and a tall glass of iced tea. That, he has discovered the hard way, is very counterproductive. The weeds love hot humid weather. They grow like a teenager during summer vacation. Weeds not only keep on growing, many of them start to go to seed. One crabgrass clump will produce enough seed to fill the whole garden next year. At least it seems like it. This means the gardener has to put on his/her big boy/girl panties and get out in the garden and deal with them. Don't put weeds in the compost if they are full of seeds, even immature seeds, as most home compost piles aren't hot enough to kill seeds.

Bunkey's Bad Day

Bunkey did a dummy! Last fall he got a load of well-rotted manure from a buddy who had just bought a hobby farm. He had it spread on his garden, and then tilled it in. So far so good. This spring, he noticed a green glaze of weed seedlings all over the garden, so he spread Preen all over it and tilled it in, then planted his seeds. Last week he noticed that George's garden was up. Nice neat rows of radishes, corn and a hint of lettuce. All Bunkey saw in his garden were the tomato, pepper, cabbage and onion plants.

"There is something wrong in my garden," Bunkey said to George. "It was short of humus so I put that old, rotted manure on it last fall. There must have been something in that pile."

“What did you do differently this year?” George asked.

“Nothing. I just tilled it up. Oh, I put some weed killer in it—Preen.”

“You didn’t read all of the label, Bunkey. Preen is a pre-emergence weed killer. That means that it kills seeds as they germinate, including your garden seeds.”

“But it didn’t kill all the plants.”

“It doesn’t affect plants that are already growing, just emerging seeds.”

Bunkey learned the hard way that you have to read ***all*** the label. A broadleaf weed killer will kill the dandelions that are blooming so prettily now. However, next fall and spring, you will have another crop. Even if the plant has not gone to seed, the yellow flowers are viable. You have to follow up the weed killer with a pre-emergence chemical. Roundup® will kill anything with chlorophyll in its leaves or stem. However, it will not kill any seeds the plant has already dropped. That’s why, even after you think you have killed all the weeds, they come back.

You need a two-pronged approach to weed murder. Corn gluten meal is not quite as effective as chemicals in killing seeds, but it will, at least, thin them out quite a bit. Read all labels, even if you have used the stuff before. The instructions may have changed. Bunkey may have to buy peas, corn and radishes this summer, but he did add humus to his garden.

Moral of the week: never put Preen in the garden before you plant. Read all labels. Never make this solution stronger than recommended—often, it won’t work as well.

Get out and get dirty. Summer is short.

It’s sneezin’ season. Your nose runs, you sneeze, your eyes itch and you’d like to get inside your ears with sandpaper. The old allergies gotcha. While there are many plants and trees that we are allergic to, one that gets blamed is innocent. It is not the goldenrod causing your problems, it's ragweed. Ragweed pollen is very light and floats on the lightest breeze. Goldenrod pollen is sticky and heavier than typical windblown pollens. Very little of it gets into the air. There are about 85 species of goldenrod. All of them are loved by bees, flies, beetles and butterflies—especially migrating monarchs—because of the heavy load of nectar the flowers hold. The bees take advantage of the heavy pollen to fill the pollen sacs on their legs. This is one reason bee keepers like to locate their hives close to a patch of the stuff. And, because the flower is so bright, the bees can continue to visit them well into the twilight hours. There are flowers and trees that are less allergenic—maples, hosta, heuchera, coleus, impatiens and pansies, for instance. The worst offenders are the oaks, fountain grass, all the artemesias and, of course, *Helenium autumnale*, more commonly called sneezeweed.

Garden Invaders

There are some plants that just love your garden. So much so that they want every bit of it. Quite often, it will be a plant that another, hopefully unwitting, gardener has passed on. "Pass-on plants" are great, but do beware. If they come by the wheelbarrow-full, politely decline. "Thank you, but I really don't care for the color" will do in a pinch. Here are a few you definitely want to pass up, that is unless you want a large area covered with plants and don't really care what they are.

- *Snow-on-the-mountain* looks so innocent. The leaves are variegated white and green, but it is a real monster. It spreads like oil on water with deep, discouragingly brittle roots that run. Dig until you are exhausted, and five minutes later it is off in a new spot. Run for the Roundup®.
- *Ostrich fern is a*nother root spreader. While it is a great plant for

the north side of a house with an ugly foundation, in a year or two, it will be off and running.

- *Common daylily*, a ditch flower if ever there was one, is another root spreader. Not only does she run, but when she is done blooming, all you have left is a chunk of long ribbon-like leaves.
- *Gooseneck loosestrife* has very loose ideas of where it belongs. Any farmer can tell you that loosestrife is a weed to avoid.

Then there are the seed spreaders. They start out innocently enough—that is, until you find their babies popping up in every uncovered bit of soil.

- *Ornamental fountain grass*, (*Pennistetum alopecuroides*) popped out of its bed in Noerenberg Gardens on lake Minnetonka and invaded the lawn.
- *Plume poppy* is quite a spectacular plant, tall and big-leaved. It took a 5-foot leap and crawled into a bed of iris at Squire House Gardens, another professional garden. They fought its sisters all summer.
- *Butterbur* was an even more obstinate plant they had to deal with. This giant hopped 7 feet, across a path no less. They dug and sprayed that one for 2 years before they got rid of it.
- *Campanula*—While the blue or white clips are quite delightful, some of its cousins are outright criminals. One looks like a chicken's drumstick, bright blue and quite attractive, but give it a home and it is "home on the range." It's very difficult to get rid of. Brush killer might do it. Another is tall and skinny with blue bells on a stalk. This spread by roots and hides a tuber deep underground.
- *Hardy geranium* sounds innocent but is another sneaker. It's short so it can hide in taller plants. You may not even notice it until it blooms either pink or blue.

Even if you must insult the giver, avoid these plants at all cost. Also beware if you see large clumps of a pretty bloomer. She may be a "Nasty Nancy" wanting every bit of soil she can get her roots into.

Are you harboring a thug in your yard? If you have a buckthorn tree, the University of Minnesota says you have. Buckthorn trees have small, oval, dull dark green leaves, and if adult are covered in small black berries. They were introduced from Asia as a good hedge tree by someone who obviously didn't do their homework. Birds love the berries, which have a laxative chemical in them. Birds who eat the berries get a bellyache and spread pre-fertilized seeds all over the place. This would be OK if the trees behaved themselves, but they crowd out native trees. There are two ways to get rid of these stinkers. If they are small, just pull them out. Bigger trees need to be cut off and the stump brushed with full-strength brush killer. It probably won't be a one-time job as the berries that fell when you cut the tree will sprout and need treatment next fall.

Nasty Nancy and Other Killers

Most people know that black walnut trees will either inhibit growth under them, or in some cases actually kill plants planted near them. However, walnut is not the only killer plant. Three trees we don't need to worry about here in the frozen north are sycamore, eucalyptus and tree of heaven. We do need to be concerned about buckthorn, butternut, hickory, hackberry, rhododendron, sumac and sunflowers. Buckthorn inhibits native plants by competition for water, minerals and light, but also by the production of allelopathic substances in the soil.

Allelopathy is a Greek term that means *to suffer from*. It refers to the inhibition of the growth and health of other plants planted near the offending plant by toxic chemicals. With black walnut, the chemical is *juglone*.

Trees and shrubs are not the only killer plants. Some grasses are, too. Fescue, rye and quackgrass are also allelopathic. Garlic mustard apparently produces a chemical that interferes with the symbiotic mycorrhizal associations of our native trees and soil fungi. That association is the reason that when you dig a tree in the wild, you should take several shovelfuls of the surrounding soil to put in the new hole. The tree has been working hard to develop these fungi and will have to start all over in new soil.

Did you know...?

Many plants are hazardous—don't let your pets or your kids eat them!

- *Daffodil*—all parts are poisonous.
- *Castor bean*—seeds are a deadly poison. Keep away from children.
- *Rhubarb*—leaves contain enough oxalic acid to kill a person. Dried, powdered roots have been used for centuries to treat bellyaches, including amoebic dysentery—just don't try this one at home! The liquid from rhubarb leaves can kill aphids on roses.
- *Tomato*—avoid leaves, stems and green fruit.
- *Grapes & raisins*—will kill a dog.
- *Lilies*—all parts of the plant are toxic to cats. Just nibbling a leaf can cause kidney failure and death within 24 to 48 hours.
- *Toxic plants*—alyssum, begonia, bleeding heart, caladium, calla lily, clematis, clivia, cyclamen, datura, dieffenbachia, dusty miller, foxglove, gingko biloba, hellebores, heliotrope, ivy, jack in the pulpit, larkspur, licorice plant, lily of the valley, lobelia, love in a mist and loves lies bleeding, monkshood and morning glory.
- *Toxic seeds*—almond, apple, cherry, peach, pear, nectarine, morning glory, plum and yew.
- *Toxic, call 911*—fritillaria, glory lily, heliotrope, Jerusalem cherry, rosary pea, squill (scilla) star of Bethlehem and vinca.

What's Bugging You?

Vacuuming up ladybugs just ticks them off.

BUGS

When Bad Bugs Happen to Good Gardens

Horrors, there are holes in the hosta leaves. The phlox leaves have white spots on them and there is some yukky looking yellow stuff on the mulch. Don't panic! The holes are probably from slugs. In other plants it is often grasshoppers. White leaves mean downy mildew and the yukky stuff is most probably vomit mold. None of these things need the gardener to be tearing his/her hair out. There are some rules gardeners need to follow to have healthy plants.

- Keep your plants healthy. Stressed plants are those that have been over or under watered, over/under fertilized, or have a recurring disease (like powdery mildew) and are more apt to be attacked by insects or other diseases. A stressed plant produces compounds that may even attract insects.
- Practice good garden hygiene. Be religious about deadheading. Remove any dead or diseased stems or leaves. Give each plant elbow room. Plants living too close together get sick more often than plants that have good air circulation. In the fall, remove any dead foliage that may conceal fungal pathogens.
- Take a stroll around the gardens at least every other day. This way, you will notice insect damage, mildew appearing, aster yellows or other problems and deal with them before they get out of hand.
- Water in the morning if possible, and never from overhead. You will lose less moisture to evaporation, leaves will dry more quickly, preventing or at least discouraging wilts, blights and leaf spots.
- Mulch! Mulch keeps fungal spores that live in the soil down there where they belong, not on your plants. It also keeps the soil cool, prevents pounding rain from compacting the soil, holds moisture, and prevents weed seeds falling on it from infesting the garden.

They either die since they can't root well, or if they don't, are very easy to pull out.

- Buy Listerine® by the gallon. Used to disinfect tools, even shovels, Listerine® mouthwash kills most pathogens and doesn't damage cutting edges like bleach or alcohol does. Plant diseases like Virus X in hostas, black knot in cherry and plum trees, and fire blight in apples, for instance, are spread on cutting edges of tools. Disinfect a tool after each cut.
- If you have a plant that gets sick every single, stinking year, throw the darn thing in the garbage and plant a resistant variety instead. Monarda and phlox are notorious for getting powdery mildew if there are two drops of dew in the air. The newer varieties are resistant and often prettier plants. Or, you can plant some other plant entirely.
- If you have had problems with tomatoes, look for the letters VFNT after the variety name. This means the plant is resistant to verticillium, fusarium wilt, root knot and tobacco mosaic virus. This doesn't mean you can have a smoke, then harvest tomatoes. The smoke left on your fingers can easily infect a damp leaf on the tomato, thus infecting the whole plant. The plant is resistant, not disease proof.
- Finally, be tolerant. A few holes in leaves, a yellow leaf or a stray insect in the garden doesn't mean the whole plant is on the way out. Most plants can stand a bit of damage, and no garden is ever perfect. Just be vigilant and never let things get out of hand. A stroll through the garden before it's hot enough to fry frogs will usually be enough to nip most diseases in the bud.

The "Green" Way to Get Rid of Bugs

What is a "green" pesticide? In most cases, it's organic. That means that it is made from natural ingredients, it is easier on the environment than the "non-green" counterparts, and it breaks down quickly after application. It won't hang around in the water or soil for long periods of time.

However, not all organic products are safe. For instance, some recommend using tobacco juice to kill bugs. It does that, but it is a poison. If it gets on you or your pets, it can make you ill. It can also hurt susceptible plants. So, what should you use instead? *Bt* (*Bacillus thuringiensis*). Get a specific strain for each of these pests: caterpillars–*Bt kurstaki*; beetle larvae–*Bt tenebrions*; fly larvae and mosquito larvae –*Bt israelensis*. Bt comes as a spray, dust, or for mosquitoes, a dunk. It is a soil-borne fungus that breaks down in sunlight so you will need to reapply every three days or so.

Horticultural oil is a highly-refined petroleum oil combined with an emulsifying agent. It suffocates aphids, insect eggs, mites and scale. It is used most often on trees. There is a light weight oil for summer and a heavier one for winter application. Beneficial insects are bigger and usually faster than the target insects, so they can get away before being coated. The oil needs to cover the bug to be effective.

Horticultural soap, a specifically-formulated soap with lots of fatty acids, causes the bug to dehydrate. It works on aphids, boxelder bugs, mealy bugs and Japanese beetles. Good bugs are not as susceptible as they often have a protective outer shell or an exoskeleton.

Neem is new to most gardeners. It is a broad spectrum killer, meaning it kills all insects. It works by interfering with hormones, preventing eating and growth. It is a good fungicide as it smothers fungus spores. Be aware that some people are allergic to it and it can kill fish and other aquatic life. In other words, don't use it near your fish pond or the lakeshore.

Pyrethrum is another broad spectrum killer. It affects the brain of the bug. It breaks down quickly in sunlight. However, it can cause a rash, allergic reaction or asthmatic reaction in sensitive people.

Spinosad is the last "green" killer. It kills caterpillars, flies, leaf miners and thrips. It is used for lawns, fruit trees, ornamentals and vegetables. It is an oil-borne fungus like Bt. However, unlike Bt, it will kill bees. Therefore, use it either very early in the morning or late at night so it is dry before bees become active. It is also toxic to fish.

Most "green" pesticides don't work as rapidly as their chemical counterparts, so the gardener needs to be patient and put up with a little damage.

Always Read the Label

Bunkey was sorting through his box of garden sprays and powders trying to decide if there was enough in the containers to store them for the winter, when his neighbor George popped over for coffee and to see what kind of mess Bunkey had gotten himself into this time.

"How do I know which of these to toss and which ones will be good next spring?'" Bunkey asked George. George pointed out that if he just read the labels, he would know what to keep.

Federal law requires consumers to read and follow the label directions of regulated products. They are prohibited from using the product in ways not described on the label, that is, off-label use. If Bunkey had taken time to read the labels on the cans and boxes he was planning to store, he would have found that they told him not only how to store the product, expiration dates, how often to use and how to use, but also a list of precautions needed to protect himself, his pets, food and plants. For instance, grub controls are effective only at certain times of the year. Some products need to be watered in and others need specific rain-free hours to be effective.

There are signal words every gardener who uses insecticides, fungicides, herbicides or miticides needs to know. These words indicate the degree of acute or long-term chemical toxicity of these products.

- *Caution*—This indicates that should you be stupid enough to eat this product, inhale it or dust yourself with it, the product is slightly toxic and can cause skin or eye irritation.
- *Warning*—This means the product is moderately toxic in the same conditions and causes moderate skin and eye irritation.
- *Danger*—This is the strongest warning. Any product thus labeled is highly toxic by at least one route of exposure. It may be corrosive, causing irreversible damage to skin or eyes. It may be even more toxic if eaten or absorbed through the skin. If this is the case, the word *Poison* will be on the front panel of the products' label.

While these signal words tell Bunkey how dangerous the product is, he needs to read further. He needs to read all of the label for the active ingredients. This tells him which chemicals are in that product so he can do a little research and decide if he really wants that chemical in his food or flowers.

For instance, he has a container of Sevin®, the third most used pesticide in the U.S. in our home gardens, commercial agriculture, forestry and rangeland. The active ingredient in Seven is carbaryl, a cholinesterase inhibitor. This chemical is classified as a likely human carcinogen by the EPA. It is banned in Canada, the U.K., Austria, Denmark, Sweden, Germany and even Iran. It is extremely toxic to honey bees and many other beneficial insects. The signal word on its label is *Warning*.

Even manure can be fatal to your pets if they eat it. Composted manure and other animal-based products may not have a signal word, but can cause nausea and dehydration if not caught and treated promptly. Products listed as *pet safe when used as directed* can be toxic not only to your pets, but also to your kids if ingested in concentrated form.

After reading some of the labels on his sprays and powders, Bunkey was so spooked that he bagged about half of them up and took them to a place to be destroyed. The rest is now in a kid-proof box in a locked closet.

This next section contains many snippets about bugs, alphabetized for your convenience.

Ants—Petunia hates bugs, so when she opened the dishwasher and discovered it was full of very lively black ants, she went screaming for Bunkey. "Do something! Get them out of here!" Perhaps, knowing more about ants would change her feelings about them. Or maybe not. At any rate, if you are a gardener, ants are very important to you. Most ant species are predators. Without millions of ants in your garden, you would be overrun with beetles, caterpillars and grasshoppers eating everything in sight. Plants rely on ants. Their tunnels get air, water and organic matter directly to the plant's roots. The tunnels also loosen the soil so it's easier for the roots to expand and feed the plant.

Ants help spread plants. The seeds of trilliums, violets, Dutchman's breeches, trout lilies and datura have fleshy, nutritious appendages called *eliasomes* that lure the ants. They feed the eliasomes to their larvae, then chuck the seeds in nutrient rich midden heaps outside the colony where they often germinate. Now that you know what those funny lumps are on seeds, you can confound your friends by picking up a seed and remarking, "The eliasome on this one is quite thick!"

Ants are very social and have a tremendously efficient division of labor. A colony can have foragers, warriors, hunters, nannies, janitors, engineers, gardeners, herders, undertakers, guards, queens and even ants that turn their bodies into food storage units for other ants. They communicate by chemicals called *pheromones*. Some species lay scent trails to food sources. The more ants that use the trail, the stronger the scent. When squished, some species release a pheromone that causes its brothers to attack, or maybe run.

So, other than drowning them in the dishwater, what is Bunkey to do to get back in Petunia's good graces? Soak some bread with a mix of 3/4 cup water, 1/4 cup sugar and 1 tablespoon of borax. Put the mix in a plastic container with holes in the sides for the ants to get in. They will carry the stuff back to the nest and eventually the whole nest will die—but they will still come in from outside. To deter that invasion, use an insecticide like *Tempo* sprayed in a path 3 feet wide from the foundation out all the way around the house.

Tiny ants found roaming around the house are usually thief or grease ants. They are yellow to light brown. They feed on live and dead insects and any greasy food they can find. While they don't carry any diseases, a butter dish full of ants would put most anyone off their food. If you can find where they are coming in (admittedly easier said than done), you can seal up the crack or hole. Or you may be able to find their outdoor nest—again, not very easy. They will eventually go away at the end of the summer, but that is definitely not soon enough for Petunia. The best way to deal with the invasion is to treat the outside of the house. Usually baits take weeks to eliminate the pests. The ants don't take bait long enough to kill the colony. For Petunia, the news just gets better and better. Ants until freeze up. Just great!

Ants: Carpenter Ants—You notice a line of big black ants charging up the trunk of your tree. You have carpenter ants feeding on dead wood. This can be very bad and it is a good idea to have an expert examine the tree. The tree may have a structural weakness. The next wind storm can bring it down on your new Cadillac. When they nest outdoors, they get ready for winter by building up body fat (fat ants—who knew?) and increase the glycerol in their blood, a natural antifreeze. They will become dormant and not eat or drink for up to six months in our climate. If, however, they are sharing your house, they will become less active in the fall. If they are well insulated or in a warm spot, they can start bugging you as early as January. You will most often see them in the kitchen or bathroom. They particularly love the dishwasher, where they can get both food and water. If you do see carpenter ants, it is both good and bad news. Their presence so early in the year means that the house is infested, but it does simplify treatment. In the summer you will have to inspect both inside and outside. In the winter, you know they are inside. At this point, you can either call an exterminator or try to find the nest yourself. The ant you see is probably a forager looking for sugar and water, so give it to him. Put a small dish or sugar water near where you saw the ant. It will eat, and then go back to the nest to share the food. Follow the ant. There are several good deterrent sprays on the market that are very helpful.

Aphids—Take a good look at your houseplants. Winter is the time of year that aphids and mealy bugs flourish. (Guess they are getting ready for spring, too.) If they are really heavy, spray the plant with rubbing alcohol, paying special attention to the growing tips and the undersides of the leaves. And then there are aphids. Occasionally you will find them on a houseplant but more often outside on a garden plant. You are dealing with more than 1,200 species of aphids known to occur in North America.

Aphids survive the winter as eggs. In the spring, all the eggs will produce only females. Each female will produce 50 to 100 live babies. Even though they only live about a week, the babies will start to produce up to 150 babies in the next month. There will be several generations in a growing season. Most of them will be wingless, but a few will have wings. This is necessary as many species need one plant for eggs, another for food for the adults. Near the end of the year, winged males will hatch. They mate with wingless females who lay eggs for the next year. All in all, that is a lot of aphids. They damage plants by sucking the sap out. This can cause misshapen flowers, leaves and fruit. Usually all the gardener needs to do is hit the plant with a strong spray from the hose. They are too weak to crawl back onto the plant. Neem oil or an insecticidal soap works too, but try the hose first. It's a lot cheaper.

To determine if damage to a plant is aphids, look for a curling leaf. Aphids feed on the underside of leaves, causing them to curl.

About the only other thing that causes a leaf to curl is chemical damage. To dispose of aphids, encourage ladybugs and spiders to live in your garden. Ladybugs in particular like umbrel flowers like dill and Queen Anne's Lace. Their larvae look like small red and black dragons and eat every bug they meet. Don't use much nitrogen, as soft growth attracts aphids. Plant calendula near aphid-favored plants. Blast them with a shot from a hose, or for more tender plants, spray with a soap solution, a few drops in a quart of water. If the plant is so damaged it can't be saved, bag or bury it. Aphids not only suck the sap out of your plants, they also spread many plant viruses.

Apple Maggots—This is the most common pest of apples in our area. You may have eaten the maggot all unknowing. Apple maggots emerge in mid-July. The females insert eggs just below the skin. The eggs hatch into larvae that begin burrowing through the flesh. If you look very closely, you will be able to see a small scar on the apple with a trail where the maggot left. There are no holes left when the maggot feeds and the maggot itself is very difficult to see in the flesh of the apple. Leave a soft-fleshed apple at room temperature for a few days, then you may be able to see the brown streaks in through the flesh. If there are a lot of maggots in the apple, the fruit will be stunted with a knobby surface. Don't eat that one. Apples with a few maggots are considered to be eatable or you can cook them. McIntosh and Haralson have either high acidity or very firm flesh. The maggots may lay eggs in these two, but they won't hatch. No so in Chestnut, State Fair and Honeycrisp. They could be crawling with the little critters. Eat with caution, unless you don't mind a little meat with your fruit.

Asian Lady Beetles—To deter the Asian lady beetles from wintering in your house, repeat the spray when you see them getting together and planning an invasion. This is usually the first part of October, but an early frost will speed that up. Because horizontal and vertical lines look like cracks to the beetles, it is a good idea to spray around windows and doors and around any cracks in the foundation or other opening that they could sneak into. The chemicals usually need to be renewed every two to three weeks. READ THE LABELS AND FOLLOW DIRECTIONS EXACTLY. More is not necessarily better.

Bedbugs—You've heard the old poem, "Sleep tight, don't let the bedbugs bite." Unfortunately, they are biting more than ever. More and more people are sleeping in homeless shelters and for some reason that leads to more bedbugs. We used to think that freezing weather killed the little blood suckers, but only if it is cold enough for long enough. The eggs are very cold tolerant and need to be exposed to freezing temperatures for one to two months!

There is little research that looks at how long you need to freeze bedbug-infested furniture. The U.S. military believes if you expose furniture to 0 degree temps or less for four days, that MAY be sufficient. But there are other factors to consider. The temperature where the bed bugs are hiding may not be as cold as you think it is. So if you are concerned that you may have furniture that is infested, what should you do? Leaving things outside in the cold will immobilize the little monsters at least until you decide what to do with it. If you want to save the furniture, be safe and call a pest control service. Then you will know the bugs are dead. After all, no one wants to pick up hitchhikers. It just isn't safe.

Ridding clothing of bedbugs is another matter. Just wash and dry them at the highest temperature the fabric will allow.

Beetles: Drugstore Beetles—If you have discovered a small brown oval beetle dashing around in your pantry, you probably have drugstore beetles, and a major problem. This guy is about 1/8 inch long. Its head is pointed down, hidden from above by what looks like a hood. The immature beetles are small, whitish C-shaped larvae. These little monsters commonly infest cereal products, spices, seeds, beans and dry pet foods. They have been known to eat drugs (including strychnine), red pepper and book bindings, and have chewed through tinfoil and sheet lead. They will even tackle wool, hair, leather and dead insects.

Not a bug you want in your house.

The key to controlling drugstore beetles is finding their food source and disposing of it. Bird seed and dry pet food can be wrapped and stuck in the freezer for 4 days, or put outside for that long if the temperature is 0 or colder. Unopened dry foods, older than 2 months, should get the same treatment. Any infested product should be wrapped and chucked, unless the wild birds will eat it—put it out for them, they love fresh bugs in the winter. Vacuum up any beetles you see. Spraying them is neither practical nor necessary. It will not eliminate them. Check dry food that is not eaten regularly. Remove any spilled food or crumbs. Look in the spice drawer, toaster and any other place that might harbor a food source for the beetles. If you wonder about a package, dump it out and examine it carefully. Disinfecting these areas doesn't bother the beetles at all. Get the vacuum out and suck out any cracks or hard-to-reach spaces that might have beetle food in it. The stinkers will die without a food source. If, however, you see them again after all this, you will have to start all over again—there is still some of their favorite food someplace.

Beetles: Japanese Beetles—Apparently it hasn't been cold enough here in the frozen north to deter Japanese beetles. They used to be found only in the Eastern states. They should have kept them. They attack trees—crabapple, Japanese maple, linden, mountain ash, Norway maple, pin oak, and most fruit trees. All trees that grow here, with the exception of the Japanese maple. They also like sweet corn, grapes, strawberries, raspberries and Virginia creeper vine. They skeletonize the leaves. If the season is long enough, however, the leaves will grow back, smaller and fewer. Of course, this depletes the plant's energy and can lead to death if repeated often enough. Their favorite flowers are roses, dahlias, hibiscus, hollyhocks, common mallow (the first cousin of the hollyhock) and evening primrose. You can just forget these flowers and plant others, or go to war. Start by controlling grubs in the lawn. This is where they start. Apply a grub killer before they become active. You can try nematodes. It comes as powder that you add water to and spray on the grass. There is a milky spore powder that has been effective, or try Bt (*Bacillus thuringiensis*). If you aren't too sissy, you can simply pick the beetles off your plants and drop them in soapy water. Be prepared. Put on your bug repelling clothes, your bug repelling bracelet, a big floppy hat (even if you look like a dork), grab a spray bottle of bug killer and go get 'em.

Beetles: June Beetles—Petunia is having a hissy fit. She absolutely abhors insects of any kind, and now the yard is full of June beetles (you can call them June bugs, they don't care). What can Bunkey do to soothe her feathers? Nothing. Petunia will just have to put up with them for now. They are armored, so save your spray. They have laid their eggs and will soon die. Next year Bunkey will have to treat his lawn to kill the teen-aged grubs. If you had damage 2 years ago, treat your lawn this year. If you have grubs this year, it is too late. They are too big to kill.

Beetles: Picnic Beetles—Have you ever bitten into a nice ripe raspberry and felt a CRUNCH?! Yuck. You have just bitten into a picnic beetle. They are everywhere in the garden. Look for a small, ¼ inch long oval black beetle with four orange/yellow spots. They are attracted to fermenting smells, including overripe/rotting fruit and vegetables. If you are having an outdoor picnic and serving wine or beer, beware. Crunchy drinks will not make you the host of the year. You see them most often on corn, berries, tomatoes and melons. It is very disheartening to cut into a beautiful melon and find the inside crawling with beetles. They found a soft spot and took advantage of it. They typically don't attack healthy, sound fruit or vegetables, but once in the garden they will go for ripening fruit and vegetables. To prevent damage from picnic beetles, pick your garden produce as soon as it is ripe. And never, never leave any damaged or rotting fruit or vegetables in the garden that will attract them.

Boxelder Bugs—Another invader is boxelder bugs. They have much the same habits and are looking for a place to winter, preferably indoors. If they congregate on your house, spray them with soapy water. This dries up their skin and they die. If they do get inside, just vacuum them up. If you squish them, they leave a nasty orange stain.

Borers—It seems that every tree has its own borer. There is the emerald ash borer, the Dutch elm borer and now the pine bark beetle, also a borer. Symptoms of borer attack show up in late summer. Leaves will suddenly wilt and turn brown, but will stay on the tree. Removing some bark will reveal larvae and borer galleries. Only part of the tree may die, but it may be attacked again. Infestations may occur in pockets and look like oak wilt. Preventives are good watering and avoiding root damage by cutting roots, changing soil grades or drainage. Systemic insecticides are not always effective because of problems of timing and getting good coverage in large trees. What the heck, every tree has some disease or bug, but we plant them anyhow. We need tree shade to live in this extreme climate.

Borers: Ash borer—Another tree not to plant is any ash. The experts say any ash is "toast," a real scientific term. It may not happen next year, but so far there is no treatment to stop the ash borer. The only good thing about this is ash trees make good firewood. It splits easily and burns hot. A nice side effect with the price of heating oil and gas so high. The emerald ash borer is unstoppable at this time. Yes, there is a chemical you can have injected into your tree but it is very expensive ($1,000 or more), and it needs to be done every year. It is going to take thousands of our ash trees before it's done. Your mountain ash is safe, however. It is not an ash but a cousin of the apple tree. That means, like the apple, it can be killed by fire blight. If it is not one thing, it's a bunch.

Borers: Iris Borers—If you have irises, you may well have iris borers. How do you know? The leaves will have brown streaks starting at the top of the leaf. That leaf will either fall off or be easy to pull off. Another good diagnostic indication is if your irises smell like rotting potatoes. The borer didn't cause the rot, he just made it possible by boring into the rhizome of the plant. You can reduce the amount of damage by removing all the dead leaves in the spring and exposing the rhizomes to the air. If you smell rot, dig up that clump of iris three to four weeks after it blooms. Remove any rotting parts, and cut the leaves to about 6 inches. Before you replant the rhizomes, sprinkle the hole with an insecticide powder like *Garden Guard*™. In the fall, after the first touch of frost, cut all your irises down to about three inches and bag the leaves. While these treatments will not totally eliminate the borer, it will reduce it. Continuing these steps for several years should eventually clean up the problem.

Borers: Pine Bark Beetle—Another troublemaker is the pine bark beetle, which usually attacks drought-stressed pines. They like red, jack, Scots, Mugo and Austrian pine, but may also come after white pines and spruces. The beetle overwinters in the duff layer of needles under the tree. The tiny, ¼-inch-long red-brown or black females lay eggs in the spring. The resulting larvae burrow into the bark of stressed trees or freshly cut logs. A sign of their attack is the pin head-sized holes they leave in the bark as the adults emerge. Control them by doing your thinning or pruning in the late fall or winter and removing any damaged branches and logs and burning them. Keep the trees well-watered and fed, as chemicals aren't a practical control for the beetle. We love our trees and don't want them damaged.

Milkweed Bug—If you see a black and red beetle, your first thought is boxelder bug. They are only attracted to female boxelder trees. If you see the bug on milkweed, it's a milkweed bug, where more than likely it is sucking milkweed sap. It is about 1/2 inch long with a red body and black wings. The head is black with a red spot on the back.

Borer: Squash Vine Borer—Last June, Bunkey noticed some of his squash vines were dying. "Hey, George, come take a look at this and tell me what is killing my squash." It only took a glance for George to diagnose squash vine borers. He pointed out a wasp-like moth with an orange abdomen and coppery green wings buzzing around. He suggested Bunkey get one of Petunia's yellow bowls and fill it full of water to attract and kill the moths. The dummies fly into the pan and drown. George pointed out the borers' eggs around the base of the affected vine. They are disk-shaped and brownish and are easily picked off. About a week after the eggs are laid, white larvae with brown heads tunnel into the stem of the squash vine. They feed for 4 to 6 weeks until they are about an inch long, then exit the vine and burrow into the soil and form a cocoon. They will overwinter there, getting ready to attack next July. The first symptom of a squash vine borer attack is the sudden wilting of part of the vine. There are a few things the put-upon gardener can do to prevent the squash killer next summer. The best thing is to prevent the borer from laying eggs at the base of the plant. A collar of tar paper, shingles or a hunk of carpet wrapped around the base of the vine will keep the moth away from the vine. A yellow container full of water will attract and drown any moths flitting around the vines. Rotate your crops each year and pull up and destroy all vine crops to help prevent the cocooned larvae from overwintering.

Cabbage Worms—Did you find protein in your cabbages last summer? Nothing is worse than finding little green worms floating in the water you just cooked your cabbage in, unless it's finding one hidden in the raw broccoli. This happens because early last spring you were visited by that little white butterfly, or perhaps a dusky brown moth. Both are the culprits who lay eggs on cabbages, broccoli, and Brussels sprouts. The little green worm is the offspring of the white butterfly. Yuck!! If you like the cabbage family, but not the worm poop or the worms, you will need to take action now. Start by finding and destroying any wild mustard or shepherd's purse weeds. They can harbor the caterpillars. As soon as you put your plants in the ground, cover them with a floating row cover, a very lightweight white fabric that lets in sun and rain but excludes insects IF PROPERLY APPLIED. Encourage the tiny wasps that parasitize all caterpillars by planting sweet alyssum or other small-flowered ornamentals in the garden. Don't forget the dill. It is a favorite of the ladybugs larvae. While these little red dragons don't kill caterpillars, they do eat many small insects, especially aphids. If a cover is not practical, head for the poison row in your favorite nursery. You are looking for *Bt kurstaki*. The trick with this spray is that you need to spray the whole plant, including the bottom leaves. It is only effective for 24 to 48 hours and must be reapplied after a rain. In the fall, clean up all residues of the cabbage family as soon as you harvest them. This will help reduce pest eggs, pupae or larvae that have been hiding in the crops.

Caterpillars: Horn Worm Caterpillar—Petunia had quite a scare when she was picking tomatoes and discovered a huge green caterpillar on the plant. What scared her was what appeared to be a big stinger on one end. Actually, the "stinger" is the horn on the horn worm caterpillar. It loves tomato leaves and can partially defoliate a plant in no time. Simply remove the caterpillar to another plant. It grows up to be a beautiful sphinx moth that pollinates wildflowers. This caterpillar does not need to be controlled as it does little or no damage to the landscape. That is, other than scaring the pants off an unsuspecting tomato picker.

Caterpillars: Eastern Tent Caterpillars—Petunia hates any kind of creepy crawly and now she has caterpillars crawling on her house and dropping from the trees and tents of them in the chokecherry and plum trees. It's an altogether icky situation. However, Bunkey has it under control. He called the Extension office and got a list of worm killers. The chokecherry trees in Petunia's yard have tents from the eastern tent caterpillar. First he has to make a hole in the tent before he sprays anything. Then he has to get up with the chickens—the worms are active during the day so he wouldn't kill them all if he sprays then.

In the early morning or late at night, they are all cuddling in the tent. Of course, for the tents he can reach, a gloved hand can simply rip the tent down and squish the worms. Spraying the leaves with Bt, a bacteria readily available at most nurseries, will kill them by paralyzing their gut so they starve to death. Bt is environmentally safe.

Caterpillars: Forest Tent Caterpillars—The forest tent caterpillars (a.k.a. Army worms) are spinning webs in Petunia's aspen, birch trees and fruit trees. Bunkey learned that an aerial spray is the way to go. He contacted the local airport to have that done. If you do not have them (and you don't want them), shut off all outside lights from now until the end of July. As they mature, the worms spin cocoons. About two weeks later they emerge as moths. As anyone who has an outside light knows, moths are attracted to lights. Even though the moths live only about five days, they lay 100 to 350 eggs every day up in the tops of your trees. They will overwinter and hatch next summer. Its cycle is about 13 years, with outbreaks lasting three to four years. A cold damp spring or early summer weather is supposed to reduce this population.

Centipedes—If you have found the dry, brown curls of centipedes in your basement, usually with your bare feet in mid-winter, you might want to exclude them. Pull any mulch, wood piles or plant material away from the foundation and caulk any cracks. Pay special attention to the place where the house meets the foundation. Centipedes are very small and don't need much of a crack to sneak inside.

Caterpillars: ***Linden Looper***—Even our tough basswood trees have a worm that eats their leaves. The linden looper will also attack maples, oaks, apples, birches and hawthorn trees. It has a rusty-brown head, yellow body with wavy black lines. The young ones eat holes in the leaves. As they get older, they eat all but the mid-ribs of the leaves and can defoliate a tree. Spraying with *Bt kurstaki* is effective on the young worms, but infestations are usually small enough so that is not needed.

Caterpillars: Milkweed Tussock Moth Caterpillars—Male milkweed tussock moth caterpillars sing to attract females by making lovely clicking sounds. You may find him feeding on your butterfly weed. Probably have to listen pretty hard to hear that song.

Caterpillars: Woolly Bear Caterpillar—The second generation of woolly bear caterpillars are out and about in the fall. Their host plants are mostly weeds, dandelion, dock, plantain, aster and goldenrod. To make it through the winter, they produce a type of antifreeze, and hibernate under dead plant debris. They are as accurate predictor of winter weather as your grandfather's arthritis.

Cockroaches—If you travel over the holidays and stay in motels or hotels, leave your luggage outside for two to three days in the freezing weather after you get home. (Take your freezables out first.) This will kill any cockroaches you may have picked up. The little stinkers have become resistant to many of the insecticides in use today. They take anywhere from 21 to 120 days for eggs to develop to adults, so you may bring them home and not know it for three months. Leaving luggage in the cold garage for three days seems like good insurance. There are other ways you can become a host to these guys. Stuffed furniture, mattresses and even used drapes can be hosts to cockroaches. If you buy used furniture, leave it in the garage for a few days. You may have to scrape frost off the car window, but it beats bug bites.

Flies: Drain Flies—Petunia has been chasing flies all week. Bunkey made the mistake of asking her what kind they were. "Well, there are red-eyed ones, pale brown ones and some kind of dark fuzzy ones." Drain flies are the dark fuzzy dudes. To check for them, lay a sticky mouse trap sticky side down on the drains and garbage disposal. If it has flies on it in the morning, you need to go to work. First, you will probably have to clean the sticky stuff off the sink. Try nail polish remover. Then flush the drain out with about a gallon of boiling water and try to scrub the drain with a brush. Drains hold all kinds of goop.

Grease, skin cells, hair, bits of food and all the other yukky stuff the flies are eating. If the hot water doesn't do the trick, you will need a biological drain cleaner. Regular drain cleaners won't remove all of the organic goop. One brand is *Bio Clean*®. You can usually get this from a plumber.

Flies: Fruit Flies—The red-eyed flies are fruit flies. They often come into the house as eggs on fresh store fruit. The eggs are on the surface of the fruit, so either wash all the fruit with soap and water or promptly peel it. The little monsters can lay 500 eggs that hatch in about a week. While they love overripe and rotting fruit and vegetables, they can also breed in drains, garbage disposals, mops and damp cleaning rags, and in empty bottles or cans that haven't been rinsed. If you brew your own beer, make wine or apple juice, be sure the bottles have a tight-fitting cap—the flies can lay eggs under a loose cap and the larvae can then drop into the bottle. Nothing like a little protein in your wine. Yuck! Just one rotting spud or onion forgotten in the back of the drawer, a dribble of fruit juice under the fridge or a recycling bin full of unrinsed containers and you are infested.

Don't bother to spray them, it doesn't work. First, find and eliminate all breeding areas. Then, put out traps. A shallow dish with a drop of dish soap in it will attract and drown the little stinkers. Fruit flies must be a worldwide pest. Why else would so many scientists be working to eliminate them by learning how to shut down the flies' mating behavior? Female fruit flies with their chemical shut down are too busy grooming themselves to pay any attention to courting males. Males don't attract females, either because they can't smell the female or can't produce the necessary signal to tell the girl fruit flies, "Hey cutie, here I am."

Flies: Fungus Flies/Gnats—Do you have a flying circus around your houseplants? Fruit flies? Nope. You have fungus flies. Fruit flies are brown with red eyes. These stinkers are brown. Having fungus flies is an indication that you are overwatering your plants. Now, to get rid of them. Let the top 3 inches of soil get dry between watering. They lay their eggs in the damp soil. You can put a 2- to 3-inch layer of colored rocks, the type used in aquariums, on the top of the potting soil for a dry layer. If the soil is old, chuck it out, scrub the pot with a solution of bleach and water and repot with fresh soil. You can hang a sticky fly strip near the plant to catch the fliers. A yellow square of stiff paper with something sticky on it hung or stuck in the soil can catch some of them when they are in the flying stage. This is the time when each flyer can lay 200 or more eggs.

To determine if you have so many larvae to actually damage the plant's roots, lay some raw potato cut into 1-inch pieces on the soil. The larvae will collect under the spuds telling you how bad the infestation actually is. Some people have had luck watering with a solution of 4 parts water to 1 part of 3% hydrogen peroxide. Insecticides usually aren't needed, and why would you spray a poison in your house? Both you and the bugs will be inhaling it. The simplest solution is to let the soil get quite dry, almost to the plant starting to wilt. To prevent another infestation, don't water so much. Use the finger test. If the soil is damp at the end of the first finger joint stuck in the soil, it's wet enough for now.

Flies: House flies—Petunia was furious. "The house is full of flies! You must have had the door open or there is a screen with a hole in it," she yelled at Bunkey. "It wasn't me and I just fixed all the screens," he replied. Cool it girl. The flies didn't come through the door or the screen. They sneaked in either early this spring or last fall and laid eggs that are hatching now. The flies are quite metallic and very slow. Just swat them. While they are a nuisance, they'll disappear shortly.

Flies: Spotted Wing Drosophila—Did you have the misfortune of finding protein in your raspberries last summer? The culprit was spotted wing Drosophila. She is a tiny fly, only about 1/8 to 1/2 inch long and looks much like a fruit fly. Her joy in life is laying eggs in ripening fruit—not only in raspberries but in blackberries, blueberries, strawberries, grapes, plums and cherries. Not sure if this includes our native chokecherries.

The male flies have clear wings with a dark spot near the tip of each wing. The females lack the dark spot but have an ovipositor with teeth at the tip of her abdomen to help deposit eggs in our fruit. These busy ladies can start laying eggs one day after hatching from a pupa. The eggs hatch into 1/8-inch-long white worms that hide in your fruit. The fly can complete its life cycle in a week. This means there are multiple generations and multiple populations of the little stinker during the summer. Feeding larvae can leave sunken areas in the damaged fruit, or you may not see any signs of larvae until you take a dish of fresh berries out of the fridge and find it crawling with tiny white worms. Yuk to the max. To add insult to injury, the damaged fruit is more susceptible to bacteria, fungus and other insects like hornets or picnic bugs, both of whom love ripe fruit.

What to do? Keep ripe berries picked, every day if need be. Never leave overripe fruit on the ground around the berry patch. You can spray spinosyn or organophosphate insecticides on your berries, but they must be sprayed once the flies become active. This will probably keep you busy, considering how often another batch of flies hatches.

A better option for organic gardeners (and people who would rather not ingest any more chemicals than necessary), is to trap the adult flies. Find a 32-ounce clear plastic cup with a cover. Punch holes in the side for a hanger, then punch small 3/16th- to 3/8th- sized holes along the sides of the cup. This will let the flies get in but not get out again. Bait the cup with about an inch of apple cider vinegar. Then put a bright yellow card, covered in something sticky in the cup. It should be the full height of the cup. Now pop the top back on. The fly is attracted to the yellow card and, hopefully, gets stuck to it. Hang the trap in the shade close to the plants to be protected, or put it on the ground in the case of strawberries. Check the traps a couple of times a week. Dump the vinegar well away from the trap and replace it each time you check the trap.

With any luck, you may be spared the bowl of worm-covered raspberries for breakfast.

Galls—Did your tree's leaves look like it had pimples this summer? Don't panic, the tree is fine, just the target of a miniscule insect. These lumps or pimples on the bottom of the leaves are properly called galls. They are tree specific—in other words, an oak gall will not be found on a maple tree. They can be found on any part of a plant, not just the leaves. Each species of insect, midge, moth or wasp chooses a particular part of a plant to lay her eggs. Scientists are not sure if the resulting gall is formed in response to the chewing action of the caterpillar or to chemical secretions produced by the insect. Whatever the cause, the result is a hard, usually round lump on the leaf or stem of the infected plant. The insect encased in the gall will eventually tunnel its way out, usually in the spring, then start the whole process all over. How interesting that a tiny insect can force a tree or plant to build a home for its offspring. If you pile leaves on your gardens, the developing insects inside the galls will hatch and provide food for the spring birds, reducing the "bug" load on your trees next spring. Although these galls look terrible, they don't damage a tree unless they totally infect every leaf. This will slow down photosynthesis but won't kill the tree.

Grubs—How do you know if you have white grubs as opposed to southern masked chafer grubs? You turn them over and look at their back end. White grubs, under a 10X lens, have a pattern of hairs called rasters that have a V shape. If you have the right kinds of friends (who don't run squealing), they will be impressed with your vast knowledge. When you are done looking, they squish very easily. Or call your local fisherperson. Grubs are great bait. The old adage made new: if you give a man a fish, he will eat for a day. If you teach him how to fish, he will sit in a boat all day and drink beer.

Honey Locust Plant Bug—This tiny green insect is so small that to find it you will have to shake a branch over a piece of paper. It overwinters as an egg under the bark of 2- and 3-year-old twigs. They hatch soon after bud break and begin to feed on the unfolding leaves. The nymph appears first as a pale green oval crawler. As it ages it will develop yellow spots on its back. They will become adults in about a month. They and the nymphs feed until mid-summer. They cause severe leaf distortion, dwarfed leaves, chlorosis, and yellow and brown leaf spots. A heavy infestation can cause a failure to leaf out or leaves to fall off. To get rid of the critters, spray the tree with a strong spray of water while the bugs are small. You may need insecticidal soaps or an insecticide if you don't get them early and they get bigger and tougher.

Mealy Bugs—Bunkey's houseplants spent the summer vacationing on the shady corner of his deck. The morning the weather man predicted frost that evening, he gave the plants a lick and a promise with the hose, then brought them inside. This morning, while he was having breakfast, he noted that the hoya had a few more spots on it than it should. A closer look at the plant, and horrors—mealybugs! If there are only a few, a Q-tip dipped in rubbing alcohol and touched to the bug will kill it. Repeat weekly. If you have a heavy infestation and it is above 45 degrees outside, a strong stream from the hose should get rid of quite a few of them. Of course, this won't work on hairy leaves. You may have to stoop to an insecticide. It can be very difficult to totally eradicate. Bunkey has been known to throw a favored plant in the trash if it is too heavily infested. This is a good lesson to all houseplant lovers. Inspect your plants any time they have been outside. Never put a plant from another house, greenhouse or neighbor right next to your clean plants. Isolate it for a few weeks to be sure you are not bringing a disastrous infestation or disease into the house. While it is easy to chuck a small plant in the trash, it can really hurt to have to discard the orange tree that stood in Gramma's parlor for years, even though the darn thing sheds leaves like a pole dancer's clothes.

Mosquitoes—Mosquitoes can do more than bite, they can hijack your body's first responder cells and infect your whole body. European researchers discovered the mechanism that mosquito-borne viruses use to infect the rest of the body. This is what they THINK happens. When a mosquito bites you, your body sends immunity cells to the area, causing the skin to get red and itchy. A virus carried by the mosquito saliva gets through the skin and infects some of the immunity cells. The virus then has an opening to spread throughout your body, giving you Zika, Dengue Fever or West Nile Disease. One solution is bat houses. Bats love mosquitoes and are active at the same time of night. Forget purple martins as skeeter eaters. They don't fly at night and prefer dragon flies. Now aren't you so much smarter than a few minutes ago?

Slugs—Slugs love wet, cool weather. They also love hostas, and most any other plant they can crawl up to. Nothing is more off-putting than picking a nice red tomato and finding a slug hole in it, with the slug still in the hole. Yuck! Even though they make good fish bait, most people would rather do without the little slimers. The question is how to do it. There is no one-size-fits-all to get rid of the little slimers. If you can stand the ick factor, simply lay a board on the soil in the area where you have had damage. Put it down in the evening and lift it up the next morning. Now peel the slugs off the board and from the soil under it and drown them in soapy water. Or bury a tuna or cat food can in the soil. Leave a lip above the soil, then fill it about half full of beer. The slugs lean over to take a drink, fall in and die singing *Show Me The Way To Go Home*. This is still a bit icky, as you need to dump the can occasionally. Or if you'd rather drink the beer, warm water and yeast will work, too. The object is to have the slug crawl up a lip, lean down to get a drink, fall in and not be able to get out. If it rains and fills up the container, the slugs will be able to crawl out again, drunk or not.

Use any method you can to reduce humidity around the attacked plants. Water with a soaker hose, not an overhead sprinkler, for instance. Leave space around plants to improve air circulation. Remove some lower leaves or prop the plants up so they don't touch the soil. If the weather stays dry, *diatomaceous earth* can be a reasonably effective barrier. It scratches the cuticle (skin) of the slug, causing them to dry out. Copper and slugs don't agree. The slime contacting with the copper gives them a shock. They promptly head for less dangerous territory. A strip of copper weather stripping, on edge, or a Kurly Kate copper scrubber pulled apart will do the trick here. If you want to go the chemical route, there are several granular sprinkles that kill slugs when ingested. They are based on iron and are safe for both your soil and your animals. Here's a tip from a gentleman who was inundated with slugs big enough to choke a frog this summer. He sprays the critters with a mix of half ammonia and half water. Says the mix doesn't hurt the plants, but is deadly on slugs. Of course, you have to find them first.

Spiders—Bunkey has a "thing" about spiders. While he insists he isn't afraid of them, Petunia has to dispose of them. His job, as he sees it, is to point them out for her to remove. Lots of spiders indicates lots of small bugs for spider food. As long as there is food for them, the spiders will return. Petunia bought an Osage orange (also called hedge apples). Her neighbor said it would chase away all the spiders she had been dealing with all summer. Actually, nobody has done a scientific study to show that these ugly, warty yellow/orange balls do anything but remove money from your pocket. To get rid of spiders, get the broom out and sweep them down. Or if you are more modern than that, suck them up with the vacuum cleaner. If you are an *arachnophobe*, that is afraid of spiders, be aware that there are probably 100 species of them in your gardens and probably another 10 in your house. Be nice to them—they are excellent predators.

Spittle Bugs—You are out walking among your pine trees and see what looks like someone spit on a few of the twigs. Spittle bugs can be found on most any growing plant, including trees. You can dislodge them with a strong blast from the hose or a squirt of insecticidal soap. On trees, use horticultural oil.

Ticks—We have all heard how much Petunia hates any variety of insect, so you can imagine how horrified she was when she found a tick on her ankle late this fall. They were supposed to be hibernating by now. Unfortunately, deer ticks didn't get the message. They can be active and biting down to 39 degrees. Deer ticks, also called black-legged ticks, are a vector for Lyme disease. That is the bad news. The good news is that the tick has to be biting (the head embedded in the skin), for at least 48 to 72 hours to transfer the spirochaete to a person. The other good news is that not all deer ticks are infected by the spirochaete. The other bad news is they are very tiny and easily overlooked. Petunia has had no symptoms yet, but she has a list of them. Symptoms at the outset of Lyme disease can include (but are not limited to): a red area (sometimes with a clear center like a bullseye, fatigue, headache, muscle pain, sore throat, nausea, vomiting and generally feeling yucky! Sound familiar? An awful lot of illnesses start with some or all of those same symptoms, other than the red areas. The moral for this week: have your partner do a full body scan after you have been tromping through the brush.

Wasps—Wasps in the garden do a bit of good by removing caterpillars to feed to their larvae. However, that is not a ringing endorsement if you get stung. Grab a tomato or potato leaf to rub on the area. The venom is very acidic and the leaves of the nightshade family are alkaline. Remove any overripe fruit from the garden as soon as possible—it attracts wasps like the call of free beer attracts your neighbors. If you see wasps flying into a crack or a space in a building, you may have a problem bigger than you can handle. Try the dust treatment. If that is unsuccessful, you may have to call in a professional. Whatever you do, don't seal the hole up. It may drive the wasps inside your house. Don't spray into the hole either as that will have the same effect. It is no fun dancing with yellow jackets. They always want you to lead.

Wasps: Sphecid Wasps—This is the time of year Bunkey is most apt to see *sphecid* wasps around the yard or on his flowers. They are very different looking from most wasps. They are called thread-waisted for a good reason. The abdomen of these insects looks as though it is connected to the rest of the critter with a thick thread. These are solitary wasps, unlike the yellow jackets. Thread-waisted wasps belong to this family. So do ***mud dauber wasps***. (They are the ones that build those hard to remove mud nests in the most inappropriate spots.) This family of wasps eats spiders and other insects. In other words, these are the good guys. They are nonaggressive. If you don't bug them, they won't sting you. Since they do eat a lot of insects you would rather not have in your gardens, do tolerate them if at all possible.

Wasps: Yellow Jackets—Yellow jacket nests are gray, paper-like ovals. They may be under your eaves, in a tree, in the voids of cinder block or in the cavity in a wall. If they are in the area of human activity, you will probably want to remove them to prevent stings, especially if a family member or friend is allergic to stings. If you have access to the nest, wait until evening to spray it as they are not very active in the dark. Spray the insecticide into the hole in the bottom of the nest. Check next day and treat again if you see activity. If the nest is in the ground, forget the spray. Get a dust that is labeled for insects in the grass. Look for active ingredient *bifenthrin*. (However, from personal experience, the spray is more effective.) Once you are sure all the wasps are dead, fill up the hole or you invite another family to move right in.

Weevils: Flea Weevils—This weevil eats holes in elm leaves. Heavy feeding can cause the leaves to wither and turn brown. The adult lays an egg in a cavity she makes in the leaf midvein. This shows up as a blotch at the tip of the leaf and can be controlled by an insecticidal spray. If the tree is 40 feet high, however, you may have to rethink that.

Weevils: Granary Weevils—These little stinkers have a snout and will get into your flour and make webs. While this will not hurt you, it sure isn't appetizing. If you suspect you have granary weevils in your cupboard, put all flours and other grain products in the freezer for a week. This will kill the eggs that might be in that product. The theory being, I guess, *if you can't see it, it can't hurt you.*

Weevils: Strawberry Root Weevils—Bunkey is having bug problems. He's finding little black bugs have seemingly taken over his house. He wants to know what they are—Petunia just wants them gone. The little black bugs are most probably strawberry root weevils. They are small enough to creep through the smallest crack in the foundation or window frame. While they are harmless, they really are not the best house pet. These guys have a hard black shell, a bulb-like belly and are only 1/8 to 1/4 inch long. While they don't damage food, clothes or furniture, or hurt your pets, most of them go away on their own.

Did you know...?

The best tool for removing ladybugs, spiders and weevils is the vacuum cleaner. Just suck the little critters up and dispose of the bag outside—the trip through the machine doesn't kill them, it just puts them in a fighting mood.

And did you know that just plain dish soap is deadly to any soft-bodied insect? It dries them to death. A few drops in a quart of water spayed on the offending crawler will do it in. Try it on that house wall of boxelder bugs. It also works on those white, green or red aphids. Follow it up with a strong spray from the hose. They should just drop off dead.

Milk is another handy liquid in the gardeners' box of tricks. A cup of whole milk and a few drops of liquid soap in a gallon of water, sprayed on downy mildew, will stop it in its tracks.

CRITTERS

To keep cats from using your flowerbeds as litter boxes, scatter anything prickly—pine cones, bottle caps (sharp side up)—or lay chicken netting on top of the soil.

Not Tonight Deer

Bunkey has been fighting deer ever since he moved to his house. They ate the top branches off his small apple tree and the bark off an older one. One attempted to join him for breakfast by running into the glass door. (The deer survived, the door didn't.) They lunched on his hostas, knocked down the corn and ate it, totally reshaped a yew (and not for the better), and reduced the spring tulip bed to a blanket of compost. He was almost ready to reduce his landscaping to grass until he talked to his neighbor George. George had a thriving garden, flowerbeds and undamaged trees—and he lived nearly right next door. Here are the tips George gave Bunkey.

Deer are creatures of habit. They will take the same route each time they come to visit. Plant plants deer don't like on either side of the path. If you have a lot of cover close to where they walk, remove it. Even tall grass will be enough cover to make them comfortable ambling in for a feast. Steal some of Petunia's panty hose, preferably after she has worn them so they have her scent on them. Cut them in half and put bar of Irish Spring® or other highly scented soap in the toe. Hang them 6 feet apart and about 3 feet from the ground in your apple tree. They are effective for about 3 feet. Replace them as they dissolve.

Plant deer repellent plants in with the plants the deer love. They will have trouble distinguishing the good-tasting stuff from the yukky ones. Never leave apples on the ground or on a tree. The exception, of course, is the crabapple you planted for the birds. To keep Bambi from standing up against the trunk to reach the fruit, plant steel fence posts several feet away from the trunk. This should keep her far enough away so she can't reach the fruit or the branch tips.

Make a "pee pot." Pour predator urine in a container like a cottage cheese tub. Poke holes in the top to let the smell out and set it near the plant or shrub you want to protect. Selling predator urine has gotten to be quite little micro-industry. Bunkey is not prepared to attempt to collect bear, mountain lion or wolf urine himself when it is easily purchased from any store that sells hunting equipment.

A radio set to an annoying talk show (think *Rush*) can spook most wildlife. A barking dog will send Bambi running, but only if it is not tied up. The deer quickly realize the limits of a tied-up dog. Instead, fence the dog in. While the deer may jump the fence, they won't stay long. If you are worried about "dog spots" (that dead spot of grass where she peed), teach the pup to use a specific spot mulched with pea gravel for easy flushing. If it is too dumb to do that, flush the spot with water, then a 1 to 10 solution of vinegar and water. Dog urine is alkaline. The vinegar is acid and neutralizes the urine. Stinky repellents work too, but better in the summer when the smell can waft on the breeze. The trick is to change the repellent about once every 2 weeks, or weekly if you still have a problem. From the Use-Your-Brain department, don't put the stuff on anything you are going to eat.

Another way to deter deer is to invest in some electric fence posts, the type you push in the soil with your foot. Line the area to be defended with them. Now wrap monofilament fish line, the heaviest you can find, around the poles about 2 ½ feet from the ground. Deer run into it at night when they are wandering around looking for trouble. They run into the invisible line and it spooks them as they don't know what it is. If you have electricity close to the garden, bend throw-away aluminum pans in half and hang them over the hot fence. Butter the outside of the pan with peanut butter. Bambi smells the peanut butter, puts her damp nose on it and Wowie! Bambi flies. A lower line with this treat will send the raccoons looking for an easier place to get fresh sweet corn.

Lizards: Five-Lined Skink

We have all seen the Geico gecko. You have to admit, that for a lizard, he's pretty cute. We have a lizard in Minnesota that is pretty cute, too. It is called a five-lined skink. The first time you see one you are liable to jump right out of your underwear. They move like a streak of lightning. All you will see is a flash of what looks like a very small dark snake.

When he stops though, you can see that he has four very short legs and has claws on his toes. He has a very slim body with five narrow yellow stripes running from nose to tail. If he is a young one, he will also have a bright blue tail. He has eyelids and can move his eyes independently, and unlike snakes, he is slimy.

Now, you ask, *why would I want one of these "blue devils" in my garden?* Not only are they fun to watch, but they eat bugs and slugs. You will only see them May through August—they hibernate for the other eight months below the frostline in small mammal burrows or cracks in rocks.

One odd fact about that bright colored tail—if a predator grabs it, he goes away with just the tail and the skink runs away to grow a new one. Experts say that we don't have skinks up here because they are only found in southern Minnesota. Tell that to the pair that live in a rock wall near Underwood or the tribe that lives at the Prairie Wetlands.

Rabbits

Bunkey wants nothing to do with the Easter Bunny. He and his extended family have been using Bunkey's yard as a buffet all winter. They chewed all the bark off one small apple tree. The only one that didn't get a hardware cloth sleeve around its trunk.

Bunkey needs some defenses. If you can't fence them out, stink them out. Instead of planting onions in a row, plant them around the edge of the garden, or grind them up with some hot peppers, a few drops of soap and spray their favorite plants. Dead fish is a repellent smell for most noses (including the gardener). Fish emulsion is available at your favorite nursery. It does double duty as it's an excellent fertilizer. Rotten eggs mixed with water or the fish works too. Vinegar can be both a repellent and an attractant—rabbits hate it.

Used cat litter works great for any rodent. They smell the cat but have no idea how big or mean it is and will avoid the area. (Of course, you don't want it mixed in with your vegetables.) Predator urine will inform your problem critters that there is a bad guy in the neighborhood so they had better stay away for that area. People urine works too. However, it can be a bit problematic to apply. Especially if you have close neighbors or street lights.

If you don't have problems with strange noises, bury pop or beer bottles, necks up, around the area you are trying to protect. The sound when the wind blows over them can hurt an animals' ears if they get close. The eerie sound may have your neighbors coming after you with pitchforks, so clear that idea with them before you try this one.

Most gardeners will tolerate bugs, but Bugs Bunny makes them practically froth at the mouth. Rabbits trim shrub right down to the soil line in the spring or the snow line in the winter. They can devastate a vegetable garden. They love peas and beans, but like kids, leave spinach alone. They usually will not eat iris, peonies, astilbes, ferns, foxglove or ornamental grasses. They will eat red salvia (but not the blue variety) and tall sedum (but not the creeping types).

During the winter, a cylinder of 1/4 inch mesh hardware cloth will fence them out of shrubs, vines and small trees. Fencing the garden in the spring will do the same thing.

The University of Minnesota Extension polled a bunch of Master Gardeners on their methods of bunny protection. Here are a few of their suggestions.

- Provide alternate feed, such as corn and sunflower seeds on the ground. They will also eat the sprouted bird seed that falls to the ground.
- Stick silvery hologram pinwheels around the garden.
- Put floating row cover over the crops for a few weeks.
- Try pepper spray, but it didn't seem to work for many gardeners.
- Apply dried blood—it works, but must be applied after each rain. Keep it off plants as it is 14% nitrogen and can burn them.
- Let a cat roam around your gardens—it works, but the cat may also eat small birds, a no-no for many of us.

Rodents

It's gardening time. Rodents (squirrels, gophers, chipmunks, raccoons, skunks, moles, woodchucks, mice, voles, rabbits, etc.) can cause a lot of damage to the garden. They will eat the peas as fast as they come up, nibble any green leaf, help themselves to a strawberry dessert.

If your potted plants are pulled up at night, blame the raccoon. If it happens during the day, the culprit is either a squirrel or a woodchuck. If your grass is full of divots of dirt, blame the skunks or raccoons looking for grubs, or squirrels burying seeds and acorns.

If you find holes near stone walls, the house foundation, in your rock garden, in brush or even in open ground, look for chipmunks. They can be quite destructive.

If the hole is in areas of short grass you are looking for a 13-lined ground squirrel (a.k.a. striped gopher).

If the hole is in heavy vegetation or just under the duff in the woods, you have voles. Voles love root crops. If you dig your spuds and find that someone else has dined on them already, blame voles.

Star-nosed moles look like a mouse that ate an octopus and didn't quite get it all down. They leave multiple tunnels just under the surface that raise the soil or sod. They like damp places. If the tunnels are in dry areas, you have eastern moles. At least they don't look like a nightmare.

How do you keep the critters from eating your produce, defecating in the flowerbeds, digging up the plants in the deck pots you just got going well, and just generally protect your property?

Most of these critters can be trapped if they are causing problems. The best deterrent for these stinkers is used cat litter spread around. Just don't put it in soil where you plant vegetables or fruit.

Snakes like that messy area close the foundation too, so pull any mulch, wood piles or plant material away from the foundation and again, caulk any cracks. Pay special attention to the place the house meets the foundation. They will accidentally fall inside, but not actively attempt to get out. Meeting a garter snake in the basement is not conducive to a calm state of mind, even for people who don't mind snakes. They just do not belong indoors. Of course, if you leave them, they may catch and eat the field mice that also seem to be able to get into the tightest house.

Voles, Those Pesky Critters

Bunkey noticed tracks all over his yard when the snow finally melted. They seemed to be barely under the soil and several of them led to an apple tree he had planted last spring. A coffee klatch with George, his Master Gardener neighbor, answered the question of what the critter was: a vole.

This little creature, a.k.a. meadow mouse or field mouse, had been busy under the snow making surface runways and shallow underground tunnels all winter. Luckily, Bunkey had wrapped the trunk of his new apple tree or he would have discovered that one of the foods the voles live on is tree bark. They also eat plants, snails, bugs and dead animals. Last fall, they had been busy storing seeds, tubers, bulbs and rhizomes. Bunkey had planted a bunch of tulip bulbs last fall, but had only sprinkled a layer of chicken grit over some of them. The ones he missed, the voles didn't.

Vole damage to grass is caused by their shallow tunnels just under the grass, killing the roots. If you have had vole damage to trees or shrubs, remember to wrap those trunks next fall. If you use wire, bury it about 6 inches—voles can dig. Be sure the wrap is above the snow line so they can't crawl or jump over it.

Diseases & Remedies

Milk is not just for your morning cereal.

There's a Fungus Among Us!

It's a Fungus, Fred!

If not for fungus, we would be up to our noses in undecomposed *lignin*, the stuff bark and other woody material is composed of. While bacteria breaks down *cellulose*, the stiffener in plants, they can't work the same magic on lignin. Only after various fungi have done their work can bacteria move in and complete the job. Bacteria has a limited ability to move, while the microscopically small filaments of fungi called *hyphae* are able to travel long distances in their search for nutrients.

A single *hypha* is a round tube. A bundle of them is called *mycelium*. Only when there are huge bundles of them can the gardener see them. There may be many yards of hypha in a single teaspoon of garden soil. Their fruit pops up all over. Yes, you have seen that fruit. It's that mushroom that drives the Martha types up the wall.

Plants and fungus are interdependent. *Mycorrhiza*, (*myco* means mushroom and *rhiza*, roots) forms a mutually beneficial relationship with plant roots, bringing water and food to the plant, often from areas far from the plant. Plants can't move, and their roots only reach so far. The mycorrhiza, in the meantime, is searching distant areas of soil and bringing water and food back to the plant.

In exchange, the plant's roots exude carbons, sugars and other carbohydrates that the fungus needs. Some fungi go even further; they coat plant roots with a cover that protects the plants from bad bacteria.

Your perennials and trees not only benefit from this exchange, they prefer it. To promote fungi-dominated soil, the gardener must stop behaving like a mass murderer. Stop tilling! Tilling kills quadrillions of bacteria and chops up miles of fungal mycelia. Chemical fertilizer, fungicide and pesticide also slaughter soil life and can cause an unbalance that actually attracts bad bacteria and insects. So what should you do instead? Pull the big weeds, then mulch the soil. To plant, just dig a hole in the mulch and pop the plant in. Bacteria loves untreated grass clippings. Untreated wood chips are fungus heaven for trees and shrubs. A layer of good compost—topped with a layer of damp paper, topped with leaves, straw or hay—will not only promote soil health, it will make for a gardener with fewer aches and pains. Pulling weeds and running that tiller are tough on a body.

Bunkey's Scare

The other morning as Petunia was making breakfast, she happened to look out the window. Her scream brought Bunkey, barefoot to the eyebrows, sprinting into the kitchen. He was sure she was being dismembered.

"Just look at that yard! What will the neighbors think? Bunkey, you have to do something."

After his heart dropped back in his chest, Bunkey looked out the window, not knowing what to expect. "What did you see?" he asked, expecting a bear or a moose, or at the least the neighbor kid streaking. (He's done it before.)

"There are mushrooms all over the grass. Do something before George sees it and thinks we are hillbillies!"

Bunkey took time to get dressed and eat breakfast, then went over to George's to ask what he could do about mushrooms, thinking that George would know about a spray or powder to get rid of the eyesores. George did. He handed Bunkey a rake. "Just rake them or mow them or enjoy them. They will be there for a while."

This is what else George told his henpecked neighbor. Mushrooms pop up in mid-summer, usually after a wet spell. They are feeding on buried, rotting wood and will continue to come back every year until all the wood has been consumed. A circle tells you that they are feeding on a buried stump; a line on a root. In newer neighborhoods, the food is usually wood that the carpenters left on the ground and the landscapers buried. You can attempt to dig the wood up, but often it is several feet down. If you just can't stand the look of them, get the rake out and rake them up. Unless you are an expert on mushrooms, DO NOT PICK THEM TO EAT. Some mushrooms are easy to identify, like *morels*. Take an expert with you if you want to forage in the area. Some, like *chicken of the woods*, are fairly easy to identify—if you know what you're looking for. But leave the ones in your yard right where they are. By the way, Bunkey now puts on a robe when he shaves.

Mushrooms—some people actually eat them! Not Bunkey—he calls them toad furniture and refuses them in any form. Mushrooms are neither plant or animal. They have their own kingdom—*fungi*. They are more closely related to animals than plants, but you can grow them if you are an aficionado. Mushrooms come in every color but green, but some of them glow green in the dark. How is that for spooky? Just imagine it. You are strolling about in your yard and there in the dark is a green glow. Yikes. Like us, mushrooms make vitamin D out of sunlight. If you like mushrooms enough to grow your own, just don't invite Bunkey over for a meal of them. He doesn't even like the looks of them, let alone eat the ugly things.

Mushroom Menace & Lawn Diseases

There is no chemical that will kill mushrooms. They are feeding on buried wood, a dead root, or possibly construction leftovers that got buried. You can dig the stuff up, but usually it is so deep it is virtually impossible to find. If you leave the mushrooms, eventually they will run out of food. Most of them do no damage to the grass other than esthetically. The exception is fairy rings. The mushrooms appear in a circle. The grass on the outside of the circle is deep green. Inside the circle it is dead. Again, rake, but you will have to treat the dead stuff.

There are many kinds of fungus diseases in our lawns. Here are a few and what to do about them.

- ***Leaf Spot***—Spots on the leaves develop purplish-red to purplish-brown borders and tan centers. The tips of the leaves may be dead. This can spread rapidly, killing the grass. It is very difficult to treat at that stage. Prevention: do not over fertilize with nitrogen, don't water at night and remove excess thatch. A fungicide may stop the disease but not cure it.
- ***Necrotic ring spot***—Here you will see a mix of green, red and straw-colored leaves. Thatch can decompose, leading to sunken spots. It, too, is difficult to control and may reappear for several years. The treatment is the same as for leaf spot.
- ***Summer patch***—This disease occurs in the hot days of summer. Initial symptoms: yellow patches 6 to 12 inches in diameter, turf in patches thins and turns bronze. If it stays warm, the patch may die. This can be caused by either overwatering or not watering enough.
- ***Rhizoctonia Blight***—This fungus produces circular patches 1 to 3 feet around on lawns. In humid weather the outer edge of the patch may have a dark gray to dark purple ring in early morning when the patch is covered with dew. This disappears later in the day. At first, the grass may appear watersoaked, but dries to a light brown. This fungus is most active at 80 to 90 degrees and humid. The same treatment is recommended.
- ***Powdery Mildew***—This shows up in dense shaded areas as a white powder on the grass leaves and is more easily treated. Simply trim shrubs and trees to increase air circulation or remove the grass entirely as it doesn't do well in those areas anyhow. Replace it quickly with a groundcover before creeping charlie takes over.

Although he is a good groundcover in dense shade, if you can tolerate him.

If you have red cedar trees and apple trees in the same area, you need to be aware of ***cedar apple rust***. The fungus moves from cedar to apple and back. You can see the fungus in the spring. It looks like a glob of orange jelly hanging from the cedar. Cut it off and bag it. If you do get the rust, you may notice rusty patches on the leaves. On the apple it makes a round rust-colored lesion. It can go into the fruit. *Wealthy* is most susceptible and can be defoliated by the disease.

Oak Wilt is a fungus that causes the infected tree to plug its own water transport system in an attempt to limit the infection. The tree then wilts and dies. Any insect that visits the infected tree can spread the infection. They sit on the spore pads produced by the infected tree in the spring, then fly to another oak that has an open wound and infect that tree. Spring wood has larger openings than later season wood, so the fungus has easy entry into the tree. If there is a grove of oaks, the fungus can spread from one to the next. It can progress as far as 20 to 30 feet a year through connecting roots.

So what should Bunkey be looking for in his oaks? In the red and pin oaks, wilting starts at the top of the tree. The leaves turn a dull green, then bronze from the tip to the base of the leaf ,which then falls off. Burr oaks may have wilting branches here and there throughout the tree. They can live for several years with the infection, and some can even recover. Infected red oaks or pin oaks should be cut down before March 15th the next spring. You want the logs to dry quickly, so cut them into short lengths. If you are going to use them for firewood, cover the woodpile with 4-6 mil-thick plastic until June of the following year. Spores of the fungus rarely form on white or burr oaks, so their wood does not need to be covered if you are cutting it for firewood.

Petunia went to the garden to get some sweet corn for lunch. As she was peeling the husk off one cob, she exposed a big silver/gray mass. Yuck, yes? Actually, no. That mass is ***corn smut***, a fungus that can affect most any part of the corn. In Mexico, this is a delicacy called *huitlacoche*, pronounced wheat-la-KO-chay. It is said to have a smoky, mushroomy flavor and is added to soup, sauces and quesadillas.

Elm trees not getting at least an inch of water a week will show signs of ***Dutch elm disease*** quickly when stressed with warmer weather. Symptoms are yellowing and wilting of leaves. If you live in the city, call the city forester.

Don't you just hate ***mildew*** on any plant? Here is a pretty effective home remedy: 1 cup milk, any kind, in 1 gallon of water with 1 or 2 drops of liquid dish soap for sticker. Spray on the affected plant, being sure to get the undersides of the leaves. It will stop progression of the disease, but nothing will totally cure the ugly stuff. The milk concoction to kill ***powdery mildew*** and ***black spot*** on roses is: one-part whole milk, two parts water and a drop of liquid dish soap. Who said gardening was easy?

If you grew pumpkins this year, did you have some scary-looking ones with black velvet spots on them? While that looks pretty cool, it is a very bad thing. ***Pumpkin fungus*** is a type of the dreaded fungal disease called ***Anthracnose***, which seems to show up in one form or another on any live plant, including trees. The type that attacks pumpkins can also infect squash, cucumbers and melons. It can come into your garden on infected seed and is easily spread by splashing rain or irrigation. Another reason to mulch and cover the soil. Lots of weeds crowding the pumpkins, melons, etc., can increase the humidity, making for perfect conditions to spread fungus. This fungus usually shows up mid-season, especially when we have frequent rains or heavy dews. Since it can survive on any plant parts left in the garden, be sure to get all the vines and fruits out of the area and bagged or burned to remove some of the problem. Any area that had infected plants should not be planted with squash, pumpkins, melons or cucumbers for the next three to four years.

Did you have red or yellow grass this fall? Don't panic, the Martians haven't invaded, its' just ***rust fungus*** (a.k.a. ***red grass*** or ***lawn rust***). It's caused by lots of summer rain depleting the nitrogen in the soil, followed by a dry spell when the grasses are actively growing new shoots and roots. If you get down on your belly and really look at your grass, you will see orange tuft-like pimples on the grass blades. These pimples produce huge numbers of spores. Or, if you choose not to get that cozy with your lawn, just walk through it wearing white tennis shoes. If they turn orange, you know you have grass rust.

To treat rust fungus, remove the host plant, buckthorn. Since it can overwinter in plant debris, rake the lawn well. Apply nitrogen in the spring when the grass is beginning to show active growth. You may need to apply a fungicide next year as soon as you see symptoms. If the grass has thinned, be prepared to overseed. Wait until the soil is too cold for the seeds to germinate. The seed should sprout in the spring. Don't just scatter seed on the soil. It needs to be covered with soil. A good garden rake should disturb the soil enough to make a seed bed. Then pack it down.

Strawberry Problems

Now that you have picked all your June berries, it's time to get back down on your knees and look for trouble. There are 3 diseases to look for: ***strawberry leaf spot***, ***leaf scorch*** and ***leaf blight***. They all survive in our winters in the mature perennial leaves of the strawberry plant or in leaf debris in the strawberry patch. All three fungal diseases can infect both wild and cultivated berries. It's a minor problem if there are only a few spots or a major yield reducer if the fungus is allowed to spread uncontrolled.

Spores of the fungi are spread by splashing water or by wind. This starts the infection on new leaves early in the spring. Although it may seem like a minor infection at the time, the fungi will continue to grow and spread all season long whenever the weather conditions are favorable. (think *rainy, windy days*). Overhead watering can increase the moisture on the strawberry leaves, resulting in increased problems. The berry plants weakened by these fungi will have fewer leaves, root and crowns resulting in a poor crop next year.

Strawberry leaf spot starts out as small purple spots. As they grow, the center of spot turns light gray or white, but still has a purplish border. The spots can grow together and kill the leaf. Leaf scorch starts out the same way, but never develops the white center. Instead the tissue around and between the spots turn purple or red. The next step is for the edges of the leaves to turn brown, making the leaf look as if it has been scorched. A severe infection of this fungi will reduce the yield from 20% to 40%. The plants are also easily killed by heat, drought or very cold weather. Leaf blight also starts out as a purplish-red spot with a gray or tan center. As these spots grow, they widen out into a large V-shaped lesion with a brown center of dry dead tissue edged with a purplish-red V-shaped border. This fungus can also cause a soft rot of the strawberry. All three fungi can infect the leaf stem, the stem that connects the mother plant to the daughter plant and the fruit.

The good news is that renovation of the patch can significantly reduce fungal problems. First, mow the patch using a bagging mower to remove diseased leaves. If there are weeds or grass between the rows, mow them too. Next, till the patch. You want to have narrow rows, only 9 to 12 inches wide. This allows better air circulation through the berries. Usually the older plants produce smaller and fewer berries, so you really aren't loosing much production. Then fertilize—test your soil before this step to determine what kind and how much fertilizer to apply. There is nothing like another chore that must be done in the summer.

Tomato fungus can be slowed by mulching right after planting and picking off any affected leaves. A mix of 1 cup whole milk in a gallon of water and a few drops of liquid soap will stop most fungus.

Fungus on Your Trees—A Bad Sign

Rainy summers can cause some of our trees to take on some really scary-looking fungus. You may see a shelf fungus on the trunk of the tree, an odd fungus growing from the roots or on the root flare. All are signs of ***heart rot*** in the tree.

Trees can have several different kinds of wood within their trunk. *Sapwood* (in the outermost rings of the tree) is composed of living cells that conduct sap throughout the tree, store extra energy, close off wounds and actively fight invading microorganisms. Maple, birch, beech and poplar form only sapwood. Other trees also form a second type of wood, *heartwood*, at the core of their trunk. Heartwood cells are dead cells that mostly add structural strength to the tree. It also contains a number of toxic chemicals that protect the heartwood from wood decay fungi. Naturally, some trees are better at this than others. Redwoods and cedars are very good at this protection.

Heart rot can cause decay in both types of wood. Many different fungi can cause this disease. They can be seen on rotting logs, dead trees and live trees. Mushrooms, shelf fungi and other odd structures are the spore-producing structures of the fungus. Fungus appearing on a live tree indicates that the tree has heart rot.

So how does this bad boy get into your tree? The usual enemies—weed whips, lawn mowers, frost cracks, broken branches, rodent damage and even deer rubbings. It can even get into an injured root. Once inside the tree, the fungi use a variety of enzymes and chemicals to break down the wood for food.

Trees can survive for years with heart rot. This internal rot goes unnoticed because the tree keeps growing with no symptoms of disease or decline in the canopy because the heartwood cells are not living. If you see fungus on your tree, don't panic. The rot fungi progress very slowly, at a rate of about 3 inches a year. Do check the tree often to be sure it is structurally sound. This will vary depending on the type of tree, the extent of the decay, the type of rot and if the tree has other defects such as cracks or cavities.

One good thing about heart rot—it provides nesting sites for many cavity-nesting birds and animals. If it is not going to fall on your house, leave the tree standing. Having woodpeckers pounding on a dying tree sure beats having them drill holes in your cedar-sided house.

Other Diseases

Fire blight is a devastating apple and mountain ash disease. (Bet you didn't know that both these tree cousins are in the rose family!) Fire blight is caused by bacteria that infects either the blooms or the new growth. It moves during periods of heavy rain when splashing moves the bacteria to new growth. Once established, it moves very fast down the infected branch, causing the branch to die within a week after infection. When the branch dies, the tip bends over giving the branch the easily diagnosed "shepherds crook." There is a distinct line between infected and healthy tissue. Cut the affected branch off as soon as possible, disinfecting your tool with Listerine® mouthwash between cuts. The most susceptible apples are *Fireside* and *Honeygold*.

Seems like the best-tasting apples the homeowner grows are the ones most apt to get sick. Still, nothing is better than picking an apple off your own tree and enjoying it right there. Just don't look too closely for the little maggot enjoying the same treat.

If your peony has ***phytophtora***, there is no saving the plant. It has been given a death sentence. In this disease, the plant parts turn back and leathery. It may be spotty or whole shoots and stems may turn black and fall over. It often invades the crown of the plant causing a wet rot at the base, consequently killing the plant. If this is the case, you need to dig out not only the plant but all the soil the roots touch. Don't plant another peony there. It obviously is a bad location for one.

Raspberry Diseases

Many raspberry growers are not aware that their plants can have diseases. One disease, ***tomato ringspot virus***, produces stunted canes, poor yields and crumbly fruit. The name is an indication of where the problem arises. This disease affects all members of the *Solanaceae* family: tomatoes, peppers, potatoes, eggplant, nightshade and flowering tobacco, plus many of our flowering annuals and perennials. It is vectored through the soil by a root-feeding dagger nematode, and since it is a virus, there is no treatment. Remove the infected plants and burn or bag them.

Another problem virus is the ***raspberry leaf curl virus***. Symptoms are curling/distorting of dark green leaves and stunted and excessive branching of canes. The berry is usually small, excessively seedy and crumbly. The plant many have reduced yield, and often dies in the winter. This disease is spread by the raspberry aphid. Other hosts are dandelion and many other weeds. Another good reason to weed.

The third bad boy of raspberry viruses is ***raspberry mosaic viral complex***. As the name implies, there are several viruses responsible for this problem. This infection will cause delayed bud break, yellow-green leaf mottling, leaf blistering, leaf tip browning and/or stunting. A real ugly plant in other words. Often when the weather gets hot the symptoms disappear but the plant is not cured. If the infection becomes severe, shoot tips may die back and infected cares will produce multiple shoots from the same node. The plants usually die in a few years. To make things even more confusing, the plants can be infected and show none of these symptoms. If the plants are severely infected, there will be a reduction in plant vigor, fruit quality, winter hardiness and fruit yield. Late spring frosts, powdery mildew, mite damage, fungicide/herbicide damage and boron deficiency can also cause these symptoms. Only a laboratory test will give you a conclusive diagnosis.

The next question: how do we manage these problems? First, remove any wild raspberries that are within 500 feet of your patch. Keep the area weed free. Since aphids spread infections, practice strict aphid control. Last and most important, remove any infected plants—once they are infected there is no cure. Do not plant new canes in the same place either, as the soil may still contain the nematode that put paid to the last batch.

Perhaps you have seen ***witches' broom*** in a tree. This condition results in a big glob of branches, obviously abnormal. Bunkey has it in his arborvitae trees. It makes for a good windbreak—

the tree becomes very dense, if a bit ugly. It not only affects trees, but lately rose growers have seen a similar abnormal growth in their roses, especially the *Knock Out* series and *William Baffin* rose, but it probably can affect all roses. One would wonder if a witch has cursed the plant. The stems will grow unusually long and spiny and thorny. The leaves turn red and twist and distort. They are also abnormally small and can be a combination of red, yellow and green.

The only cure is to immediately dig the offender out. Be sure to get all roots, and it may be a good idea to include some of the surrounding soil. Bag the whole mess, then disinfect any tools you used, including the shovel, with Listerine® mouthwash.

This condition/disease is a virus, spread by a mite. Like many plant problems, this one arrived from Asia in *Rosa multiflora* roses. They have spread in our better climate and now are considered wild. Any plant, tree or shrub with *amur* in its name is of Asian descent. *Amur maples*, a small, very pretty tree, is now considered invasive by the state. Birds love the bright pink seeds and spread them, crowding out smaller, less aggressive native shrubs and trees.

But, back to roses. The ***rose rosette virus*** was first described in the 1940s. By the 1970s it had spread all across the U.S. It may be already in the rootstock of your favorite rose, or arrive with grafting buds. Or perhaps, through air currents if the multifloras are downwind from your roses. Or you or your neighbor may be harboring an infected bush. If it is a large plant, it could live for a few years with the disease. Horticultural oils and insecticidal soaps may provide some protection if sprayed every week in June and July. But why bother. The stinker is on its way to the graveyard. You don't want it to take the rest of your roses with it. Dig it out, then replace with "own root" roses. If you have one of the *Northern Accents* ™ series (a.k.a. the *Norwegian* series)—*Ole*, *Lena* and *Swen*—you are safe. An "own root" rose, if you didn't know, is one that has not been grafted onto a different rootstock.

Weather Woes

Too much of anything is never good.

Minnesota Extremes

According to a weather man who writes for the *Minneapolis Tribune*, the weather in Minnesota is the most extreme in the world, excepting Siberia. No wonder we have zone envy. Gardening is hard here. The state is divided into three zones: 4b (with temps -25 to -20 in the south), 4a (that's us, with temps -30 to -25), and 3b (whose temps range from-35 to-30).

All well and good, but what about summer? Not only do we get 90 and above, we also get temps that drop from 90 one day to 65 the next. The average number of days with a high dew point are also increasing, and we have changes in the amount and type of rainfall. Annual precipitation has increased over the last several decades and is expected to continue. If we don't get drowned, we get dried to death. It's a wonder we can grow anything.

It is tempting to try zone 5 and 6 plants when it gets so warm, but remember it also gets cold. While they may do quite well all summer, next spring you may have a nice addition to the compost pile.

Use native plants—they are adapted to our extreme weather. Add a few exotics that grow in similar conditions. Some tough plants that can handle heat, humidity and drought include bishop's cap, bowman's root, blue star ansonia, Appalachian sedge, bigroot geranium, blue sedge, calico aster, coral bells, heart-leaved aster, Japanese aster, sky blue aster, Siberian bugloss and sweet woodruff.

Another way to go is to group plants with similar water and shelter needs together. That way, you can save water in the hot dry times by letting everybody have a drink but only giving the tender plants all that they need.

The moral this week: invest in a rain barrel to water those water lovers. It keeps the water bill down.

We have been labeled zone 3B for years. Now we have had several warm winters and the "experts" have decided to move us to zone 4A. Take that with a tablespoon of salt. An open winter can be as devastating as -30 degrees. While you can flirt with zone 4 plants, it still behooves you to plant mostly the zone 3 perennials, trees and shrubs for best results. That being said, there are a few that will be reliable here in the frozen north of Otter Tail County. Remember to look for plants for Zone 3 unless you plan to treat the more tender ones as annuals. An example of a perennial we treat as an annual is geranium.

Don't Fight the Site

If you lost perennials in the spring, you may be looking for better ways to tuck your plants in for the winter. If you thought, *Well, it was just a freak winter and I don't really need to do anything different this fall*, you may need to rethink.

It takes more than one condition to kill a tree or perennial. Drought—or other stressors such as long stretches of over 90 degree temps, cold, wind or bright sun in winter—can work together to off your favorite iris or pine. The nasty cold is good for daffodils, but reduces the blooms of most other perennials.

If it was a conifer that bit the dust, you should think about our native trees for a replacement next spring. Look for the native white pine, or if you want a spruce, the *Norway* spruce. It the toughest and most adaptable of the spruces. *Uncle Fogy*, a zone 2 jack pine, is a show stopper with twisting and turning branches. *Swiss stone pine* is a zone 3 choice. It is not as wide as many pines, so it fits well in smaller yards and will tolerate some shade. If you have trouble with winter burn on conifers, you probably have them in the wrong spot in your yard. Note where the browning is—not on the north side, but on the south. That is where the killer winds come from in winter. They need to be on the north or east side of the house so a sudden rise in the winter temperatures don't have their buds swelling in mid-January.

Some plants need extra food (roses, mums, lupines and phlox). Feed them in the spring. Adding fertilizer in the fall will push them into the winter with new, tender growth. A recipe for damage, or at worst, death.

Another plant killer is frost heave. Some plants are more susceptible to this—plant them in early spring, then mulch the snot out of them. These include mums, foamflower, scabiosa, shasta daisy, foamy bells, coral bells gaillardia, coreopsis and sea thrift.

Of course, you need to know your site. Never plant trees (other than tamaracks) in a low, wet spot. Birches and dogwoods like slightly damp feet, but most trees, shrubs and many perennials will simply drown if the site stays soggy all summer. Almost all plants, whether trees, shrubs or perennials, need a soil with adequate pore space so air and water can get to the plant's roots. Adding compost or composted manure to your planting hole will increase the chances of a plant living long and prospering in its new home.

If we don't get good fall rains, do water all your trees, shrubs and flowerbeds very well. If you have been battling creeping charlie or other weed nasties, keep spraying them with a good broadleaf killer until they freeze solid. Plants preparing for winter in the fall by pulling all their food down into the roots. The spray you put on the leaves goes right to the roots, either killing the plant now or reducing its ability to pop up next spring.

You can rest after the first snowstorm—that is, until the seed catalogs show up in your mailbox. Then you start drooling over and planning where you can put that fantastic new plant.

We all know how often the long range weather forecast is correct. Makes us wonder if they throw chicken bones or check the depth of dog hair on the couch to get their numbers.

Drought-stressed trees and shrubs are more open to attack by diseases and insects, particularly wood-boring insects like the emerald ash borer, or the Dutch elm borer. Root systems may have been damaged by the shortage of soil moisture. This can limit the ability of the plant to take up enough water and nutrients from the soil. During a drought, some trees and shrubs show damage to the fine root hairs. If your plants seem to be struggling, may need to be watered more often. Don't just stand with the hose for 10 minutes—soak the soil to 1/3 wider than the drip line until the ground feels soggy. DO NOT FERTILIZE. Drought-stressed, woody plants need to rebuild damaged roots. They will do this with the food they make naturally through photosynthesis, not artificial fertilizer, which can stress the plant more. In times of drought, watering is more important than fertilizer.

Hot humid conditions promote fungi such as *pythium* and *brown patch disease.* Hotter and dryer weather will control these. They show up mostly on high maintenance turf like golf courses and in the yard of that guy next door who trims the edges of his lawn with a scissors and fertilizes it every time it rains. If you irrigate your lawn, a bit of fertilizer (half-strength nitrogen) will be beneficial. Keep mowing tall, three to three and a half inches for the healthiest lawn.

Seasonal Chores

That hired hand is at the end of your arm –
put on your big girl/big boy britches
and get to work!

When You Just Gotta Plant!

Are you getting itchy fingers along about mid-February, wanting to get dirt under your fingernails? Are your plant-starting pots only used for tomatoes? Get out of the rut. (A rut is nothing but a grave with the ends knocked out.) Start some plants that need 10 to 12 weeks to get a proper start. If we have a late spring, you may be looking at 12 to 16 weeks before you can even harden off your seedlings.

So, what can you start now? For vegetables, only celery and later, peppers. Celery takes a long time to get tall enough to repot. It needs quite a bit more moisture to do well than most seedlings. Start it in a small container—you only want 2 to 4 plants. You want celery to get tall, not bushy, so don't cut back the top leaves. There are several nice things about homegrown celery. For one, you can cut off the outside stalks and use them all summer without damaging the main plant. Second, this tastes like celery, not celery-flavored water. If you use celery in cooking in the summer or canning in the fall, you just can't beat the stalk you have just picked from your own garden. If you can any tomato products, you will love the taste of home-grown celery. It has REAL flavor. The only spray it has had on it is rain. (That is unless the dog is allowed in the garden, definitly a no-no.) Bunkey had a vegetarian dog. He dug up carrots, pulled ripe corn off the stalk and loved tomatoes. Especially just as they got ripe. He also liked to baptize garden plants.

Start peppers about the end of February. Keep them nipped off and you will have nice, bushy peppers ready to start producing long before the tiny plants are available in the spring.

If you want to have a lot of one flower, for instance a path lined with lobelia or six large planters filled with only white petunias, start your own. A clump of flowers always looks better than just one or two scattered about. There are usually 4 to 6 plants in a pack in the nursery—if you want 30 you might want to start them yourself. Here are a few you can start now for spring planting: edging lobelia, cupflower, heliotrope (these smell marvelous), ice plant, Livingstone daisy, monkey flower, wishbone flower, snapdragons and petunias.

Wait until the first of April to start tomatoes and any plant that only needs 6 to 8 weeks from seedling to garden. That 30 or whatever day to maturity isn't from when you plant the seed, it's from when you put the plant in the soil.

It's Apple Tree Pruning Time

February and early March are the best time to prune apple trees. They have already set buds for this year, but have not started any sap moving. This means that when it does warm up and the tree begins to wake up, it will be able to heal the pruning wounds quite easily. If the tree is already growing, it will take more time and energy for it to heal.

There are only a few rules to remember when pruning any tree.

1. Never remove more than 1/4 of the tree or shrub in one growing year.
2. Remove dead or broken branches at any time.
3. Remove any branches that grow straight up, including that hula skirt of them around the base.
4. Remove any branches that cross each other.

Really look at your tree. It should not be crowded with any small branches. You may have to thin out the interior of the tree. Step back from the tree and decide which branch is the best one to keep. It should add to the proper shape of the tree. In other words, don't save a branch that is sticking out of the tree at a bad angle or one that will eventually cross another branch.

Even though it may have been a very stressful winter for your tree and it may have some root damage from the lack of snow cover, it still needs pruning. If the roots have been reduced, it definitely doesn't need a huge load of leaves to feed in the summer.

If you need to prune an oak tree, you can do that now, too. Wait to do maples and birches until they are fully leafed out—they lose a lot of sap if pruned too soon in the spring. The maple syrup people depend on that fact.

Get out the stepladder, the snow is deep. As all gardeners know, gardening is a matter of your enthusiasm holding up until your back gets used to it.

Stay Out of the Garden!

Have you had problems with mildew in your flowerbed? Plants that just don't do well? A super crop of weeds every year? There are a few things you can do this spring to at least reduce some of those problems.

First of all, STAY OUT OF THE GARDEN!! If you go tromping around in the garden just because the snow is gone and it's nice and sunny, all you're doing is packing the soil down. And if it is bare with no mulch, you're driving weed seeds into the soil. If you mulched your flowerbeds (good on you), keep checking them for lumps.

Daffodils are the first flowers to start to grow. They will make lumps in the mulch as they pop up. Very carefully lift the mulch off of just the lumps. As the temperature rises you can remove a little of the mulch, but don't walk in the garden to do it. A pitch fork works quite well for this. (Just be careful you don't spear a lily stem with it.) Leave at least 3 inches of mulch on flowers. Keep removed mulch close in case the mercury takes an unexpected dive. This is Minnesota after all. Spring flowers growing close to a foundation will pop up much sooner than if they were in the garden, making them more apt to get frozen noses in a sudden temp drop. Most spring bulbs will weather a short cold snap if they have warm feet from mulch.

When the soil is dry enough for you to walk in the garden, cut down last year's dead stems. (You did leave them to stop the snow, didn't you?) Pitch this stuff out of the garden. If it was healthy, put it in the compost pile. Next, check the plants that didn't do well last year. Are they so close together that there is no air circulation around them? That can lead to mildew. Were they just kind of yucky looking? Maybe they need a little food, or if they were really yukky, a quick trip to the compost pile. If you do fertilize, use an organic fertilizer. Synthetic fertilizers reduce the load of organic microorganisms that you have worked so hard to introduce into your soil with mulch and compost.

Watch Your Big Feet

Bunkey planted a perennial flower garden last summer. The seed catalog he got bulbs from said the minor bulbs and daffodils would be blooming by mid-March, so he shoveled all the snow off the bed the first of March to speed thing along. This was a really bad idea. By mid-March nothing was showing, so he pulled up most of the mulch, another bad idea. If he had paid any attention to his neighbor, George the Master Gardener, he would have bought his bulbs from a northern catalog. He had ordered one of those "1,000 bulbs for $20.00" deals. Not only were the bulbs undersized, about a third of them aren't hardy here. To top off his mistake, the catalog was based in southern Iowa, zone 5.

Early March is not early enough for bulbs to pop out of the soil in most years. They don't grow by date but by soil temperature, and that is cold. Snow cover keeps the soil from freezing deeply and is an excellent soil temperer. Mulch keeps the soil cool also, so daffodils don't pop up prematurely and get their noses frozen off. A frozen bud will not bloom. If your tulips and daffs are showing next to the house, cover them up with snow, the branches you cut off the Christmas tree or whatever you can find to keep them cool. The heat loss through the foundation warms the soil up too early, making the plants think it's warm enough to bloom. It's not.

March is the time of year to plan your garden. If you didn't make a map of your vegetable garden last year, try to remember where you planted what. Potatoes, tomatoes, and eggplant are cousins. They need 3 years between planting where a cousin grew last year. If you have problems with lettuce and spinach bolting, plant them in the shade of a taller plant. This will slow bolting down. If you have little space and like lettuce, edge your flowerbeds with it. The red varieties are especially pretty.

Now about the title—do not go tromping through your flowerbeds looking for budding bulbs just because the snow is gone and it's nice and sunny—all you're doing is packing the soil down, and you are very apt to stomp down lily spears or other plants that are just popping through the soil. And if it's bare with no mulch, you're only driving weed seeds into the soil. Be patient, flowers are coming.

Daffodils are the first flowers to start to grow. If you mulched your flowerbeds (good on you), wait until the mulch is showing pretty big lumps where the leaves are pushing up. Very carefully lift the mulch off of just the lumps. As the temperature rises, you can remove a little of the mulch, but don't walk in the garden to do it. Leave at least three inches of mulch on flowers. Keep removed mulch close in case the mercury takes an unexpected dive. This is Minnesota after all. Most spring bulbs will weather a short cold snap if they have warm feet from mulch.

Spring Break

Late March/early April can be a really yukky time of year. Lawns are brown and covered with twigs, all the treasures the dog has dragged home from all over the neighborhood, plus the re-run dog food and a few of its poop piles. The mess bugs the gardener, especially the Martha types. If it is REALLY bugging you, grab a good book, pull the drapes and chill. Now is not the time to be raking up the mess. Until you can kneel or sit on the grass and not get up wet, stay off the grass. Raking a wet lawn, especially with a garden rake (as opposed to a fan–shaped grass rake), does more harm than good. It opens up bare spots in your lawn, which leads to weed seeds germinating. And walking on the soft, wet grass packs it down, never a good thing. Stay out of the flower garden, too. Wait until you can see plants popping up before you pull last years' flower stalks, even if it is driving you crazy looking at that ugly mess. Clean the dead stuff out of your flowerbeds if you can do it without walking in them.

This is the time of year to sit down and draw up a garden plan. You do remember where the tomatoes were last year, don't you? Any of the tomato's cousins—spuds, peppers or eggplant—should not be planted in that area for at least three years. That is why a savvy gardener has a garden map.

Hit the seed racks. Carefully read the back of the packet. If it says the plant is ripe in 120 days, leave it there. Plan for 90 days and hope we get more frost-free days. There are always new varieties of flowers and vegetables coming out. Live a little and plant a flower you have never planted before. Try a purple carrot or an orange tomato. Or just for the heck of it, plant a hill of warty gourds or pumpkins. Have fun gardening this summer.

It's too late to prune apple trees, but you can prune shrubs now. Just be aware that if you prune flowering shrubs, you may not get as many flowers this year. The exception is *Annabelle*. She blooms on new wood, so you can get her under control if she is taking up more than her share of the world. Leave the spring-flowering shrubs until just after flowering if you didn't do it last year. Don't prune your tree or shrub in rainy weather to minimize the chances for diseases. If the snow has fallen off the roof on a shrub or the snowblower damaged it, cut badly-damaged stems back to just above the soil line. If there are just a few broken stems, prune them back to an undamaged stem.

Till the garden only if it's dry enough (if you squeeze a handful of its soil, it falls apart—if it stays in a gob, wait awhile). If you do till wet soil, it makes big nasty clumps that will pretty much stay that way all summer. It's difficult to plant a pea seed in a hard glob of soil, and if you plant between the globs the rows stagger like a drunken sailor. Makes for difficult walking, too. Hang tight. Things will get dryer. In the meantime, have another cup of coffee and drool over the pictures in the seed catalogs, the gardener's *Playboy*.

April—It's Planting Time!

Planting time, really? Yes, that is if you want a tomato other than *Big Boy* or *Early Girl*. There are hundreds of tomatoes and dozens of varieties of peppers available. The time to start these are about the first of April. Remember, the 90 days to maturity stated on the seed packet is not the time from when you plant the seed. It's the time starting from when you put that plant in the garden.

Tomatoes should be transplanted at least twice before you put them in the garden. The first time shortly after the plant has 2 to 3 real leaves, then again when it starts to get leggy. When you transplant it the second time, bury the stem right up to the lowest leaves. Every bump on that stem turns into another root. More roots mean more food getting into your plant. It also makes for a stronger plant.

Nipping the top leaves off the tomato and pepper plants will make them thicker. *Auxin*, the chemical in the top leaf, suppresses side leaves. The plant just gets taller. Cutting off that top set of leaves transfers the auxin, allowing the plant to grow more side leaves. More leaves mean more sun available to feed the plant. You want as sturdy a plant as possible when you put it in the garden. It will get a head start on blooming and producing fruit.

Plants started at home are like babies. They need real T.L.C. before they go in the garden. Plan at least 7 to 10 days to harden them off before planting out, an hour a day in a protected spot to start with, adding an hour a day and eventually exposing them to a breeze to toughen up the stems. Bunkey puts a 3-pound coffee can with the bottom cut out around each transplant for about 10 days to 2 weeks. This keeps the cut worms away and keeps the wind from drying the plant out until it gets accustomed to the real world.

Are Your Evergreens Still Green?

Now that it is warm enough to get outside, people are noticing that their evergreens are brown, not green. If this is the case in your yard, don't head for the chain saw. A warm spell may have done the damage to the conifers. Because they have leaves in the form of needles, they grow all year round, albeit, very slowly in winter. When we get a warm day, the needles "sweat" (in tree language, "transpire"). Because the ground is frozen, the tree can't pull moisture from the soil as it would were the soil thawed. They are losing water through their needles that they can't replace, causing the needles to freeze dry. If the needles can't be easily pulled from the branch, it will probably recover. If, however, the needles come off in your hand, that branch is dead and can be pruned off.

Evergreens normally lose some needles in the interior of the tree each year, but browning needles on the ends of branches is damage. If you have had damage to the trunks of your shrubs or trees, again, don't panic. If the bark is totally removed all the way around and clear through the green layer, that stem will die as it can no longer transport food. If it is only part way around the stem or part way through the bark, take a wait-and-see stand.

Do not paint anything on the tree or shrub, as that simply slows or stops healing. If bunnies have remodeled the shrub, finish the job by cutting out up to 1/4 of the older branches and cutting damaged branches back to a bud. Look closely at the bud to see which way it is pointing, as that is the direction the branch will grow. Usually, you would want the bud to point up and out. This is true for any pruning you do. If the shrub is chewed to the soil line, again, don't get your knickers in a knot. If the roots are healthy, the shrub will not only come back, it will probably be better looking than before the damage. Much damage blamed on rabbits is actually done by voles. Rabbit damage is easy to diagnose—the branch will have a sharp 45 degree angle cut. Chewed bark is vole damage and can be controlled next year by putting barriers around the tree or shrub up to the level you think snow will be in that area. Go with the deepest level it has been in the past. If you see shredded branch tips, you are dealing with deer damage.

Get off the couch and go out and survey your plantings. Now is the time to repair damage before the shrubs and trees start putting out leaves.

Pruning Evergreens

Do you have to go out your front door sideways? That arborvitae just got too wide, didn't it? Can't walk up the sidewalk to the door because of a too-wide juniper? If they are not too large or too old, you can probably make good neighbors of them by judicious pruning. If, on the other hand, that tree is rubbing against the house and is taller than the chimney, your best bet is to take it down and start over. Next time, plan ahead. Trees do get taller and wider. Move them at least four feet from the house. Further, if it will be a full-sized tree.

Conifers have two types of growth. You need to know the growth habit of the tree or shrub you are dealing with. The first type is *whorled branching*. These are the pines, spruces and firs. They have branches at regular intervals along a main stem. You can't "shrink" these trees because they don't have latent buds on older wood, although some red and Scotch pines can resprout from old wood if it still has needles. You can, however, make these trees fatter or slow them down by nipping off about 1/4 to 1/3 of the new candles in the spring. These are not trees you want to plant right next to your house, unless you plan to hide the house and later enter it with a chain saw.

The other growth type is the *random branching* conifer. This includes juniper, arborvitae, hemlock and yew. Redwoods also fall into this category, but since they don't grow here we will ignore them. You prune these trees to keep them a manageable size, create a more natural appearance (or a more unnatural one, spiral for instance), or to get more light penetration. If you are shortening branches, cut deep within the plant so you don't see branch stubs. You can also shear these particular trees to make them look like lollipops, triangles, spirals or most any shape you can envision, if that's what floats your boat.

Most random branching conifers will resprout when cut back to old wood. Yew is especially forgiving. Cut it back any amount anywhere and it will soon sprout, even on very old wood. If you have a conifer hedge, be sure to make the top narrower than the bottom. If you skip this, it won't be long before you will have bare "legs" on the bottom of your hedge because it didn't get enough sun all the way down the side of the hedge. Those "bare legs" are great trash collectors.

Sharpen up the clippers and get out now before the weather gets too warm.

If that wascally wabbit has been enjoying a salad lunch in your tulips, there are several sprays that will send to back to the dandelions. If you have given up all hope, plant daffodils next fall. All of that plant is poisonous. Nothing will touch them. Another spring problem is the neighbor's cat using your flowerbeds for a toilet. Fresh coffee grounds scattered around the bed should send her looking for a new potty place. The coffee will add acid to the soil, a good thing for our alkaline soils. Your cats, of course, are more refined. They use a litter box. The used litter will send any rodent heading for better pastures. Even though spring can be a fleeting season, you really don't need to do all your spring chores in one week. What you don't get to will be there tomorrow. That is, if you can get your aching bones out of bed to do them.

It's Tree Planting Time

Late April is the perfect time to plant trees. The snow storms are done (we hope), the soil is thawed and starting to warm and there are no mosquitoes. Trees have not started to bud out very much. The soil has quite a bit of moisture in it, and we should be able to depend on rain to do much of our watering.

Plant bare root trees now (or those you dug from Grampa Pug's woods). If you are digging a tree in the wild, be sure to take some extra soil from around the tree. That soil is full of microorganisms that help the tree to feed. Don't plant it any deeper than it was. There is a flare on the stem of a tree that should be out of the soil. Dig a wide hole to give the roots soft soil in which to spread out. Don't plant it any deeper than one to two inches below the first roots.

Mulch small, just-planted trees with shredded bark. Never put rock mulch around any growing thing. It heats in the summer, heating up the roots, and is nearly impossible to keep looking neat. Mulch should keep the roots cool, help keep moisture in the soil, prevent the soil from packing down during a hard rain and eventually, breaking down and feeding the soil. Mulching trees does all this, and it keeps the lawn mower operator from hitting and scarring the delicate bark. It also keeps the dreaded weed whip a good distance away from the trunk. You will need to add some nitrogen to your tree next year as the mulch does deplete it. Do not fertilize your tree the first year. It needs time to get established before you push it.

Beware of May Frosts

This is Minnesota, and we have had frosts in every month but July in the past. Frosts in May are a real threat. *How does frost damage plants*, you ask? Actually, it's not the frost but the freezing and thawing that does the damage to the plant's cell walls. It can damage the leaves, flowers and even shoots, killing tender or zone-inappropriate plants. It is often worse in variegated, red- or golden-leaved plants. Symptoms can be as mild as few damaged leaves to complete death of the affected plant.

If fruit trees were blooming during a frost and had damaged, blackened pistils, you will get little or no fruit from that tree. Frosted annuals will have dark green, water-soaked areas on their leaves, blackening to death. You will most probably have to replace those. For other frost-injured plants: when the threat of frost is over, prune out any damaged growth back to an undamaged bud or side shoot. Damaged perennials can be cut back and should recover.

If your plants regularly get frosted in certain areas, you need to rethink your planting positions and fertilizer practices. Don't plant in frost pockets. These occur where cold air settles or becomes trapped, such as at the bottom of a slope or between buildings.

Don't plant flowering trees with a southern exposure as this encourages early flowering. Planting near a lake slows down the spring warm-up, preventing early blossom development and resulting in little or no frost damage. If you need to prune flowering shrubs, do it right after blooming as most of them set new flower buds as soon as the old blooms die. This is especially important with lilacs. If the shrub that was such a cute little thing is now in the monster category, covering the window and biting people as they walk past it on the sidewalk, cut it down to about 6 to 12 inches high. It may take 2 to 3 years to bloom again, but it will be better behaved.

Don't put out your hanging baskets or annual pots until the nighttime temperatures are regularly 50 degrees. While lower temps may not kill the plants, it will slow them down quite a bit.

SUMMER

Common Summer Questions

How do I keep the squirrels from eating the jelly I've put out for the birds? Sprinkle some Tabasco sauce on top of the jelly. Birds don't have a mucus membrane like animals do, so they don't notice the fiery taste. One try should put critters "on the wagon."

What can I do with plants that have downy mildew on them? There is no cure, but a homemade spray will stop the disease. Mix a cup of whole milk (the butterfat content is important) with a gallon of water and 2 or 3 drops of liquid dish soap, spray on the affected plants.

Can I prune my trees now? No, unless the branches are broken or dead. Apple trees should be pruned in late winter, February or March. Oak trees in early spring or late summer, August or September. Maple and birches can be pruned early summer after they are fully leafed out.

How can I get the grass to grow under a clump of oak trees? You can't. The shade is too dense and the tree is sucking up all the moisture and food from the soil. Mulch the area or try a groundcover. Even creeping charlie won't do well under oaks.

What kind of fertilizer should I put on my just-planted tree? None!

A Pinch in Time

Did your mums get so tall last fall that when they bloomed they fell over? Bad gardener. You should have been out there pinching them off, starting early in the summer. It's a simple exercise—simply let your fingernails get long enough that you can pinch off the growing tips of your mum plants about every 2 to 3 weeks until they start to set buds, resulting in a shorter, bushy plant. This works for tomato and pepper seedlings, too. If you want shorter snapdragons, pinch them off just above the top set of leaves. They too will bush out. Of course, now you won't have that tall accent to add to a bouquet, but they won't fall over either.

Deadheading is a similar gardening chore. Start with your delphiniums. They will often re-bloom if you religiously snip off the dead blooms. All annuals need deadheading to continue to blossom all summer. That is why you plant them, isn't it? Some plants just get leggy, such as alyssum, petunias and impatiens. Don't bother deadheading these. Simply shear them off about half way down. They will pop back nice and full.

Roses are a bit trickier. Cut off the stem down to the first set of five leaves. This encourages them to repeat bloom on that stem. If you have re-blooming daylilies, you must remove old blooms to get new ones. Daylilies are not one of Bunkey's favorite plants. They look too much like a clump of grass, and he hates grass. His neighbor George has a bed of nothing but daylilies. They bloom all summer as he has early, mid-season and late bloomers. He is also very quick to deadhead any spent bloom stems. George also has grasses as accents in his flowerbeds, and even though they do look nice, the mere idea of grass in flowers gives Bunkey nausea.

When your irises are done blooming, cut the blossom stem off as far down as you can reach. Do not cut off the leaves—they are feeding next years' blooms.

Daylilies need to have stems removed, too. Don't panic if they have yellow leaves early in the spring. It doesn't seem to bother the plants. Old timers call it "spring sickness," as good a name as anything.

If your plants, trees or shrubs have yellow-green leaves with green veins, they are lacking iron. (You will never see this on lilacs as they love alkaline soil.) To remedy the problem, add a sulfur/iron combo to the soil. The sulfur assists the plant to absorb the iron. No, adding a hand full of nails won't do the job, nor will pounding them into the stem of your apple tree. If this is a continuing problem for you, add Canadian peat moss to the soil to help acidify it. A mulch of pine straw won't hurt either, although there isn't much acid in it. Aluminum sulfate has been recommended as an acidifier, but if used more than once it can poison your soil, not a good thing.

The moral for the week: get to the garden and deadhead and pinch when you weed for a happier flowerbed (and gardener). You get bragging rights. "My delphiniums are blooming again, aren't yours?"

Summer Musings

June is strawberry month. Did you know that strawberries do not ripen once they are picked? You need to look sharp when you pick them. Do not pick a berry with a white tip or any lighter area on its side. That berry is not fully ripe and has not attained its full complement of sugar. Pick only fully red berries for the best taste.

Does your lawn usually look pretty sad in the heat of July? Often it is because you have been cutting it too short. Cut the grass 2 1/2 to 3 inches long. This does several good things for your grass. The taller leaves shade the soil, keeping it cooler and shading out many weed seeds that need sun to sprout. Leave the clippings on the lawn, unless they are so thick they mat the grass down. As the clippings rot, they release nitrogen—and you don't even have to pay for it.

If you have white clover in your grass, rejoice! The roots add nitrogen to the soil, the plants are short (needing clipping less often), and the bees love the blooms. They also add some texture to the grass. Well, actually plantain does too, but most people kill that weed.

If your first tomatoes have blossom end rot, you need to add calcium to the soil around them. Most good tomato fertilizers will have calcium in them. A Master Gardener suggests you grind up unflavored Tums and scratch the powder into the soil around your plants and water it in. He swears by it. Keep the fruit off the soil for a better crop. A layer of newspaper covered with leaves or grass will do the job. Don't over thin your tomatoes as they will get sunburned—really.

Do your garlic stems look like they have pretzels on their tops? That is called a scape. It's actually a flower stalk and if left will develop a small head of bulblets. These can be shared if you have friends who want to start their own patch of garlic. However, if you like the taste of garlic, cut the scapes off and use them in cooking. They can be cut 1 to 2 inches long and steamed as you would asparagus. They can also be pickled or used in stir fry. At any rate, you want to cut them off just as you would deadhead any flower to encourage more root growth.

You've got that cute garden hat, now wear it. Sunburn is bad enough, but melanoma is a lot worse. Enjoy the summer. It's darn short here in the wilds of the lake country.

What to Do in August

There are only about 50 frost-free days left in our growing season, so get hopping on some of those late summer chores.

If the spring flower show wasn't all that you desired, start ordering bulbs now. Do check the catalog for shipping dates. November is a bit too late to be digging down tulip bulbs, although Bunkey did have that joy one fall. If your grafted roses didn't bloom, dig them up. They have died below the graft and will never bloom. *Ole, Lena* and *Swen* are on their own roots, so even if they freeze to the soil line,they will come up and rebloom.

If you have plants still in their pots, plant them now. It is a good time to freshen up your "estate" with some new shrubs and trees. They will have time to get well established before freeze-up. Keep them well watered until the soil freezes, and do mulch them. Keep the mulch away from the bark.

Cut the ends off vines that are heading for the Interstate. They will freak and start to ripen any fruit left on the vine. Don't compost vines. They take forever to rot. Replant lettuce, radishes and spinach as soon as we get a cool spell. They will live well and prosper.

August is the month to do garden repairs. Start with that iris that has gotten too big for its britches. Iris need reining back every 3 to 5 years. Dig out the whole clump. Throw away all the rhizomes that don't have a good healthy fan of leaves on them. Cut the leaves off to about 6 inches and snap off any part of rhizome that points down. You only need 6 or 8 inches of healthy *rhizome* per plant. (If you don't recognize the word *rhizome*, it's that part of the plant that looks like dry dog poop.) To replant, dig up the area and add some bone meal. It may or may not do any good, but most gardeners seem to have a bag of it lying around.

Next chore is moving plants. Often shade creeps up on our flower gardens so gradually that we don't realize our sun-loving plants are now getting shaded, thus reducing vigor and blooming. Most of us don't really want to cut down a perfectly healthy tree, so that means either moving the garden or changing all the plants for shade lovers.

Cut the dead blooms off the lilies. Don't cut the stalk down. It is needed to feed the plant for now and for next year's bloom. Wait at least 3 weeks after flowering to move it—give it time to recover.

When you share your excess plants, don't present them in a wheelbarrow. Experienced gardeners are very wary of plants that are so prolific that they arrive in a wheelbarrow. They equate them to zucchini: too much of a good thing. Give them instead to the beginners. They probably need more plants.

August Gardening Tips

It doesn't seem to matter how many tomato plants you have, you hardly ever have enough tomatoes at one time to a make a full batch of anything. Here's one way to solve that problem. Pick fruit as it ripens. Wash it and remove stems and any blemishes. Now for the easy part—drop the clean tomatoes in a clean plastic grocery bag and dump it in the freezer. When you have enough frozen fruit for your spaghetti sauce, take them out the night before you plan to cook and lay them one deep in a pan. By morning, you can slip the skins off simply by grabbing the tomato and it's ready to use. Some of the liquid will have collected in the bottom of the pan. You can add this, but if you don't your sauce will be a bit thicker and more "tomatoey."

Vine crops go wild when the temperatures are high. Unfortunately, while they are growing vines they don't stop to ripen fruit. Grab the end of your vine and follow it back to either a flower or an unripened fruit. Cut it off there. This scares the plant into thinking it better get things ripened because it has been attacked. Use this technique for squash, pumpkins, cucumbers, melons and tomatoes.

Pull any vegetables that are done producing. Why let them continue to eat if they aren't feeding you? Now that you have more room, plant radishes, lettuce and spinach for a fall crop.

If your mulch is getting thin (or even nonexistent), renew it to prevent those nasty ripening weed seeds from finding a nice place to live this winter.

Keep picking garden produce as it ripens—some plants will stop producing if ripe vegetables are left on the plant. Remove any overripe fruit unless you enjoy the company of yellow jackets—they just love rotting fruit.

Many annuals are producing seeds now. If you don't mind surprises, let them reseed where they stand. Birds will spread some of them, of course, so they will pop up in unexpected places. However, if you are a Martha, collect the seeds and put them where you want them.

Now is the time to peruse your local nurseries for bargain perennials. Houseclean your flowerbed and try something new.

The Second Season

July has been hot as fried frog and usually August isn't any better. The garden is starting to look pretty sad. The peas, brown and dry if not pulled, potatoes beginning to dry up, the onions all tipped over and ready to pull. The lettuce and spinach has bolted and the one radish you forgot has gone to seed.

All is not lost. Leave the radish to ripen. It will provide you with radishes much earlier next spring than those you plant. Remove all the leafy plants and drop them on top of the mulch. Onions need to dry before you store them, so get them pulled and either dry them on racks in a cool place or hang them up to dry. Pea vines can be composted—just don't leave them in the garden. They wrap around the tiller tines, leading to blue air from the tiller controller.

Now check the calendar. You will need 6 weeks of frost-free days for your second season. "Recharge" the areas you are planning to replant by working in some compost and/or organic fertilizer like *Milorganite*. Keep the newly-seeded areas moist and the new plants well watered while the temperatures are still summer-like. Broccoli, cauliflower, kohlrabi, mustard greens, spinach, chard, turnips and carrots can tolerate a light frost (32 to 28 degrees). Beets, green onions, peas radishes and parsley can easily deal with the high 20s. Brussels sprouts, cabbage and kale will put up with temps as low as 20 and live.

As the weather cools to the low 70s, replant your lettuce and radishes. They will sprout quickly. Most seeds will be removed from shelves soon, and are usually marked down first. If you are planning a second season, get them now. Even if you don't use them this fall, most seeds are viable for several years. Look for seeds that are labeled for less than 50 days to maturity. If you have a sheltered area, you can probably get away with plants that take a bit longer to mature. Of course, all gardeners have old sheets or floating row covers for that unexpected cold night.

Once the temperatures start to drop Bunkey removes his tomato plants from their cages and lays them out on the soil. The soil is warmer than the air and will help the last few fruit ripen. A warm blanket at night to keep them toasty and he can have ripe tomatoes well into October.

If your pots are starting to look their age, head for the local nursery. They may have a few annuals left. The annual mums should arrive soon. They add a nice pop of color. A clump of red lettuce can fill that empty spot and you can eat it when it gets too big. Nothing says you can't plant a perennial in a pot. Stick it in the garden just before frost. If you can, bury pot and all. Keep it well covered until spring and it may make it through the winter. If not, you enjoyed it while it was with you. All gardeners have committed planticide, and some have actually enjoyed it. Bunkey once deliberately sprayed Roundup® on some Hollyhocks, so there.

It's Not Fall Yet!

We Minnesotans treasure fall with its cooler weather and beautiful fall colors. However, August is not fall, so why are some of the tree leaves turning color? Stress!

Actually, it is normal for some color this time of year. Shrubby sumac is quite red in many of the ditches and Virginia creeper is right on time for color change. Our native butternut tree will start coloring up as early as July, but if your maple is changing color, it's in trouble.

Trees change color because the day gets shorter. Like fall blooming mums, who only start blooming when the days are shorter than the nights, trees start to color usually in late August or early September. There are many things that can stress trees: disease, insects, storm damage, planting too deep and lack of water. When we have a dry late summer and fall, many trees go into the winter short of moisture. Dry soil freezes deeper and gets colder than damp soil, damaging tree roots. If your suspect tree is on a hill, it can be because of gravity—water runs downhill and the tree didn't get enough of it.

If your tree isn't red but pale green, yellowing or even almost white with the only green in the veins, the poor thing is anemic. Actually, in tree talk it has *chlorosis*. It can't take up the iron it needs to make chlorophyll. Feed it with a sulfur/iron mix dug into the soil and watered in well.

Fall

What to Do in September

Water, water, water if we don't have regular rains, at least an inch a week. Trees are especially at risk of premature death next spring if they go into the winter dry. The more-than-usual death of conifers is directly related to drought. Trees growing at the edge of a wetlands or lake have been subject to fluctuating water levels in a dry year. When the roots are flooded, the lowermost roots die. If it is too dry, the upper roots die. This causes photosynthesis to shut down, causing the tree to use up stored sugars and starches. The tree starves to death. This is especially true of balsam firs and the white and black spruces. The pines don't live near wet areas so they too starved—they couldn't replenish their reserved sugars and starches for lack of moisture. Our leafy trees and shrubs have the same problems. They lose water from their leaves in hot weather making the problem worse.

- Treat charlie. Apply *Trimec®* once a week until hard frost. This will at least slow him down.
- Keep weeding. Leaving one weed in the garden will result in several million next spring.
- Keep deadheading annuals, unless you want a few to reseed. Cosmos, calendula, asters and poppies will reseed readily now.
- Remove any diseased material from the garden. Don't compost it either. That will only perpetuate the disease cycle and can make it worse next year.
- If the lawn is looking a little thin in places, reseed it now. A good mix for our area is a mix of Kentucky bluegrass, creeping red fescue and perennial rye. Then add a winterizer turf fertilizer. Reseed again in October if needed. Keep the area from drying out and you will have grass.
- Take cuttings of coleus for all-winter color. You can continue to take cuttings all winter and have a whole new crop of plants to put out in the spring.
- After the first light frost, dig your sweet potato vine tubers. Cut off the vine and plant it in a pot. It will do well in a bright window until time to go out again in the spring.
- If possible, pile or bag leaves for winter mulch for the flowerbed. Leaves are great in the vegetable garden too—they have no weed seeds like hay or straw may have.

- If your foundation evergreens take a hit each winter from snow that slides off the roof, take time now to devise protection for them to apply just before the first snowfall. Yes, it is coming, sorry. Start now to get ready for cold weather. It's no fun cleaning up the gardens when it's 20 degrees and the north wind is attempting to remove your face.
- Cut off the corn stalks if you can't pull them out.
- Spuds, beets and carrots can stay in the garden for quite a long time after a hard frost. Dry onions and potatoes in a warm, dry dark place before you store them. Remove any loose skin from the onions, but don't strip them.
- If you haven't picked your early apples, get at it. *Honeycrisp* and *Sweet Sixteen* are 2 varieties that will get brown and mushy if frosted. Late apples can take temps as low as 27. If they do get frosted, don't touch them until it warms up later in the day. Otherwise, your fingers will leave bruises that can rot.

These chores should keep you busy all month. Remember, gardening is not only good for the body, it's great for the neighbors who don't have one and love to see you coming with your extras.

Bunkey's Job Jar

Petunia gave Bunkey a list of jobs long as his arm to be done before unassembled snow men start to descend on them. Here are a few of them.

- Pick up leaves as they fall. That way, the lawnmower's grass catcher won't plug up with every run. This is especially important if you are using leaves as a mulch on the flowerbeds. If you have a large bed, it takes a lot of leaves and the wind has a tendency to move them around, leaving bare spots.

- Put grass seed in the bare spots in the lawn. Cool weather is a perfect time to reseed grass. The autumn rains mean you don't have to haul the hose out as often.
- Cut the grass until it freezes up, and cut it shorter than during the heat of the summer. This helps prevent snow mold and the longer grass makes for a perfect cover for the new grass seed.
- Sprinkle annual flower seeds in the flowerbed. Cleome, poppies, bachelor buttons, marigolds and many more annuals will come back in the spring if merely sprinkled on bare soil just after a freeze. The soil should be cold so they don't start to grow this fall. This works very well for radishes, spinach and lettuce. They pop up long before the seeds you carefully plant.
- Remove all windfalls from the apple and plum trees. This keeps the hornets and wasps away and removes food for the apple maggot.
- Remove corn stalks from the garden—they are difficult to pull out in the spring and even more difficult to till up. Use them for fall décor or to hold down the leaf pile until you can use it for mulch.
- Put a layer of leaves on the garden and till it and any greens still there. Add a sprinkle of nitrogen. This gets the soil ready for spring planting. The nitrogen assists the bacteria and worms in the soil to make compost of the litter.
- Empty the flower pots into the flowerbed and wash them out with a 10 to 1 solution of bleach. Leaving soil in a pot can cause the pot to break during the winter. You can re-use the soil if you can store it in an unbreakable container. A wooden box works, or a large garbage bag. To re-use, add fertilizer and at least 1/4 new soil.
- Drain all the hoses and put them away. Bunkey had to buy 3 new hoses this spring. They had water in them, froze and broke where the water had collected.
- Clean the acorns and maple helicopters out of the gutters so they don't overflow.

This should keep poor Bunkey busy until the end of the month.

Here are a few things that tell you that it is fall planting time, besides hay fever. Soil temps drop to 55 and nighttime temps are between 40 and 50. You start to smell wood smoke, and in the country, burning leaves. You start closing windows and turn the heat on in the car. You see ads in the local papers selling firewood. The hostas lie down, the ragweed stops blooming, and the grapes are getting ripe. The birds and animals are getting ready for the cold. The hummingbirds have left. Squirrels are building nests and dropping clumps of leafy twigs all over the lawn in the process. Deer are losing velvet on their horns, the crickets are silent and you no longer have to dodge night-flying bugs to get in the door. Your garden shoes aren't keeping your feet warm any more, you bring a blanket to the football game and you pull up that blanket that has been folded up on the end of the bed all summer. There is frost on the windshield in the morning, and you put that old winter coat on to mow the grass for the last time.

Fall in Minnesota: time to start thinking about what to plant next spring. It beats thinking about 6 months of cold and nose-deep snow.

What to Do with Tender Corms & Tubers in the Fall

Whether it's a corm or tuber, it needs to be dug up and given proper care now if you want it to bloom again. It is a good idea to dust your corms and tubers with an insecticide/fungicide mix for that specific plant.

Gladiola "roots" are a corm, a flat, hard structure. They can be left in the garden for as long as 6 weeks after the first killing frost. However, unless you like digging in a snow-wet garden, earlier is probably better. Cure the corms for 2 to 3 weeks in a warm (60 to 70 degree), dry area. Do not wash them. Discard any that have insect damage or are diseased. Remove the old corm and the small cormels, then dust with an insecticide/fungicide mix that is labeled for them. They then can be stored in a labeled paper bag. For your information, the blooms do not change color. What really happens is that one color is more robust than the rest, so it lives and the more fragile-colored flowers die off.

Dahlias should be dug right after the foliage is frost killed. Be careful with that potato fork, the best tool for digging up plants. You don't want to damage the tubers. Cut the tops off about two inches above the soil line. Wash off the soil and let the tubers dry for about three days in high humidity. Store in shallow boxes filled with moist sphagnum peat or vermiculite in a cool spot.

Tuberous begonias can be treated as houseplants in the winter and left in their pot. The stems will eventually fall off but will sprout and be ready to go out in the spring, ready to bloom. If you don't like that idea, dig the root up when the foliage turns yellow or after frost kill. Leave the foliage on and store in vermiculite or peat at 40 to 50 degrees, the same temperature as the dahlias are stored.

Do dump soil out of all pots as freezing dirt-filled pots leads to pot shards. This is especially true with ceramic pots. Of course, if the pot in question is that ugly one your mother-in-law gave you: *I forgot, sorry*. Get out and get gardening while the weather holds. Remember, we live in schizophrenic Minnesota weather.

Bunkey's Fall Chores

Bunkey has been putting off fall chores, waiting for the first hard frost. Well, now we've had one. His first chore was to dig the spuds. They need to cure about two weeks before storing them for the winter. He knew better than to wash them—this can damage the skin, leading to rot down the road. Ideally, they should be stored in a cold, slightly moist dark area. A foam cooler will keep them for quite a while if you don't have a root cellar. Beets, with their tops off, need the same conditions. Bunkey has kept carrots and parsnips as long as 8 months in a cooler full of dry sand. Old timers used a crock for this, but not many of us have one now.

Next he mulched the strawberry patch, but left the asparagus standing until spring. The stems will hold snow and any stray leaves that blow into them besides the mulch you put on them.

Bunkey knew he was going to have to prune apple trees this winter, so he marked the branches with a shot of spray paint. That way, when the snow is 14 feet deep in February, he can see which branches need to come off. Now that all the chores are done, Bunkey is having a cookie and coffee and planning next summer's gardens. Smaller ones probably. He is getting older (and wiser).

Leave It Messy

This time of year, new gardeners get the "Martha syndrome." They pull out all their annuals, cut down all the perennials, and rake the whole garden. They want their gardens to look neat in the winter. On the other hand, experienced gardeners know a messy garden will be a healthy garden next spring. Bunkey learned that the hard way when 5 of the 6 mums, 2 of 3 roses and about 1/4 of his other perennials froze out one "open" winter.

This is Bunkey's new fall regime. After the first hard frost, he pulls out any diseased plants and bags or burns them. He cuts the iris down to about 4 to 6 inches and bags or burns the leaves. Then he picks up leaves and mulches the flower garden with about a foot of them. Next, he puts a fence of hardware cloth around the roses as tall as the plants are and half again as wide and fills it with dry leaves or straw.

Leaving a garden messy saves Bunkey enough time to enjoy a football game. Not having to pull out all those volunteer asters, cleome and zinnias is easier on his aging frame. He also gets to watch the winter birds feast on all the seed heads left standing. In the spring, messy gardens have all sorts of surprise plants popping up, saving money for seeds and filling in bare spots with no effort on Bunkey's part. Bunkey is all for saving effort and Petunia likes the money-saving part.

The moral this week: be a Martha about the lawn but a Bunkey with the flowerbeds.

There Is Still Time

Well, Minnesota did it again. The weather changed so fast we nearly got whiplash. Unfortunately, because of the quick change some gardening chores just didn't get done. There is still time to do some of them.

If, like Bunkey, you left the hose connected to the outdoor faucet, get it off there as soon as you can and hope the pipes didn't freeze. If you left a hose on the ground, get it in a heated area and get the poor thing thawed out so you can put it away. Do it carefully so you don't end up with 20 pieces, three feet long. While sometimes you want a short bit of hose, most people don't have much use for multiple short hunks.

There is still time to mulch. If the soil is frozen, so much better. If you planted trees this year, they need to be mulched, as do your strawberries. Mulch on trees prevents frost heaves. You planted the tree in an upright position, one would hope. A good frost heave will leave it listing like a drunken sailor and kill any roots that end up exposed to the weather. The reason to cover strawberries is to prevent the buds from freezing, either late in the fall or early in the spring. Mulch can be the leaves you bagged up. If you don't have leaves, a straw bale is an option. The only problem with straw in the garden is that it may contain weed seeds. Hay is a better choice. If you don't have access to any of these, cardboard will work, if not too well, for trees. However, it would probably smother strawberries.

If you didn't get all your leaves picked up, you will discover that it is rather difficult to shovel them. If we get a thaw, rake like mad. Leaves left on the lawn promote snow mold. This fungus comes in several colors, pink, gray and tan. While this may hit you as very decorative, it can and will kill the grass under. Next spring you'll be on the phone to the Extension office wondering what the heck happened to your grass and what you can do about it. Not that we mind your call. It makes us Master Gardeners feel good that we can help.

Hope for a thaw so you can get your belated chores done, or next spring you may have a hose split end to end, frozen pipes, no strawberries and a very stressed tree leaning at a drunken angle.

Winter

Winter Protection

Our warm spell is probably over. Now that the ground is frozen, there are a few garden details to take care of. Mulch flowerbeds if you haven't already. Do leave the dead flower stalks standing. They do double duty by helping to hold the mulch in place and feed the birds in the winter. The birds do a great job of spreading seeds, resulting in plants springing up in all sorts of unexpected places in the spring.

Mulch the roots of your young fruit trees. It can be piled as high as the graft union. Pull it away from the stem of the tree, however. Damp mulch can damage the bark, and mice and voles just love to operate under the cover of mulch to snack on the tender tree bark.

Protect the bark of thin skinned trees like young fruit trees, mountain ash and small birch trees. The commercial white tubes with holes in them, white reflective wrap, insulated wrap or even white latex paint thinned and painted on the trunk are the way to go. On the frugal side, prop up a board against the south-southwest side of the tree and fasten it in place. This will protect against sunscald. However, you will still need some type of rodent protection, such as hardware cloth.

If your evergreens are dropping inside needles, relax: it's needle drop and perfectly normal. However, if one side of the tree is naked, you do have a disease.

Christmas Trees

Bunkey and Petunia have the same arguments every Christmas time: what to add to the tree to keep it fresh. Petunia heard aspirin works well. (Use it only if the tree has a headache.) Bunkey advocates 7Up®. "The citrus and sugar feed the tree," he says.

Petunia counters with, "I never knew a spruce tree that fed on lemonade."

"Well," Bunkey, counters, "how about that stuff you put in flower vases to keep the flowers fresh?"

"A dozen roses are hardly equal to a 10-foot fir tree," replied Petunia.

How should you keep your live tree fresh? Cut off the stump just before you put it in the stand, and keep the stand full of water—just water. Never let the tree dry out as then the cut stem sort of "heals over." The tree is no longer able to get enough water to keep from dumping needles all over the floor.

This is the season of the *poinsettia*, a plant that outlives Christmas and often Easter—if you don't expose it to cold on the way home. Even a few seconds of frost can kill it. If you only want it for the Christmas season, keep it in dim light. For a longer life, expose it to 6 to 8 hours of bright light daily. Tough as it is, it will not tolerate either hot or cold drafts. Slice a hole in the bottom of that fancy wrap it came in to prevent root rot from overwatering. It likes cool nights, but no cooler than 55 degrees. If you plan on keeping it for the winter, begin fertilizing it monthly. Plant it outside once all chance of frost is over. It will not bloom again. Greenhouses have a very elaborate system to get the plant to bloom. Enjoy your poinsettia for the holidays, then compost it.

If you bring home a *cyclamen*, it will keep blooming until Easter—if you treat it right. It needs to be deadheaded regularly and kept from direct sunlight, but in a bright spot and out of drafts. They like cool nights, 50 or so, and 70 during the day. Fertilize about once a month with a water-soluble fertilizer at half strength. Since they grow from corms (think *gladiolas*), water from the bottom to prevent rotting the corm. Let the soil nearly dry out between watering. If you can't bear to let the plant die, dig up the corm and replant it just under the soil in the partial shade in the flower garden. If you have no garden, leave it in the pot and stop watering once the leaves turn yellow. When all the leaves are dead, re-pot in a larger pot and start watering again. If this doesn't work, you are not a bad person. It doesn't for everyone. Take a deep breath and enjoy the smell of Christmas from that fresh, REAL tree. Buy a locally grown real tree. It's good for the economy and smells like Christmas.

Bunkey's in the Doghouse

Bunkey got that 8-foot tree in, nearly dismembering the chandelier in the dining room, knocking several pictures askew and totally demolishing a glass Santa sitting on the coffee table on the way in.

Now he is eyeing the needle-dropping monster, wondering how he is going to get it back out without further destruction.

Here's how: dismemberment. Bunkey gets out the pruning saw and clippers and cuts the branches off—after Petunia takes the ornaments off, of course. He put a sheet down first to collect all the needles, then cut off the branches and stuffed them into the bag he bought to haul the tree out in. A bag of branches is much easier to haul through the house than a tree. (Remember how much fun it was to get in the house to start with?) Now all he has to take to the curb is the trunk.

A wreath made from real evergreens can be dismembered and used this way too, or just propped up on the south or west side of a small tree or shrub. It shades the stem from the sun and keeps the trunk from heating up.

Bunkey is no longer in the doghouse, now that the tree was removed in pieces and nothing more was destroyed in the process.

So your lighted Christmas deer died. Don't put him in the trash—instead, tuck him away until spring. He will make an interesting addition to a flat flower garden. Plant a vine around him (nasturtiums for instance). Or tie 2 half baskets together and hang them over his back. Hang a half basket from his neck or put a wreath around it. Any garden can use a bit of whimsy. Your neighbors will either praise your artistic talent or wonder about your mental health.

Winter Care for your Trees

Oh, look! It's snowing again! The evergreens look so pretty with the snow on their branches. That is, until the snow load starts breaking those branches. What should you do? First, DO NOT beat the snot out of them. Think you should take the broom and brush them down? Nope. Use your broom to gently lift the branches to get the snow off. Putting more pressure from the broom or bat or whatever you grab just adds to the weight on the branch, making it much more apt to crack or even break off. Trees don't heal this time of year, so you are setting the poor thing up for disease or bug invasion in the spring.

Most deciduous trees easily shake off snow, but if they don't just wiggle the stem a bit and the snow will all come down and slide down the collar of your jacket. At least it's off the tree. Of course, if the tree is 100 years old, this will not work, but that tree has dealt with snow and ice for a long time. Heavy ice will break branches even if you shake some of it off. Be very careful after an ice storm, as branches can fall on you with just a bit of wind. Tempting as it is to go out and get it off the trees, if you have large trees stay away from them until the ice comes off by itself. Enjoy the snow, but don't overdo the shoveling. Save the energy for next summer's gardening.

Late Winter Chores

If you hear grumbling, it is probably Bunkey as he dons his snowmobile suit and boots and heads outside with his pruners and saw. Why? Even though the snow is chin deep to a professional basketball player, winter is the perfect time to prune or thin trees and shrubs, and Bunkey has quite a few of both that have been long ignored. One nice thing about pruning trees when there's lots of snow: Bunkey won't need quite as tall a ladder, he can just stand on the snowbanks.

Don't say you don't know how to prune a tree. It is quite simple. Remember, you only want to remove 1/4 of the branches in any one year. With that in mind, take a good look at your naked tree. You can easily see branches that are crossing each other, that are shooting up from the top side of a horizontal branch or are dead. Any or all of these branches should be pruned off. If you get your hat knocked off every time you walk under your tree, then you may have to cut some of those branches off, too.

If you have red-twigged dogwood, cut off the older branches to the soil line to keep the shrub the best color it can be. Only the newer branches are bright red. Older ones tend to have a gray cast.

Bunkey had just gotten into the house and was removing the layers when Petunia reminded him that he had put off sharpening the lawn mower blades when he put the mower away last fall and he better do it now as long as he is already dressed for the weather. There are chores every season for gardeners.

When he finally got back in the house again, Bunkey decided to start planning his next garden. The perfect gardener plans by blocking out, on a sheet of paper, where each row of veggies or each new flower is going in the garden. Bunkey is doing his planning by napping with the newest catalog open on his chest. Close enough for most of us.

Tools & Toys

If it doesn't fit, give it to a taller neighbor.

Garden Helpers

While it would be nice to have a crew of garden helpers (including a few weightlifters to help you), it probably isn't going to happen. There are, however, helpers available. Here are a few every gardener should have.

Trenching Spade—This tool has a short handle and a long narrow blade. It's perfect for cutting hostas or other fibrous-rooted plants apart or for digging a narrow, deep hole for planting.

Potato Fork—Use it to dig iris, peonies, dahlias, potatoes of course, or any tuberous plant. It will not damage the roots like a spade would.

Hand Trowel—Get a good one. Petunia has chucked dozens of hand trowels after she used them to pry out bricks or dig out plants in clay. Look for one made of stainless steel with a cutting edge on one side and a forked bottom. It is nearly indestructible.

Garden Rake & Leaf Rake—Use one in the garden and the other on the lawn.

Hoe—The hoe is only for making rows in the garden. If you don't mulch, it is also for hoeing out weeds week after week all summer.

Long-Handled Hand Fork—This is for getting under shrubs to remove all the debris that ends up there.

Hand Clipper—Get a good one (usually expensive) to use for trimming small tree branches and tough flower stems.

Folding Hand Saw— This is for the bigger tree branches.

There are a few other tools that are nice to have.

Thermometers—One for the compost pile and another to check the soil temp. The latter tells you when the soil is the proper temp for peas, corn, tomatoes, etc. Of course, the old way of sitting on the soil with as few clothes on as is decent in your neighborhood will tell you when it's warm enough to plant tomatoes and the vine crops.

Floating Row Covers—These are great to keep insects out of cabbage and protect the plants from the cold on a cool night in the fall.

Compost Maker—This would be super!

Tall Stakes/Tomato Cages—Stakes and supports for flowers are nice, but tomato cages do a good (if not fancy) job for most plants.
Gloves—Get a soft leather pair and a pair with a nylon back and rubber front (look for the *Atlas* brand). The first for pulling weeds, the other for planting. There are gloves especially for rose growers with a long leather cuff that goes to the elbow to prevent thorns from ripping skin or clothes.

A few things that are not worth your time or money.

Garden Seat with Wheels—Unless you can grow crops on cement or a tar road, forget it. They just get bogged down in the vegetable garden and are too wide to get between plants in most flower gardens.
Wheeled Garden Seeder—Bunkey finally put his on a garage sale. Even if all but one of the holes in the planting disks are plugged, it still plants the seeds too close together. You end up thinning everything you planted. A waste of seed and time.
Fancy Fertilizers—Forget them all. Compost or composted manure adds micronutrients to the soil, not chemicals. If you till in your mulch and add just a touch of nitrogen, you will be making your soil lighter and more productive next year.
Christmas is coming and it is not too soon to start thinking about gifts for your favorite gardener. Petunia has been leaving gardening tool catalogs all over the house. Bunkey should get the hint sooner or later.

Tools to Try

Every gardener has a few favorite tools. Even if you have been gardening for years, here are a few you may not have heard of or just haven't tried yet.

If you have been blessed with unwanted shrubs or small trees that you are determined to remove, you might think of investing in a ***weed wrench***, also called a ***woody plant puller***. This is an L-shaped device made of heavy steel. Its handle is about 5 feet tall. At the bottom end is a grasping jaw. You fit this jaw around the plant or shrub you want to remove, push down on the handle and the offending shrub pops right out of the soil. It comes in different sizes, so you can use it to pull up thistles or trees with trunks up to 2 inches thick. What a neat way to get rid of buckthorn. Beats attempting to dig the stinkers out.

If your hands aren't as strong as they used to be, or if you are susceptible to repetitive motion injuries, look for a ***Fiskars pruner***. It's recommended by the Arthritis Foundation. When you squeeze the handles together, leverage rotates the head of the pruner. Another easy-on-the-grip tool is the ***Florian ratchet pruner***. It cuts by building incremental power, much like a car jack. With either, it is a good idea to get a ***holster*** to put on your belt. Tripping and falling with open pruners in your pocket can lead to damage to sensitive body parts. It could be a bit embarrassing to explain to the E.R. doc how you got stabbed there.

Plumbers and carpenters know how handy a ***reciprocating saw*** (think *Sawzall*®) is. The blade slides back and forth. It's fast, lightweight and makes nice clean cuts.

A ***folding pruning saw*** is one that folds the blade into the handle. This one you can stick in your pocket and not worry about damaging any important body parts. The typical saw is about 14 inches long (folded), with a 6-inch blade and weighs about 5 ounces.

If you garden on your knees and don't mulch, a ***circle hoe*** makes quick work of small weeds. It just a sharp-edged metal circle attached to a wood handle. Another hand tool is a ***cobra***. It may be called a ***Cape Cod weeder*** or a ***Japanese weeder*** in your catalog. This tool has a wood handle attached to an L-shaped steel rod that ends in a triangular tip. The only down side to these is that after you have dug the weeds with them, you will need to pick up the uprooted results.

One tool you can leave in the store is a ***bulb planter***. It doesn't make a deep enough hole and if you have any sense of gardening style, you never plant one bulb at a time. You get out your handy ***ditching spade*** and dig a hole big enough for 5 to 50 bulbs at least 8 to 12 inches deep. After all, if they are tulips and you don't plan on feeding the squirrels fresh bulbs, you are going to put 2 inches of chicken grit on top of the bulbs before you cover them with soil.

Most of these tools will be found in our local stores or in one of the many seed catalogs that fill up our mailboxes this time of year.

A handy way to hang hand tools is to fasten an old garden rake head to the wall. The tools with strings hang on the tines, the others fit between them. You can see which one you want at a glance. It's a good idea to paint the wood handles with a florescent paint. It makes it easier to find them after you absentmindedly leave them in the flowerbed overnight.

Tough Gardening

Ladies, did you ever wonder why it is so much work gardening with long-handled tools? MEN! That's right, men. Long-handled tools are designed for a man's shape, even the ones with the pretty pink handles. Women use long-handled tool differently from men. The reason? A wider pelvis means a woman's center of gravity is closer to her hips. A man's broader shoulders puts his center of gravity higher. Proportionally, women have greater lower body strength than men, but less upper body strength. This means women rely on the power of their legs, not their arms, for strenuous jobs like digging. Most gardening tools are designed for men, by men. They are too large for most women. Using too large a tool leads to strain, fatigue and injury. Women may not realize just how unnecessarily hard they are struggling because there have been no other options.

These problems led Ann Adams (a 67-year-old former nurse) and Liz Brenisinger (53, who worked in public health administration), to design a shovel/spade for women. The two had been market gardeners for 13 years, so they knew the kids of stresses gardening puts on the female body. The tool they design is ergonomically engineered to maximize the power of a woman's body and make digging less strenuous.

This didn't mean just taking a big tool and making it smaller. They studied what actual changes were needed so it compensated for the woman, rather than the other way around. It acknowledged a woman's lower center of gravity and lower body strength, crucial when bending and lifting. They also had to take into account a woman's narrower shoulders, smaller hands and weaker grip. Regular long-handled tools were too heavy, too long and too awkward for women to use comfortably.

They designed and tested all sorts of shapes and handle lengths, and came up with the HERS™ shovel/spade. All parts are sourced and made in the U.S. The name of Liz and Ann's company is *Green Heron Tools*. Their goal is to bring more women back to the land, and to let women garden without pain or risk of injury. Let's hope our local stores will soon be carrying their tools. Husbands would love to hear less complaining about backaches and being too pooped to cook after a long day in the garden.

Gifts for Lady Gardeners

Today we will discuss gifts for your lady gardener. The guys go out and buy whatever they need, so we will stick to the girls. First of all, know your gardener. If she hates cutesy-poo, don't get her a garden gnome. If she has rabbit statues all over the place, she may or may not want another one.

If she starts her own seeds, a bag of seed starter and a heating tape would be much appreciated. Wonder Soil® is one brand to look for. It is made from coir (fibers from coconut hulls). It is more "green" than peat as it is renewable. There is only so much peat in the world.

Another "green" gift is sea weed or fish fertilizer. A barrel that sits under the rain gutter to collect rain water for her plants is a great gift—some even have a faucet on the bottom for easier access. How about a compost pail for the kitchen? There are some pretty fancy ones.

If she likes to do crafts, there are kits to make stepping stones, word stones or walks that look like stone. You may need to give a bag of cement with those gifts. If she likes books, get a garden book for Zone 3 or short season growing.

Several pairs of Ajax gloves are great, especially if she has never worn garden gloves. They are very tight fitting and the palm material is so dense that she can pull out thistles with ease. If she is an apron wearer, a garden apron to hold tools and her cell phone would be a hit.

One thing that isn't worth the money are the blooming flowers-of-the-month. The plants are shipped from someplace south by air to Minneapolis, then to Fargo. Ten minutes on the tarmac between planes in mid-winter will damage or kill the best packaged plant. If they are not transported in a heated truck from Fargo...well, you can guess what that does.

Check out her hand tools. If she has a trowel that bends every time she uses it to pry out a rock from the garden, it needs to be trashed. A long-handled hand rake is great for getting the dead leaves and stalks from under shrubs during spring clean-up. A stool with wheels sure beats kneeling for an older gardener. For the younger ones, a kneeling mat is nice. Knee pads will be tried once, then left in the closet. They are clumsy and make walking difficult. Do not, under any circumstances, buy her wind chimes unless you know she likes them.

If she is a bird watcher, a heated bird bath is a super gift. Or get a small heater for the bird bath she has. A squirrel feeder will lure the little thieves away from the bird feeders.

Make your garden girl's life a little easier with the proper tools and fun gifts.

Toys for the Tech Gardener

Do you have a nerdy gardener on your Christmas list? One with a phone that does everything but bring you your slippers after a hard day in the garden? If so, here are some ideas for you to think about.

Orbit® has a hose-end timer—perfect for the office worker who doesn't have time to water during the early morning, the best time. It has a digital clock that allows for very specific watering settings, while the manual dial keeps the programming very easy. You can set the start time, frequency and duration in a manner of seconds. It even has a rain delay button to stop the flow during a rainstorm.

For the computer nerd, Black and Decker has PlantSmart. You put it in the garden and it tells you what is best planted in that spot by measuring sunlight, temperature, soil nutrients and moisture. It takes all the fun out of it for the rest of us.

If your techie is into houseplants, look for WaterStik and LiteStik, both from Fertile Earth. The LED light on the end of the WaterStik flashes if the plant needs water or is too wet, with a range of colors representing the different water needs. If it is always showing too much water, check to see what is in the bottom of the pot. If it is a layer of gravel or pot shards, dump them out. A coffee filter will cover the drainage hole quite nicely until the soil settles. The gravel/shard layer holds water, making for too-wet roots. The LiteStik sticks in the plant and turns its LED lights when it senses the natural light from the day is gone. This is for plants that need 16 to 18 hours of light a day to prosper. Use it with an artificial light.

If your gardener is a plant starter, Gardener's Supply has a heat-mat thermostat with a probe to determine if the potting mix is too warm or cool.

Now for the phone apps, available in the iTunes store. GardenPilot has videos and plant info for 15,000 plants and a database of local retailers.

Eden Garden Designer lets you inexpensively design a virtual garden by taking pictures of your space and adding digital plants. It can prevent garden goofs like a big rock or fountain plopped in the middle of the yard, unconnected to anything else.

It's not too early to think about Christmas, just too early to do anything about it for most of us.

If you are absolutely at your wit's end, a gift certificate at a local nursery or from a seed catalog that specializes in seeds and plants for northern climates is always welcome. Still don't know what to get that favorite uncle for Christmas? Get him started birdwatching. He will need a squirrel-proof feeder or two, a suet feeder, a heated birdbath and seed. Black sunflower seeds, nyjer seed and suet will do it. Next year, you can get him some good binoculars so he can watch distant birds, or maybe his neighbors.

Leftovers

Articles, not food...

What Kind of Gardener Are You?

THE NORMAL GARDENER

You won't leave town when your tulips are in bloom.
You have an account at the local garden center.
You value all living things, great and small.
You have a compost heap.
You can't believe you ordered so many bulbs last fall.
You love to grow and cook your own vegetables.
You are proud of your baby carrots.
You can crush a Japanese beetle with your bare fingers.
You would never kill a ladybug.
You have dirt under your fingernails.
You know the pH of your soil.
You had your soil tested.
You buy composted cow manure to top dress your garden.
You know the virtues of weeding.
You teach your kids the wonders of gardening.

THE OBSESSED GARDENER

You won't leave town when your tulips are in bloom. Or your daffodils, lilies, lilacs, clematis, hydrangeas, roses, asters...
Your spouse and kids buy all your Christmas, birthday and Mother's Day gifts at the local garden center.
You cheered when Bambi's mother died.
You take your compost heap's temperature every day.
It wasn't enough—you should have ordered more bulbs.
Cook? Who has time to cook?
You carry pictures of your baby carrots in your wallet.
You love the sound when you crush a Japanese beetle.

You bring ladybugs inside for the winter.
Who has fingernails?
All of your friends also know the pH of your soil.
You studied for it before you had your soil tested.
You don't buy composted cow manure, you buy a Jersey cow.
You know the virtues of weeding.
Kids? Who has time for kids?

Mistaken Identity

There seems to be some confusion among the populace about the difference between Master Gardeners and the members of the garden club. While there is some crossover between the two groups, they are separate entities.

Garden club members are gardeners who enjoy socializing with other gardeners, meeting to listen to informative speeches about gardening from their own members and from guest speakers. They sponsor the plant sale where their members sell plants from their own gardens. There is no education required to join garden club, nor are they obligated to donate time to the club.

Master Gardeners, by contrast, must have 48 hours of college level classes taught by professors from the University of Minnesota. After taking the classes, they still are not officially Master Gardeners. They must first put in 50 volunteer hours. Even then, they can't just sit on their laurels. They must have another 25 hours of volunteer work and 5 hours of education each year to keep their titles. While some Master Gardeners work at nurseries, those hours are not included in their volunteer hours. The hours must be unpaid hours.

The official description from the University of Minnesota is: "Master Gardeners are University of Minnesota trained volunteers whose job it is to educate the public about a variety of horticulture subjects using readily available up-to-date research-based information. This education effort is designed to enhance the public's quality of life and promote good stewardship of the environment."

Quite a job. Garden Day is one way the Master Gardeners get their yearly hours. The planning starts in October and usually ends late March or early April. They assemble 35 to 40 speakers who hold classes on everything from starting your own plants to how to prune your apple tree for the biggest crop of healthy apples.

There are other ways to get the required hours. Some of the braver members are available to speak to groups interested in gardening. Others answer questions in the Extension office, at the county or state fair and on the local radio. Some of the group specialize in various sub-garden subjects, such as trees, vegetables, perennials or seed starting. Some act as advisors, for instance at the community garden. Members of the garden club are also involved in that garden.

So, next time you buy a plant from the plant sale, thank the garden club. When you attend Garden Day, thank the Master Gardeners. They are easy to spot that day—they wear flashy purple T-shirts. Both groups are an asset to the community, just don't confuse one for the other. While members of either group may not have a hissy fit if you confuse the two, just remember: Garden Day, Master Gardeners; plant sale, garden club.

Garden Gnomes

Garden gnomes seem to be making a come-back in the United States, mostly in miniature gardens. Even though J. K. Rowling, the author of the Harry Potter books, says they get up to all sorts of mischief in the garden at night.

Gnomes are not everyone's idea of artistic beauty. Some people (with too much imagination or eggplant where their brains should be) see them as an oppressed minority whose civil rights have been violated by unscrupulous landlords.

The first garden gnomes were introduced into England in 1847 by Sir Charles Isham. He brought 21 of them from Germany and decorated his gardens with them at his home (Lamport Hall in Northamptonshire). The only survivor is named Lampy and is on display there. It-he-she, whatever, is insured for a million pounds. The owners must be aware of the habit of travelers gnome-napping garden décor and taking pictures of them in often strange locales the gnome-napper traveled to.

In France, there is an underground movement known as the Liberation Front of Garden Gnomes, and there is a similar group in Italy. These activists (as they call themselves) have been using the cover of night to remove hundreds of gnomes from people's gardens and putting them in city centers to bring their plight to the attention of the public. Some of these suburban terrorists deposit the gnomes in wooded areas. They call it *de-ridiculizing*, feeling that the gnomes belong in a more natural environment. This only proves that there are screwballs in every country.

Most garden centers have gnomes in multiple sizes. If they are your thing, the larger ones can be an accent for a peculiar (or particular) plant, your choice, or a smaller one a surprise hiding under a hosta. The very small gnomes are usually found residing in miniature gardens, either outside or in table-sized gardens in the house. House gnomes have not been known to misbehave as do the hardier outdoors types.

If you are fed up with fairy gardens as being a bit too froo-froo, maybe gnomes are more your thing. After all, the French, English and Italians have been having fun with them for years.

A garden spoof by Bev the Gardener, a.k.a. Bev Johnson M.G.

Eat It—It's Good for You!

How many times have you heard your mother say those words? Usually it is because the food is new to you. Some foods you know well that are especially good for you. The team of Dr. Paul Limburg, a Mayo Clinic M.D. and Vince Fritz, an Extension horticulturist, have been studying fruits and vegetables. They share their findings in events called Chemopreventive Cafes. Since everyone's genetic makeup is different, the phytonutrients may not work the same way for you. This is only a partial list:

- Apple skins, blueberries, cranberries and red grapes contain *quertian*. This helps protect against oral cancer and leukemia.
- Broccoli, cabbage and cauliflower contain *glucosinolates* that help protect against prostate, esophageal, colorectal and breast cancer.
- Bugs Bunny's favorite treat, carrots, contain *beta carotene* (as do most orange vegetables). This helps reduce chemotherapy toxicity.
- Cranberries and red grapes also contain *myricetin* for preventing prostate cancer and prevent other tumors.
- Raspberries (all colors) contain ellagic acid that protects against breast, skin colon prostate and pancreatic cancers.
- Tomatoes are full of *lycopene* and protect against prostate, lung, bladder, cervix and skin cancers.
- All grapes (not just red ones) and peanuts have *resveratrol* in them. It protects against all cancers.
- Even spices have their place on this list. Ginger, the sea sickness preventive spice, has *(6)-gingerol*, which protects against skin, colorectal, pancreatic and ovarian cancers.

The take away is—make your next smoothie with cranberries, grapes, raspberries and ginger. And add carrots and apple skins to sweeten your tomato sauce.

Better living through chemistry.

About the Author

I am a perfectly average woman. I can shingle a roof (I've done three), design and help build a house, and set a toilet (I was a plumber's helper for years). I raised four gardeners (Christa, Kelly, Melissa and Kala) and stayed married for 61 years. I can answer most gardening questions, butcher a deer, raise/can/freeze enough food to last for two years, keep two-and-a-half acres of lawn and several gardens in pretty good shape, and now, write a book. In between, I had enough time to go to college at 51, get an R.N. degree and work in a psych hospital. Not bad for an old broad.

I became a Master Gardener in 1999, and began writing gardening articles for my local newspaper about two years later. This was prompted by a gardening insert I saw in the newspaper. The information in it was all wrong for our zone, so I marched into the newspaper office, demanded to see the editor and handed him an article I had written about black knot on plum and cherry trees. The phrase that turned the tide for him was "black knot looks like poop on a stick." My gardening articles now reach over 61,000 people.

A few years later I began to host a call-in gardening program at my local radio station—it has been a blast. I told one caller to, "Water the snot out" of his newly-planted tree. The announcer dubbed that as a "Bev-ism." They aren't planned, they just pop out. In my spare time, I knit, sew or read—often all at the same time. That has resulted in a sweater with one sleeve two inches longer than the other. Since my daughter wasn't built that way, I had to redo the sleeve.

If you ever visit me, you will get a slice of homemade bread and jelly with your coffee. That is, if you can wait until I get done with whatever I'm doing in the yard or garden. You may find me up a tree (sawing off an offending branch), in the greenhouse (usually with my shirt off—it's hot in there!), or in the winter hauling wood for the stove.

Bev Johnson